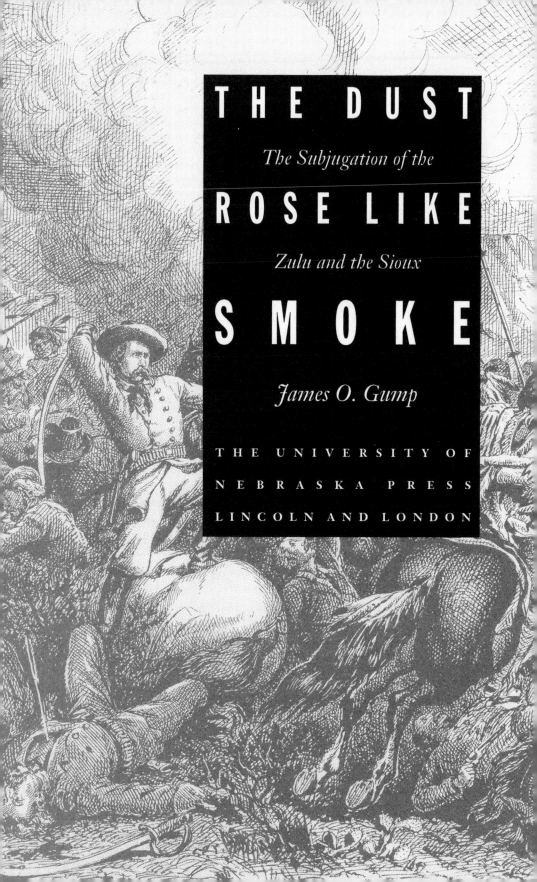

THE DUST

The Subjugation of the

ROSE LIKE

Zulu and the Sioux

SMOKE

James O. Gump

THE UNIVERSITY OF
NEBRASKA PRESS
LINCOLN AND LONDON

© 1994 by the University of Nebraska Press
Manufactured in the United States of America
The paper in this book meets the minimum
requirements of American National Standard
for Information Sciences—Permanence of
Paper for Printed Library Materials,
ANSI Z39.48–1984.
Library of Congress Cataloging-in-Publication Data
Gump, James O. (James Oliver)
The dust rose like smoke : the subjugation of the
Zulu and the
Sioux / James O. Gump.
p. cm.
Includes bibliographical references and index.
ISBN 0-8032-2152-5 (alk. paper)
1. Dakota Indians—History—Cross-cultural
studies. 2. Dakota
Indians—Wars—Cross-cultural studies. 3. Dakota
Indians—
Government relations—Cross-cultural studies. 4.
Zulu (African
people)—History—Cross-cultural studies. 5. Zulu
(African people)—
Wars—Cross-cultural studies. 6. Zulu (African
people)—Government
relations—Cross-cultural studies. I. Title.
E99.D1G86 1994
323.1′1975—dc20   93-10893 CIP

For Lee Ann and Scott

CONTENTS

MAPS & ILLUSTRATIONS

Maps

Illustrations

ACKNOWLEDGMENTS

number of individuals, to whom I am most grateful, contributed significantly to the development and completion of this project. Most important to thank are Robin Winks and Roger Louis, whose NEH Summer Seminars, "Comparative Imperialisms" and "The History and Literature of the British Empire" respectively, provided the inspiration to initiate and consummate this book; and Howard Lamar and Leonard Thompson, who sparked my own interest in comparative history, encouraged me to follow through on this book, and provided continuous support. In addition, I wish to thank the following persons for assisting me with their insights and criticisms at various stages of my work: John Cell, Ray DeMallie, George Fredrickson, John Galbraith, Fred Hoxie, Richard Killblane, Pete Maslowski, George Miles, Joe Miller, Clyde Milner III, and Donald Morris.

To carry out research abroad and throughout the United States I relied on the generous support of the National Endowment for the Humanities, the Newberry Library, and the University of San Diego. In addition, I benefited considerably from the assistance of the librarians and support staffs at the Bancroft Library, Bienecke Rare Book Library, Bodleian Library, Huntington Library, Killie Campbell Africana Library, Library of Congress, Natal Museum, National Archives, Nebraska State Historical Society, Newberry Library, Public Record Office, Rhodes House, Sterling Memorial Library, the University of California at San Diego Central Library, and the University of Texas Library System.

Finally, I would like to thank a number of individuals in San Diego for their assistance in this work. In the University of San Diego's Copley Library, Devin Milner handled interlibrary loan requests and other research support needs in an efficient and professional manner. Several graduate students at USD, including Bob Milota, Chris Nelson, and Jackie Palid, assisted generously in bibliographic searches, photocopying, and editing. Freelance computer artists Tom and Stephanie Gould produced excellent maps for the manuscript. In addition, I would like to thank Lee Ann Otto, a member of the Political Science Department at the University of San Diego and my wife. Without her support, I doubt the project would have ever made it this far.

N January 1879 a British regiment repulsed a Zulu assault at Rorke's Drift, a mission station converted into a central store to supply Britain's army during the Anglo-Zulu War. Britain's defense of Rorke's Drift, which cost the Zulu two thousand casualties, earned British soldiers eleven Victoria Crosses. Almost twelve years later the United States government dispatched five thousand troops to Pine Ridge, South Dakota, to pacify Sioux "hostiles" involved in the Ghost Dance. In an ensuing confrontation at Wounded Knee Creek, the soldiers killed or wounded most of Big Foot's Miniconjou camp. The government awarded twenty-four Medals of Honor to its troops for the Wounded Knee "pacification."[1] Rorke's Drift and Wounded Knee have become powerful metaphors, evoking images of Thermopylae in the first instance, and systematic genocide in the latter. For the purposes of this study, these battles serve as symbolic benchmarks, representing the prelude and denouement in the subjugation of the Zulu and Sioux.

The inspiration for this book derives from Robin Winks's NEH Summer Seminar on "Comparative Imperialisms" in the summer of 1984. During the seminar, I made use of earlier research on the origins of Shaka's Zulu kingdom[2] as a basis from which to take up some of the issues raised by Howard Lamar and Leonard Thompson in their book *The Frontier in History: North America and South Africa Compared.* Lamar and Thompson define *frontier* as a zone of interaction between two or more previously distinct peoples, and the process by which relations among peoples begin, develop, and crystallize. The frontier "opens" when these peoples initially make contact, and "closes" when one of the peoples gains ascendancy over the other. Their model places primary emphasis on processes of interaction—to paraphrase one of their sources, to understand why one society advances, we must understand why the other society retreats.[3]

This book is influenced as well by Winks's definition of *imperialism* and historian Ronald Robinson's model of the collaborator. According to Winks, imperialism is "that set of human interactions that arise from the impact of a high-technology society on lesser-technology societies."[4] These interactions may remain informal, as in the United States's relations with Latin America, or become explicitly formal, as in America's annexation of Sioux territory in the nineteenth century. In the latter case, American imperialism involved conquest and resistance, as well as mutual accommodation. The Sioux, like the Zulu, were political actors in their own right, not pawns to outside forces. Their concerns often transcended the "white threat." During the first half of the nineteenth century, for example, both societies were engaged in their own subimperialisms, dominating and subjugating such groups as the Pawnees, Crows, Ndwandwe, and Ngwane.

Therefore, when indigenes chose to cooperate with the western imperial powers they often did so from what they perceived as positions of relative autonomy. Robinson argues that imperialism begins when a high-technology society gains influence in a lesser-technology society by linking itself to a collaborating group. The mediators do not act necessarily out of self-interest, but may well accommodate to establish equilibrium between the encroaching and responding societies.[5] Accordingly, the form of imperial control evolves to a large extent through this collaborating relationship, and the point at which one form of imperialism becomes another is shaped as much by conditions "on the spot" as at the metropole. For example, the decisions of Red Cloud, a principal Sioux mediator, fundamentally shaped Sioux-white relations in the 1860s. Further, the betrayal of the Zulu king Cetshwayo by imperial agents in South Africa led directly to the demise of the Zulu kingdom in 1879.

A major purpose of this study—which compares two expansive indigenous societies in frontier contexts and their relations with imperial agents and white settlers—is to issue another challenge to American "exceptionalism." Although some facets of American history are indeed exceptional, many others are not. Comparison serves to clarify what is and what is not unique to a given historical experience. In the words of the historian George Fredrickson, comparative history "can be valuable as a way of illuminating the special features or particularities of the individual societies being examined—each may look different in the light of the other or others—and also useful in enlarging our theoretical understanding of the kinds of institutions or processes being compared, thereby making a contribution to the development of social-scientific theories and generalizations."[6]

By way of comparison, the Zulu and Sioux represent two expansive, aggressive preindustrial societies, each of which gained hegemony in their respective regions during much of the nineteenth century. In addition, each experienced considerable social transformations during the eighteenth and nineteenth centuries, based on their adaptation to changing ecological, economic, and political conditions. Each also developed highly effective military systems and became widely feared, hated, and respected among other indigenous peoples. Each also confronted western imperialism at approximately the same time, scored significant military victories over their western opponents—Little Bighorn and Isandhlwana—and, in the aftermath of their own defeat, disintegrated in factionalism and civil war. Finally, the Sioux and Zulu came to be represented in popular culture as quintessential "noble savages" by the late nineteenth century, an image that continues to prevail in our own times.

Comparison also enables one to view Little Bighorn as more than a unique episode in the history of the American frontier. In a broader perspective, the events leading to Custer's Last Stand occurred in the context of late nineteenth-century global economic expansion, an era marked by the escalation of conflicts between the West and less technologically developed peoples over land, labor, and resources. Furthermore, the firearms used at Little Bighorn, like those at Isandhlwana, manifested the revolution in weapons technology emanating from Europe and the United States between the 1860s and 1890s. The Sioux could purchase Winchester repeaters and, as illustrated by the Custer battle, subdue American troops. But the Sioux could not manufacture Winchesters, just as the Zulu lacked the industrial capacity to construct breechloading Martini-Henrys. The capability to manufacture millions of complex weapons on short order gave the West a decisive edge in its wars against indigenous foes, regardless of whether these groups resided in the North American Great Plains or in Africa.

In point of contrast, however, the Zulu and Sioux experienced different economic fates at the close of the historical frontier. The difference goes to the heart of the British and American imperial "missions." The subjugation of the Zulu transformed agriculturists into migrant laborers, a conversion that squared perfectly with Britain's imperial objectives. In other words, a dependent Zululand, serving as a reservoir of plentiful, cheap labor, represented the logical outcome of British policy toward independent African chiefdoms in South Africa in the nineteenth century. Sir Alfred Milner, the last British high commissioner to South Africa, offered the clearest articulation of the British position in 1899: "The *ultimate* end is a self-governing white Community, supported by *well-treated* and *justly* governed black labour from Cape Town to Zambesi."[7] For the Sioux, whose remote, sparse population remained marginalized, the reservation represented a paradox—a place to be temporarily segregated, from which the Sioux might eventually be integrated into the American cultural and economic mainstream. The reservation policy, in the words of the historian Richard White, was crafted "the way survivors of a shipwreck might fashion a raft from the debris of a sunken vessel. Reservations evolved on an ad hoc basis as a way to prevent conflict and enforce a separation of the races."[8]

The contradictory nature of American policy contrasts with the more deliberate, even Machiavellian formulations by the British. What accounts for the contrast? American Indian policy was driven by contradictory impulses. The Americans wished to liberate the Sioux from their communal "bondage," thus opening the West to capitalist development, even if this required their subjugation. Moreover, Americans believed it possible and essential to integrate the Sioux—converting seminomadic, equestrian buffalo hunters into sedentary, God-fearing farmers—by placing them on remote, dependent reserves. The British, on the other hand, who sought the establishment of a stable, prosperous white confederation in South Africa, held more focused and attainable objectives. The immediate British task was to denationalize the Zulu in order to successfully exploit their labor potential, not to facilitate Zulu acculturation to a standard white model. Therefore, in terms of Britain's imperial logic, the subjugation and segregation of the Zulu kingdom bore no contradictions.

The ensuing chapters have been organized to bear out the similarities as well as differences in these historical experiences within the methodological framework outlined above. The first chapter, "The Little Bighorn in Comparative Perspective," is a detailed narrative of the immediate events leading up to the Custer battle and Isandhlwana (1876 and 1879, respectively). Rather than romanticizing these events, the chapter intends to convey their Pyrrhic as well as transient nature. After June 1876 the Lakota, never to be united again in such a way, were rapidly relegated to a state of dependency. For the United States, the U.S.-Sioux wars of 1876–77 signal the final phase of a series of armed conflicts with

North American indigenes dating back to the seventeenth century and foreshadow a more forward phase of imperialism, culminating in the annexation of the Philippines and Puerto Rico in 1898. Like the Sioux, the Zulu victory proved fleeting. Following their defeat at the hands of the British army in July 1879, the Zulu people experienced a rapid transition to dispossession and dependency. Great Britain's thrust into the heart of the Zulu kingdom coincided with its more aggressive posture in southern Africa in the late nineteenth century. Britain's imperialistic momentum peaked chronologically with America's, reaching its zenith in the Anglo-Boer War of 1899–1902.

The next four chapters attempt to place these battles in a broader historical context. Chapters 2 and 3, "Frontiers of Expansion" and "Indigenous Empires," examine the social, economic, and political transformations of the Sioux and Zulu peoples from the early seventeenth to the mid-nineteenth centuries. Much of the popular historical literature on these societies treats them as timeless, static entities. This tendency is due largely to the nature of our sources. Much of what we take to be the pre- and early contact history of the Sioux and Zulu is based on the uncritical rendition of the accounts of late nineteenth-century informants. While these recollections still constitute an important historical source, they fail to describe convincingly the profound sociopolitical changes that accompanied the ecological and economic transformations of that era. This study attempts to reconstruct a more dynamic portrait of these societies, based on the insights of archaeology, the scattered fragments of travelers' and explorers' journals, and oral traditions.

Chapter 4, "Collaborators of a Kind," analyzes Sioux-American and Zulu-British relations in the mid-nineteenth century, focusing on the collaboration of the Oglala chief Red Cloud and the Zulu king Mpande. The chapter examines why these leaders collaborated with whites, when their collaboration turned to resistance, and the political and economic factors that constrained their decisions. The following chapter, "Agents of Empire," explores the other side of the collaborating equation. It examines the relative significance of decisions made at the Office of Indian Affairs and the Colonial Office, as compared to those of military and political officials on the spot, in fomenting a diplomatic crisis in the 1870s. It considers the careers of Philip Sheridan, William Sherman, and George Custer in North America, and Bartle Frere, Theophilus Shepstone, and Frederick Thesiger (Lord Chelmsford) in South Africa. The chapter also examines the role of capitalist expansion in leading to the deliberate fabrication of a *casus belli* in 1876 and 1879. Viewed in this light, the wars of conquest against the Sioux and Zulu, in the words of Paul Kennedy, "were in many ways the military concomitant to the economic penetration of the overseas world" by Europe and North America. These penetrations "occurred as much in the centers of continents . . . as [they] did up the mouths of African rivers and around the coasts of Pacific archipelagoes."[9]

The sixth chapter, "Patterns of Imperial Overrule," explores the aftermath of Little Bighorn and Isandhlwana. It compares and evaluates the settlement policies of the United States and Great Britain, and contrasts the economic marginality of the Pine Ridge and Rosebud reservations with the central role of Zululand as a reservoir of cheap labor. It also describes the deliberate efforts by the United States and Great Britain to promote and exploit factionalism in the Sioux and Zulu polities, the subsequent political disintegration in the indigenous reserves, and the events leading up to the partition of Zululand in 1887 and the Wounded Knee tragedy in 1890.

Chapter 7, "Images of Empire," considers the ways in which the fatal confrontations with the Sioux and Zulu came to be represented in the press, literature, and later, film, constructing mythological images that continue to inform our understanding of these societies. The Lakota, entangled in a web of popular attitudes regarding the significance of Custer's "Last Stand" and the nature of the American frontier, became the audacious if duplicitous "noble savage." The Zulu, characterized by Bartle Frere as "celibate man-slaying gladiators," became immortalized in the novels of H. Rider Haggard for "their superstitious madness and blood-stained grandeur."[10] Each western culture simultaneously dehumanized and glamorized the Sioux and Zulu, a product of the racist ideologies of the late nineteenth century as well as the guilt and compassion associated with the bloody costs of empire building.

CHAPTER 1

The Little Bighorn in
Comparative Perspective

N early June 1876 Sitting Bull called together one of the largest Indian camps ever assembled on the Great Plains for the annual sun dance. Most of those who gathered in the ceremonial circle on the west bank of the Rosebud River belonged to Sioux bands, yet some northern Cheyenne allies participated as well. For the Sioux, no occasion held more significance than the sun dance. The anthropologist Clark Wissler, writing in 1911 to James Walker, a physician at the Pine Ridge agency, described the sun dance as "the one great unifying ceremony of the Plains Indians toward which all other ceremonial activities converged."[1] Sioux informants told Antoine Herman in 1896 that the "Sun Dance is the greatest ceremony that the [Sioux] do. . . . If one has scars on his breast or his back that show that he has danced the Sun Dance, no [Sioux] will doubt his word. He is eligible for leadership of a war party or for chieftainship."[2]

The sun dance offered warriors an opportunity to demonstrate personal heroism in the interests of tribal unity, yet more importantly, it brought Sioux together to seek favor from Wakan Tanka. For the Sioux, *wakan* connoted everything that was sacred. They believed that all life forms of the universe were one and embodied *wakan*. The Sioux also held that everything in the natural world was circular, and therefore regarded the circle as sacred. Seeking harmony with this natural order, the Sioux pitched circular tipis in circular camps and conducted rituals in ceremonial circles. "The wholeness of the circle . . . represented the wholeness and oneness of the universe." *Wakan* was the animating force of the universe. The totality of this life-giving force "was called *Wakan Tanka*, Great Incomprehensibility, the whole of all that was mysterious, powerful, sacred, holy."[3]

A number of Sioux men entered the sacred circle of the Sun Dance Lodge, seeking to demonstrate their courage, generosity, fortitude, and virility.[4] Holy men gashed the votaries' breasts, inserted skewer sticks just beneath the muscles, and suspended them from a twenty-foot pole with a tautly stretched fifteen-foot rawhide lariat. Thus fastened, the warriors danced, staring constantly at the sun, deprived of food, drink, or sleep. The dance ended when the skewers tore through the flesh. Successful dancers had prepared themselves for a prophetic vision.[5]

Sitting Bull, who bore many scars from past sun dances, participated enthusiastically in the painful ritual. He offered one hundred pieces of flesh to Wakan Tanka, cut methodically from each arm by his adopted brother, Jumping Bull. Blood streaming, he danced. Eighteen hours later Sitting Bull fell into a trance and experienced the vision for which he had hoped. He saw soldiers and Indians falling upside down into the Sioux camp. This could only mean that the Sioux and their Cheyenne allies would destroy the bluecoats.[6]

Sitting Bull's vision heartened the camp, dispelling the lingering anxiety. Cognizant of soldiers entering Powder River country from the east, west, and south, the Sioux recognized the gravity of the situation. The U.S. government had identified the Powder River Sioux as "hostiles." The Sioux knew, therefore, that they faced severe reprisals, even extermination, at the hands of the army. Yet with Sitting Bull's vision of a favorable spiritual dispensation, Sioux warriors looked forward to such an encounter with unbounded enthusiasm. When the sun dance ended, the camp shifted westward toward more plentiful supplies of game in the valley of the Little Bighorn River, where new arrivals from the agencies would join them. By the third week of June, the Sioux and their allies could place from fifteen hundred to two thousand warriors in the field.[7]

On June 24 the Seventh Cavalry, commanded by Lieutenant Colonel George Armstrong Custer, discovered the abandoned sun dance camp. Lieutenant Edward S. Godfrey, one of the expedition diarists, wrote disparagingly of "a large 'Sun-Dance' lodge" that contained "the scalp of a white man."[8] Custer's Arikara scouts, who had carefully studied the camp the night before, did not miss its significance. One of them, Red Star, noted:

> Here there was evidence of the Dakotas having made medicine, the sand had been arranged and smoothed, and pictures had been drawn. The Dakota scouts in Custer's army said that this meant the enemy knew the army was coming. In one of the sweat lodges was a long heap or ridge of sand. On this one Red Bear, Red Star, and Soldier saw figures drawn indicating by hoof prints Custer's men on one side and the Dakota on the other. Between them dead men were drawn

lying with their heads toward the Dakotas. . . . All the Arikara knew what this meant, namely, that the Dakotas were sure of winning.[9]

The Arikaras now concurred with Mitch Boyer, the famous Sioux scout on loan from Colonel John Gibbon's column, who told Godfrey on the eve of the ascent up the Rosebud that the Seventh was "going to have a damned big fight."[10]

The Seventh Cavalry commenced its ascent at noon on June 22. Custer commanded a regiment totaling 31 officers, 566 enlisted men, and 35 Indian scouts. Several quartermaster employees, the *Bismarck Tribune* reporter Mark Kellogg, and Custer's nephew Autie Reed accompanied the regiment.[11] Alfred Terry, the brigadier general commanding the Powder River expedition, had issued written instructions to Custer on the morning of the twenty-second to guide the regiment's movement up the Rosebud. Terry told Custer to "proceed up the Rosebud until you ascertain definitely the direction in which the [Indian] trail . . . leads." He added that "should it be found (as it appears to be almost certain that it will be found) to turn toward the Little Big Horn . . . proceed southward perhaps as far as the headwaters of the Tongue, and then turn toward the Little Big Horn." Terry hoped the Indians might be enclosed by Custer's column, moving northward, and Colonel Gibbon's column, moving southward from the Yellowstone as far as the forks of the Big and Little Bighorn rivers. The general told Custer to conform to these instructions "unless you shall see sufficient reason for departing from them. [I place] too much confidence in your zeal, energy, and ability to wish to impose upon you precise orders which might hamper your action when nearly in contact with the enemy."[12] Afforded such latitude in pursuing the Indians, Custer feared that contact with the enemy might not be made in time to prevent the "hostiles" from escaping to the Bighorn Mountains. Failure to engage the Sioux—this was Custer's only concern.

In 1878 the Zulu king Cetshwayo kaMpande called his age-grade regiments—his *amabutho* (singular *ibutho*)—to Nodwengu, his father's capital, to take part in the annual *umkhosi*, or first-fruits festival. Cetshwayo's own capital was at Ulundi, yet he reckoned the more traditional site would enhance Zulu morale. The *umkhosi*, performed before each harvest in either December or January, functioned as the Zulu's most important ritual occasion, serving a host of ideological and practical functions. For example, it provided a forum for the expression and reinforcement of values, beliefs, and goals; it reasserted the connection between the ancestral spirits, the true foundation of the polity, and the living king; and it allowed the king to form and review his *amabutho* and reward his supporters with gifts of cattle and marriage partners.[13]

Zulu kings also invoked uNkulunkulu, the great mystery and source of all life, only at the *umkhosi*. Directly seeking uNkulunkulu's influence required the utmost reverence, and therefore the skilled efforts of *izinyanga* (doctors). Typically, the Zulu sought uNkulunkulu's influence more indirectly through intermediaries, such as recently departed kinsmen. Ancestors were praised, cajoled, and scolded into acting on behalf of the living. Such a cosmology linked the generations and provided continuity and predictability in the Zulu social universe.

A Zulu informant, Lunguza kaMpukane, told the Natalian magistrate James Stuart in 1909 of a great *umkhosi* at Mgungundhlovu under the Zulu king Dingane (1828–40). The ceremony commenced at sunrise when Dingane entered the main cattle kraal with his doctors. The *amabutho*, which had gathered several days before, encircled their king and led him out of the kraal. "Immediately before the sun rises," Lunguza recollected, "the King takes a mouth full of water, flings [calabashes] with his right arm holding at full length toward the sun the instant it appears above the horizon and then squirts the water from his mouth at the sun." As his regiments sang national anthems and shouted Dingane's praises, the king then reentered the cattle kraal and disappeared into his compound.[14]

Following the king's performance, his *amabutho* washed in a nearby river. The king returned in the afternoon to issue proclamations and grant permission for members of female *amabutho* to marry male veterans. As another informant, Ndukwana kaMbengwana, told Stuart, since "men were not permitted to [marry] whilst still young, girls were obliged to marry old or elderly men." The actual marriage might not take place for three years, and even then the men were obliged to exchange cattle for their spouses.[15]

For Cetshwayo, the *umkhosi* in 1878 offered the king a chance to revitalize his own power and to renew the allegiance of his people. Two factors, however, mitigated the king's optimism. First, conflict was brewing among his *amabutho*. The women of the Ngcugce regiment refused to marry into the Ndlondo regiment after ordered to do so by Cetshwayo, because many had taken lovers among the Dlokwe *ibutho*. As Magema Fuze recalled, this event "became a very serious matter to the king, because such a thing had never happened to the Zulu kings, that a king should be defied by a troop of girls."[16] Another schism, sparked by intergenerational tensions, erupted between the Ngobomakhosi and the older

Thulwana regiment, leaving at least seventy dead. This conflict also led to the disaffection of Thulwana's *induna* (commander) Hamu, Cetshwayo's elder brother, who withdrew to the northwest with a number of his warriors. As Fuze said, "[it] was perfectly plain that nothing would be right at this *umkhosi* ceremony."[17]

Another, even more serious issue, faced Cetshwayo. The British had seemed bent on war with the Zulu kingdom since 1877, and by the end of 1878 such a war appeared inevitable. Cetshwayo could not know that on December 10, 1878, South African high commissioner Sir Bartle Frere drafted a memorandum to the British colonial secretary arguing for "the necessity for now settling this Zulu question thoroughly and finally."[18] Four weeks later, the British army invaded the Zulu kingdom in three columns, intending to destroy the Zulu military system.

Frederick Thesiger, who became Lord Chelmsford when his father died in October 1878, commanded the British forces. On the eve of the invasion Chelmsford wrote Frere that "our cause will be a good one . . . and I hope to be able to convince [our critics] before many weeks are over that for a savage, as for a child, timely severity is greater kindness than mistaken leniency."[19] Chelmsford's plan was to sweep toward Ulundi in three columns, holding a fourth in readiness at Middle Drift on the Thukela River. He placed the northern column under the command of Colonel Evelyn Wood, the eastern column under Colonel Charles Pearson, and the center column under Colonel Richard Glyn. He placed the reserve column under the command of Colonel Anthony Durnford and, much to Durnford's chagrin, ordered it to remain in limbo, on the Natal border. Chelmsford and his staff accompanied Glyn's column, which struck out from Rorke's Drift on January 11, 1879. Nine days later it made camp at the base of Isandhlwana Mountain, approximately ten miles east of Rorke's Drift.

Donald Morris, a noted scholar of the Anglo-Zulu War, argues that Isandhlwana was the best campsite in the vicinity, with ready access to wood and water. In addition, "the view of the approaches was as good as could be expected in a hilly country, and there was no cover for an attacking force within a mile and a half of the camp."[20] For this reason Chelmsford dispensed with the impedimenta of entrenching the camp, although he had been warned of such a necessity by a number of experienced advisers. Even the Boer nationalist Paul Kruger, who felt little empathy for the British, impressed upon the general in 1878 "the absolute necessity of laagering his wagons every evening."[21]

Glyn's column consisted of his own Twenty-fourth Regiment, first and second battalions, the Natal Mounted Police and Mounted Infantry, 120 irregular cavalry troopers, (the Natal Carbineers, Buffalo Border Guard, and Newcastle rifles, under the command of Major John Dartnell), a rocket battery from the Royal Artillery, the Third Regiment of the Natal Native Contingent under Commandant Rupert Lonsdale, and the Natal Native Pioneers. Chelmsford, with a few mounted volunteers, left camp at noon on 20 January to scout the terrain to the southwest. He returned to camp at 6:30 P.M. without encountering Zulu, yet "far from satisfied that the Nkandhla Hills were empty, or that the Malakata Hills and Inhlazatye Mountain were not masking the approach of a large force."[22] Early the next morning Chelmsford dispatched Dartnell to the Nkandhla Hills with mounted volunteers, and Lonsdale southeast to Inhlazatye with sixteen companies of the Natal Native Contingent.

By the evening of January 21, Dartnell encountered a Zulu force near the Mangeni River. Staff officer Henry Harford later wrote that "it was very evident that we were opposite a very large *impi*, if not the whole Zulu army,"[23] but in fact this force consisted of only approximately fifteen hundred men. The main Zulu army, numbering twenty thousand, had advanced to within five miles of the Isandhlwana camp without detection. As the writer J. Y. Gibson pointed out at the turn of the twentieth century, "the army had advanced in the day time across open country, and ought, with proper vigilance, to have been discovered."[24] Chelmsford failed to find it. By the evening of the twenty-first the Zulu army was resting, waiting for the new moon of the twenty-third. The Zulu did not wish to attack on the twenty-second, for as Stuart's informant Mpatshana later said, "it was not customary to fight [when] . . . the moon had waned."[25]

By the time the Seventh Cavalry reached the deserted sun dance camp on June 24, it had advanced forty-five miles up the Rosebud. It traveled slowly along the east bank until it reached Muddy Creek, where Custer called the noon halt. Just above Muddy Creek the Indian trail signs seemed to be changing, and Custer extended the halt to four hours to interpret the variation. A well-defined trail, broken periodically by a large campsite, no longer existed. Instead, "the valley was now covered from one side to the other with innumerable lodge-pole trails, and campgrounds appeared in profusion. And many of the signs were suddenly much fresher. It was puzzling."[26] Custer, fearing that the village might be scattering, ordered his scouts to pay close attention to any diverging trails. When his scout George Herendeen reported spotting a trail splitting off to the left at Muddy Creek, Custer dispatched Lieutenant Charles Varnum with a party of Arikaras to investigate. Herendeen wrote in 1878 that "Custer said he did not want to lose any of the lodges, and if any of them left the main trail he wanted to know."[27]

Custer's regiment moved out at 5 P.M. and in less than three hours reached Busby Bend, the site at which Crow scouts had recently discovered evidence of the next major Indian encampment. At 9 P.M. the Crow scouts returned to report that the village had not scattered, but had crossed the divide into the Little Bighorn valley. They also reported the existence of a promontory at the divide called Crow's Nest, from which they might catch sight of the village at dawn, on June 25. Custer ordered Varnum to accompany a contingent of scouts to Crow's Nest. The Seventh, he told Varnum, would move out at 11 P.M. to be near the scouting party by morning. Varnum wrote to his father two weeks later: "At 2:30 o'clock we reached the hill, and lay there in scrub bushes until daybreak, when we discovered the smoke of a village, and by 5 A.M., I started the Rees [i.e., Arikaras] back with a dispatch to General Custer. The Crows said there were about two or three thousand ponies on the plain twelve miles off, but I could not see them."[28] Mitch Boyer told George Herendeen that "it was the biggest village he had ever seen."[29]

Shortly after leaving with Varnum's note the scouts espied two mounted Sioux to the west, gave chase, yet failed to engage them. Upon arriving in camp Red Star handed the note to Custer and sat down for breakfast. Custer read the note, nodded, and then assembled the scouts in haste to accompany him to Crow's Nest. Red Star scrambled to his mount, kicking over his coffee, and joined Custer.[30] At Crow's Nest Custer peered in the distance but, unlike his scouts, could not make out the Indian village. While he was scanning the distant terrain the scouts informed Custer that his regiment had been detected by Sioux spies. According to Red Star, Custer responded that "this camp has not seen our army, none of their scouts have seen us." When contradicted by another Crow Custer apparently shouted angrily, "I say again we have not been seen."[31] Edgar Stewart, who has written one of the most authoritative works on the Little Bighorn battle, argues that "there can be little doubt that both Sioux and Cheyenne warriors watched the command from the time it left the camp at the mouth of the Rosebud."[32] Custer raced back to the main command and upon arrival received three independent reports that the regiment had been detected by Sioux. The lieutenant colonel could no longer afford to remain skeptical.

Now that his force had been discovered, Custer believed he must alter plans radically. Terry had ordered Custer to move his command farther south up the Rosebud, yet left him the discretion to adjust that strategy as circumstances dictated. Custer already made one significant adjustment—turning west to follow the Indian trail just above Busby Bend—because he believed that delaying the pursuit, as Terry advised, might give the Sioux time to scatter their village. In modifying Terry's instructions, Custer decided evidently to move his command to some point near the divide, keep it concealed on June 25, and launch a dawn raid on the twenty-sixth. But the new circumstances seemed to require a more expeditious advance; rather than surprising the enemy at daybreak, as he had eight years before at the Battle of the Washita, Custer opted instead for a daylight march and afternoon assault.[33] The Seventh moved out at 11:45 A.M.

Shortly past noon on a very hot Sunday, June 25, Custer halted his regiment and assigned battalions. He placed three troops under Captain Frederick Benteen. In a narrative written fifteen years later, Benteen claims that Custer ordered him to "move to the left to a line of bluffs about 2 miles away. Sending out an officer and a few men as advance guard, to 'pitch in' to anything I came across, and to notify him at once." According to Benteen, Custer subsequently instructed him to continue to the second line of hills and, if no Indians were found, then to the valley. If found there, he should likewise "pitch into" them.[34] Custer assigned three troops to Major Marcus Reno and kept five under his own command. These columns moved respectively toward the left and right banks of the adjacent Middle Fork of Reno Creek. Custer assigned a support column to command the pack train in the rear.

Why did Custer divide his command? Critics argue that Custer acted recklessly—he had yet to identify the strength, temper, or location of the Indians.[35] But obviously, Custer believed the division of his forces would hasten an encounter with the Sioux, his principal objective, not weaken his capacity to fight them. And what *if* Custer had kept his regiment together? Fewer Indians had stopped General George Crook with more troops at the Battle of the Rosebud only one week before.[36]

Benteen's battalion and the pack train with all the spare ammunition (twenty-six thousand rounds) faded quickly from sight, as Custer and Reno trotted on. At 2 P.M. Custer waved Reno's battalion over to join him on the right bank. A few minutes later Custer's scouts spotted a heavy dust cloud four or five miles down the Little Bighorn Valley. "There go your Indians, running like devils," shouted Fred Gerard, an interpreter for the Arikaras. Custer, as well as many of his officers, now became convinced the Sioux were already in flight.[37] While Reno was riding up, Custer told Lieutenant William W. Cooke to order Reno's troops to move ahead to attack the enemy. Gerard and Herendeen later testified that Custer delivered the order to Reno in person. Reno, however, claimed that Cooke delivered the order. In any event, Reno recalled that he was "to move forward at as rapid a gait as he thought prudent, and to charge afterwards and that the whole outfit would support." Giovanni Martini, Custer's orderly, remembered that Custer also told Cooke that "he (Custer) would go down to the other end of the village and drive the hostiles, and that he would have Benteen hurry up and attack the center." [38]

Custer followed Reno for a few paces, then veered to his right. He halted briefly at the North Fork of Reno Creek to water his mounts, and then proceeded a mile and a half along the eastern slope of the bluffs. At this point Custer left his command momentarily to ride up to a promontory on the bluffs. For the first time he saw the Sioux village, "far larger than expected, and extending along the bottom for miles. It numbered nearly a thousand lodges, harboring some two thousand warriors. And it was anything *but* fleeing." [39] Custer dispatched Sergeant Daniel Kanipe to the pack train commander, to bring the train straight across country as hurriedly as possible. He then proceeded another mile to an even higher lookout, and from here could see Reno forming a skirmish line in the valley. At this point Custer may have fulminated, "Where in hell is Benteen?" [40]

Custer singled out Martini to deliver a message directly to Benteen. Martini, an emigrant Italian who had once served as a drummer boy for Garibaldi, still struggled with his English. Therefore, Lieutenant Cooke scribbled the message: "Benteen, come on — big village — be quick — bring packs. P.S. — Bring packs." As Martini galloped away, Custer searched for an expeditious route to the lower end of the Indian village. Around 3:30 P.M. he found Medicine Tail Coulee. At about the same time, Martini later testified, "I was back on the same hill again where the General and I had looked at the village; but before I got there I heard firing back of me, and I looked around and saw Indians, some waving buffalo robes and some shooting. They had been in ambush." [41] Some of the surviving members of Reno's battalion heard firing shortly after 4:20 P.M. But by 4:45 P.M. the fighting ceased. [42] In the space of one hour, the Sioux had annihilated Custer and over two hundred of his troopers in the hills above the Little Bighorn River.

Lord Chelmsford awakened at 1:30 A.M. on January 22 to an alarming message from Dartnell, who had been skirmishing with Matshana's people ten miles to the southeast. Dartnell reported the presence of more than two thousand Zulus in the Nkandhlas several miles past Isipezi Hill. Chelmsford believed the main Zulu army to have finally arrived. He promptly set about devising a plan "on the assumption that the Zulus were where they ought to have been and not where they actually were."[43] This assumption pointed to an unavoidable necessity—the division of his central column. Chelmsford reasoned that

> the reinforcement for Dartnell would be in greater danger than the force left in the camp; it would in all likelihood intercept the main impi before it reached the camp and thus be in action first, and it would have to fight in the open and not in the defensive position at the camp. There were five companies of the 1st/24th Regiment in the camp and seven of the 2nd/24th. . . . He would take the 2nd Battalion out with him and leave the 1st Battalion under Colonel Pulleine in the camp.[44]

Chelmsford decided to reinforce the Isandhlwana camp with Durnford's reserve column at Rorke's Drift, and sent Lieutenant Horace Smith-Dorrien with a message to Durnford telling him "to march to this camp *at once* with all the force you have."[45] The general now believed an attack on the camp by the main Zulu army, an unlikely scenario in his view, could be resisted successfully nonetheless.

Chelmsford, accompanied by Colonel Glyn, led the reinforcement out of camp at 3:30 A.M. Reaching Dartnell two and a half hours later, they found him dismayed. As Lieutenant Harford recalled, the Zulu campfires Dartnell had watched burning throughout the night "were only a blind to mislead us as to their intentions, and the few men that we had seen exposing themselves and moving about had only been left there to make us imagine that the place was occupied by a large force."[46] For the next three hours, the combined forces scouted the Mangeni plain, engaging in sporadic action. Yet the main Zulu force had not been found, so Chelmsford ordered a halt for breakfast. During this halt, a messenger rode up with a note from Colonel Henry Burmester Pulleine: "Staff Officer—Report just come in that the Zulus are advancing in force from left front of the camp. 8.5 A.M."[47]

Chelmsford expressed little concern. He dispatched Lieutenant Berkeley Milne of the Naval Brigade to a nearby hill to scan the Isandhlwana camp by telescope. Milne "reported that he thought the oxen had been moved closer to the encampment, but that everything else appeared normal."[48] Several hours later, when Harford fixed his binoculars on Isandhlwana, he "could only see two tents standing not far from the 'neck,' and these looked partially black as scorched by fire"; he could not see "a living creature of any sort."[49]

Smith-Dorrien delivered Chelmsford's message to Durnford's column around dawn on January 22, having made the perilous night journey, as he later recalled, with "the valour of ignorance." He remained behind briefly to breakfast at the mission station at Rorke's Drift, then, growing restless with the inactivity, gained permission to ride off to join Durnford at Isandhlwana. He arrived in the midst of a discussion between Durnford and Pulleine. "As far as I could make out," Smith-Dorrien recollects, "the gist of Colonels Durnford and Pulleine's discussion was that the former wished to go out and attack the Zulus, whilst the latter argued that his orders were to defend the camp, and that he could not allow his infantry to move out."[50] Prior to Durnford's arrival, a messenger rode into camp reporting large numbers of Zulu approaching from the northeast. Durnford, on the other hand, was receiving seemingly reliable reports that the Zulu were moving eastward to attack Chelmsford.

Chelmsford's military secretary John Crealock later testified to a court of enquiry[51] that Durnford had received specific orders to take command of the camp. In this line of reasoning, Durnford inherited orders from Pulleine to defend the camp and had clearly disobeyed them. Therefore, the blame for the subsequent disaster, at least hypothetically, rested with Durnford. Chelmsford's attempt to blame Durnford for the Isandhlwana defeat was especially ironic. Unlike Chelmsford, Durnford harbored doubts about the justice of the Anglo-Zulu War and had worked tirelessly in the late 1870s to preserve peace.[52] The colonel expressed a patronizing yet sympathetic view of Africans, whom he regarded as "honest, chivalrous, and hospitable."[53] As the war neared, however, Durnford turned his efforts to what he regarded as his soldierly duty. He assembled the Natal Native Horse, a regiment made up of over five hundred Sotho and Ngwane soldiers. Durnford was a kind commander, showing respect for his men and receiving their utmost loyalty. Customarily, British officers commanding Africans at the time admonished their troops with demeaning epithets and punished them with frequent floggings. Durnford scorned such practices.[54]

Furthermore, these accusations against a dead man, made principally to exonerate Chelmsford, contain several flaws. First, Smith-Dorrien, who carried the orders, remembers nothing in them about taking command of the camp—in fact, Crealock later admitted he was mistaken about this. Second, as the senior officer in camp, Durnford automatically assumed command,[55] so the accusation is immaterial. Durnford's decision to venture beyond camp constituted a technical violation of Chelmsford's orders, yet undoubtedly, Durnford believed he remained faithful to their spirit. New circumstances compelled Durnford to deviate from the general's original directives and to take some calculated risks.[56]

At 11 A.M. Durnford sent out Captain George Shepstone with a detachment of the Natal Native Horse to the Nquthu plateau. Durnford followed with several companies of the Natal Native Horse and Natal Native Contingent, as well as a rocket battery. While moving along the high ground, some of Shepstone's troops gave chase to several Zulus herding cattle, pursuing them to the edge of a deep ravine. Peering down from here, the surprised scouting party discovered the main Zulu army — twenty thousand warriors, in total silence, literally covering the floor of the ravine. The Zulu *izinduna* wished to avoid fighting on the twenty-second, yet their discovery by Shepstone's men forced them into action. The umCijo *ibutho* led the charge.[57]

Shepstone, utterly horrified, raced back to camp. When he arrived at Pulleine's tent he was "out of breath and for the moment could only gasp incoherently and point toward the sound of the firing from the invisible forces on the plateau."[58] When he finally managed to blurt out his report, Pulleine remained skeptical that Shepstone had seen the entire Zulu army, believing instead that no more than six hundred Zulus occupied the Nquthu plateau. Nonetheless, Pulleine scribbled a note for Chelmsford and ordered a camp fall-in. The time was 12:15 P.M. Less than two hours later, the camp lay in ruins and all organized resistance to a Zulu attack had ended.

Members of all seven Lakota tribes, along with a large Cheyenne contingent and some Yanktonais, Santees, and Arapahos, resided in the Little Bighorn village on June 25. The Oglala chief Crazy Horse described the composition of the camp circles to a *Chicago Times* reporter a year after the battle. Sitting Bull led the Hunkpapas; Crazy Horse the Oglalas; Fast Bull the Miniconjous; Red Bear the Sans Arcs; Scabby Head the Sihasapas, Brulés, and Two Kettles; and Ice Bear the Cheyennes. The Hunkpapa Black Moon was charged with general direction of the alliance.[59] The village population numbered over seven thousand.[60]

The Sioux and Cheyennes detected Custer's movement along the bluffs, the division of his command, and his descent into Medicine Tail Coulee, which provided them time to plot strategy in countering the impending attack.[61] They seem, however, not to have anticipated Reno's assault on the upper end of the village. When the dust cloud from upriver gave Reno's position away, panic swept through the Hunkpapa camp:

> Old men were yelling advice, young men dashing away to catch their horses, women and children rushing off afoot and on horseback to the north end of that three-mile camp, fleeing from the soldiers. They left their tents standing, grabbed their babies, called their older children, and hurried away, frightened girls shrinking under their shawls, matrons puffing for breath, hobbling old women, wrinkled and peering, with their sticks, making off as best they could, crying children, lost children, dogs getting in everybody's way and being kicked for their pains, nervous horses resisting the tug of the reins, and over all the sound of shooting." [62]

Gall, a Hunkpapa headman, led a small force of Hunkpapas and Sihasapas out to meet Reno's three companies. When Reno encountered the Sioux he ordered his troops to dismount and form a skirmish line. As Reno later testified, "they were running toward me in swarms and from all directions. I saw I must defend myself and give up the attack mounted. This I did." [63] In all likelihood, Reno encountered less than a fourth of all warriors in the Little Bighorn village.[64] The Sioux routed Reno's troops, forcing the survivors back across the river into the bluffs. Surviving Sioux then sped downriver to join in the fight against Custer. Low Dog told Colonel Nelson Miles in 1878 that "if Reno and his warriors had fought as Custer and his warriors fought, the battle might have [gone] against us." [65]

Most of the warriors prepared for Custer. Crow King led several hundred followers across the Bighorn and up the gully to the south. Crazy Horse led the main body of Oglalas and Cheyennes farther downriver, fording just below the Cheyenne camp circle, moving up a long coulee to outflank Custer from the north. Black Moon, joined by Gall, positioned a force at the ford opposite Medicine Tail Coulee.[66] Whether at this point, as Gall claimed, the Sioux moved to intercept Custer about a half mile up the bed of the coulee,[67] or whether Custer proceeded all the way to the ford, is a matter of historical debate. It does seem probable, based on the testimony of Custer's Crow scouts, that his command was at least moving down the coulee with the intention of crossing the river.[68]

Having met such unanticipated resistance, Custer's command turned to its right, moving toward higher ground and a more defensible position. Brave Wolf, a Cheyenne chief, told George Bird Grinnell that Custer's "soldiers began to retreat up the narrow gulch . . . shooting well and fighting hard, but there were so many people around them that they could not help being killed. They . . . kept fighting and falling from their horses — fighting and falling. . . . I think all their horses had been killed before they got to the top of the hill." [69] As Custer's command approached the ridge, Crazy Horse's force struck unexpectedly from the north. Two Moon, part of this group, recalled that "the smoke was like a great cloud, and everywhere the Sioux went the dust rose like smoke. We circled all round them — swirling like water round a stone. We shoot, we ride fast, we shoot again." [70]

In addition to bows, arrows, knives, and hatchets, the Sioux and Cheyennes fought with forty-two different kinds of firearms, including a number of .44/40-caliber Model 1873 Winchester repeating rifles. [71] Custer's command fought with Springfield single-shot carbines and Colt six-shot revolvers. The Springfield carbine, plagued by a faulty extractor, often jammed after the second or third firing. The problem apparently beset Custer's troops at the Little Bighorn fight. According to Gall, "the soldiers got shells stuck in their guns and had to throw them away." [72] In addition to their superior numbers, the Indians probably outgunned Custer's command. Recent ballistic studies at the Custer Battlefield National Monument by archaeologists reveal that Sioux and Cheyennes circled at will about relatively stationary soldiers, overrunning one position after another. [73]

After Custer's command had been annihilated, a number of warriors turned upriver. Until noon on June 26 they lay siege to Reno's entrenched troops, now reinforced by Benteen's and the pack train, at what later became known as Reno Hill. Crow King thought the Sioux "could have cut Reno's command to pieces" had it not been for Sitting Bull. Sitting Bull told his warriors to "let them go. . . . We did not want to fight. Long Hair [i.e., Custer] sent us word that he was coming to fight us, and we had to defend ourselves and our wives and children." [74] They also retreated from Reno Hill because of word that soldiers (Terry and Gibbon's columns) were advancing up the Little Bighorn. By late afternoon the village had been dismantled and the grass in the valley set afire. By sunset Reno's men could see the Sioux and their allies moving upriver toward the Bighorn Mountains in one vast column:

> That the [Sioux] showed no desire to stay and fight Terry was not surprising. They had had enough fighting for one summer. Their defeat of Crook, their great success in the battle with Custer, and the immense amount of plunder they had taken seem to have satisfied

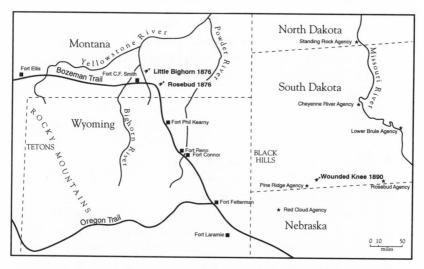

Map 1. U.S.-Sioux War, 1876. Adapted from James Gump, "The Subjugation of the Zulus and Sioux: A Comparative Study," *Western Historical Quarterly* 19, no. 1 (January 1988): 24.

them. They had fought hard, and now they wished to be let alone, to dance and feast, to gloat over the plunder, and to quarrel over its division. Occupied with these ideas they left the Little Bighorn and headed for the mountains, seeking seclusion and a period of freedom from military annoyance.[75]

Unfortunately for the Sioux, once the shock of Custer's debacle turned to anger, the Army would redouble its efforts to rid the Powder River country of all "hostiles." Consequently, the Lakota triumph at Little Bighorn was followed by a rapid descent into economic marginality and political impotence.

On the day of the Isandhlwana fight, the Zulu deployed twelve *ama-butho* in a vast crescent, with the intention of encircling the camp. The left horn, made up of the Ngobomakhosi, uMbonambi, and uVe, moved across the plain to envelop the British right flank. The right horn, consisting of the uDududu, uNokhenke and uNodwengu, moved along and behind the high ground to the north to the rear of the mountain, seeking to cut off any retreat across the saddle. The center, which included the umCijo, uMbonambi, and umXhapho, moved down the escarpment toward the British center. The *izinduna* held the uThulwana, uDloko, and inDluyengwe in reserve, following behind the right horn. Ntshin-gwayo and Mavumengwana commanded the force. Their troops pos-sessed short-hafted broad-bladed spears, cowhide shields, wooden clubs, and a few relatively ineffective firearms. The Zulu had imported thou-sands of guns through Delagoa Bay over the previous two decades, most of them low-quality muzzle-loaders, but had not effectively incorporated this weaponry into their style of warfare. The distance from the point of their detection on the Nquthu plateau to the camp was five miles; the Zulu army ran the distance to engage the British forces.[76]

Pulleine formed his troops into an angled line, placing three compa-nies on a north-facing side, three companies on an east-facing side, and two companies of the Natal Native Contingent at the angle. Durnford, who learned of the movement of the Zulu left horn when he was three miles east of camp, began a perilous withdrawal. He retreated to a donga (a dried-up water course) and turned his men around to hold up the ad-vance of the Zulu left. The attack of the Zulu center and left stalled under British fire, yet resumed by 1 P.M.[77] Smith-Dorrien, who escaped the en-suing disaster, wrote that the advance of the Zulu line "was a marvelous sight, line upon line of men in slightly extended order, one behind the other, . . . bearing all before them."[78]

The umCijo advanced against the angle. The three hundred mem-bers of the Natal Native Contingent positioned there possessed only thirty firearms among them. In contrast, each British infantry soldier was equipped with a Martini-Henry breech-loading single-shot rifle, fitted with a triangular sword bayonet. Britain adopted Martini-Henrys in 1869, taking advantage of the gun technology made available by the "breech-loader revolution" of the 1860s. The British weapon was faster and far more accurate and durable than the previous generation of firearms—a dazzling testament to industrial technology.[79] Nonetheless, the effective-ness of all firearms deteriorated steadily because of the activity back at the supply wagons. Quartermasters jealously guarded ammunition packets for their own battalions; on two occasions, for example, Durnford's des-perate requests for ammunition were denied, and his runners told to find their own supplier. Furthermore, soldiers lacked enough screwdrivers to open the tightly strapped ammunition boxes. Chelmsford had requisi-tioned spare screwdrivers for such a contingency, but the order fell victim to bureaucratic inertia.[80] As a result, ammunition supplies became dear.

As umCijo advanced yelling the war cry "Usuthu," the poorly armed Natal Native Contingent broke and fled, leaving a three hundred yard hole in Pulleine's wedge. UmCijo charged forward into the gap, killing

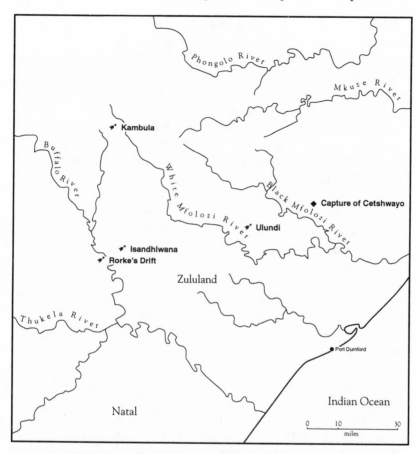

Map 2. Anglo-Zulu War, 1879. Adapted from Sonia Clarke, ed., *Zululand at War, 1879* (Johannesburg: Brenthurst Press, 1984), p. 172.

many British troopers before they had time to fix bayonets. The right horn continued its wide sweeping movement, and the left horn began to outflank Durnford, forcing him back on the camp. He died trying to hold open a line of retreat to Rorke's Drift. Pulleine perished after handing the Queen's Colour of the First Battalion of the Twenty-fourth Regiment to Lieutenant Teignmouth Melvill. By late afternoon the Isandhlwana camp lay in smoldering ruins and the Zulu reserve, under the command of Dabulamanzi, was proceeding toward Rorke's Drift.[81] The British death toll—1,329 men—represented for the British the greatest military catastrophe since the Crimean War.[82]

For the Zulu, Isandhlwana constituted a Pyrrhic victory. The death toll likely exceeded 1,000, and as Mpatshana of the Ngobomakhosi *ibutho* later said, "the wounded were very numerous from Isandhlwana."[83] Cetshwayo told a reporter from *MacMillan's Magazine* in 1880 that the Zulu "army that had fought at Isandhlwana had lost very heavily. It remained encamped close to the battle field for three days, chiefly owing to the large numbers of the wounded."[84]

Hours after the Isandhlwana battle, approximately four thousand Zulu warriors under the command of Dabulamanzi, Cetshwayo's half brother, attacked the mission station at Rorke's Drift. Situated on the Natal side of the Mzinyathi or Buffalo River, Rorke's Drift had been the original supply base for the central British column. Lieutenant John Chard of the Royal Engineers commanded the post on January 22. The camp consisted of a hospital, storehouse, cattle kraal, and 140 troopers, over thirty of them incapacitated.[85]

Dabulamanzi led the uThulwana, uDloko, and inDluyengwe regiments in the military engagement with the British at Rorke's Drift, but in doing so violated Cetshwayo's order not to attack inside Natal. In defense of this strategy, the Zulu king argued that "it is the whites who have come to fight with me in my own country and not I that go to fight with them."[86] Furthermore, because the British succeeded in constructing a defensive perimeter prior to the Zulu assault at Rorke's Drift, Dabulamanzi's forces could anticipate heavy casualties from the concentrated firepower of British rifles.

The battle raged for ten hours, ending at dawn on January 23 following a Zulu withdrawal. Dabulamanzi ordered a retreat after a series of futile offensive charges that left over half his army dead or wounded. "The Zulus died in heaps there," observed Magema Fuze, "killed by those white men in the building. They went on killing them until dawn, and in the early morning the Zulus withdrew defeated, leaving behind heaps of dead on the ground."[87] Chard's forces, bolstered by Martini-Henry breech-loading rifles and ample supplies of ammunition, sustained fifteen deaths. In recognition of their valiant defense at Rorke's Drift, Chard and ten of his men each received a Victoria Cross, the highest honor to be bestowed on a British soldier in the late nineteenth century.

In the aftermath of Rorke's Drift, the Zulu people could expect Britain to dispatch troop reinforcements to South Africa, bringing with them the mechanized destructive power of an industrial state. Short of sabotaging British supply lines, which the Zulu never tried, Cetshwayo's army could not compete. In contrast to the well-supplied British military, the Zulu

1. *Dabulamanzi, Brother of King Cetewayo, Commander of the Zulu Army at Isandhlwana.* In *The Illustrated London News*, vol. 74, 12 April 1879, p. 333. N. 2288 b. 6. Courtesy the Bodleian Library, University of Oxford.

army often faced starvation during the war.[88] The Zulu "were merely an *armed people*," the bishop of Natal wrote in 1880, "not a 'standing army.'"[89] Consequently, although the British might regard Rorke's Drift as their Thermopylae or Alamo,[90] to the Zulu, this battle marked the first stage in their road to national ruin.

The battles of Little Bighorn and Isandhlwana bear a number of similarities. In each conflict, armies considered inferior made use of superior tactics, numbers, and in the case of the Sioux, weapons, to crush the adversary. The western armies, in each instance, counted on the military support of indigenous collaborators—the United States relied on Crow, Pawnee, and Arikara scouts and the British made extensive use of African troops.[91] Officers divided their commands in each encounter, thus weakening their forces in the face of an enemy of unknown strength and inviting a multitude of retrospective criticism. Finally, in both situations, officers failed to exercise adequate reconnaissance and thereby seriously misjudged the size, strength, location, and temper of the enemy.

In addition, by scoring such unlikely victories, the Zulu and Sioux each passed quickly into popular culture as the quintessential "noble savages." Stripped of this romantic imagery, however, the aftermath of victory was anything but glamorous for these indigenous societies. On July 4, 1879, Chelmsford's forces burned Ulundi and banished Cetshwayo to Robben Island by the end of the year. The British did not annex Zululand until 1887; in the meantime, the Zulu people experienced civil war, partition, and the death of their king. By early 1877 the U.S. Army had scattered recalcitrant Sioux bands, Crazy Horse surrendered at Red Cloud Agency in May of that year, and Sitting Bull capitulated at Fort Buford, Montana, in July 1881. During the 1880s the Lakotas withstood a concentrated assault on their political system, culture, and land resources, culminating in the Wounded Knee disaster in December 1890.

Shortly after Isandhlwana, a British newspaper asserted that the Zulu should be forced to "pay dearly for their triumph of a day,"[92] and like the Sioux, so they did. Ironically, these societies "paid" for defending their independence and for wars initiated by their adversaries. Why did the United States and Great Britain prosecute wars against the Zulu and Sioux in the first place? What does a comparison of these wars and their aftermath tell us about the nature of Anglo-American imperialism? The remaining chapters seek to answer these questions by comparing the historical transformations of the Zulu and Sioux and the processes of interaction between these groups and whites in the nineteenth century.

C H A P T E R 2

Frontiers of Expansion

 T Little Bighorn and Isandhlwana, the United States and Great Britain fought expansionist societies that had waged successful wars of conquest in the past. Conquered enemies feared the Zulu and Sioux for their militarism and despised them for their ruthlessness. Why did these societies follow an aggressive course? What accounts for their successful expansion? In film, fiction, and popular history, the Zulu and Sioux are portrayed traditionally as the prototypes of martial virtuosity among "primitive" peoples, the "noblest of savages."[1] In these characterizations, warfare need not be explained because it is taken to be a "natural" condition—the Zulu and Sioux, inherently "bloodthirsty," apparently thought of war as a sport and excelled at it.

Such popular stereotypes are misleading. The Sioux and Zulu arrived at positions of predominance because of their success in controlling livestock, land, trading rights, and people. Wars for conquest were motivated principally by these practical considerations, not driven by aggressive instincts. Their success in this respect rested on significant socioeconomic transformations in the seventeenth and eighteenth centuries: the Sioux adapted their traditional institutions to an equestrian buffalo-hunting economy, and the Zulu modified their traditional circumcision sets into multifunctional age-set regiments. For the Zulu, these transformations were accompanied by a process of political centralization that culminated in Shaka's Zulu kingdom by the mid-1820s. In contrast, the Sioux experienced political decentralization during their movement onto the prairies in the seventeenth and eighteenth centuries. Some political consolidation occurred during the nineteenth century, but only *after* the Lakota had achieved predominance in the northern central plains. The remainder of the chapter examines the pre-nineteenth-century history of the Sioux and the Zulu.

The Lakotas or Tetons represent the largest division of the Dakota people. *Lakota* refers literally to a dialect of the Dakota language. *Teton* derives from *t'inta t'unwan*, "prairie dwellers." The Dakotas, the largest division of the Siouan-speaking peoples, became known popularly as the Sioux to Europeans in the seventeenth century. *Sioux* is a French corruption of the Chippewa word *Natowesiwck*, which means "snakes" or "adders."[2] In recent history the term *Sioux* has become identified with the Tetons, yet it remains synonymous with *Dakota.*[3]

According to the oldest Dakota traditions, the Lakotas formed the western division of seven gentes or "council fires."[4] The number seven is sacred to the Lakotas and represents an ideal understanding of how their society should be classified.[5] During their expansion into the northern central plains, for example, the Teton divided themselves into seven sub-bands: the Oglalas, Brulés, Miniconjous, Hunkpapas, Sans Arcs, Two Kettles, and Sihasapas. The seven council fires were governed by hereditary chieftaincy, and of the seven, the Mdewakanton, members of the eastern or Santee division, occupied a position of primacy. Even after the Lakotas became autonomous plains dwellers, they continued to pay deference to the eastern Sioux.[6] In earlier times the Sioux inhabited the central Ohio Valley region.[7] By the time of French contact in the second half of the seventeenth century, the Dakotas occupied the forests of central Minnesota.

The earliest French accounts suggest that the Dakotas gathered wild rice and hunted forest animals such as beaver and deer, yet also roamed the plains periodically to hunt buffalo. The French traders Pierre-Esprit Radisson and Jean-Baptiste Grosseliers, for example, the first white men actually to visit the Sioux around 1660, referred to them as "the Nation of the beefe."[8] Approximately forty years later, the trader Pierre-Charles Le Sueur distinguished the "Sioux of the West" from the "Sioux of the East." He described the Tetons, representatives of the western Sioux, as "wandering and without villages," living "only by the hunt," and roaming the prairies between the Mississippi and Missouri rivers.[9] In Le Sueur's time, however, the western Sioux did not wander about the prairies indefinitely. During the winter they returned to the forests to hunt beaver, and in the spring exchanged beaver pelts for firearms and ammunition.[10]

The migratory economy that Le Sueur identifies with the western Sioux had probably become institutionalized by the late seventeenth century as a result of two interrelated factors: (1) increasing warfare over hunting territories with the armed Cree and Assiniboin peoples to the northeast, and (2) the ecological and economic transformations catalyzed by the European demand for furs. The historian Gary Anderson argues that this trade

> acted as a stimulant in the western Great Lakes region creating insatiable highs and inevitable withdrawals. The reasons for these cyclical extremes were closely tied to expanding and contracting European markets as well as colonial wars that cut all western trade lines. During periods when traders increased their efforts, the Sioux pursued prime furs such as beaver and martin, animals found in a woodland environment. Depression, on the other hand, produced native disenchantment and undoubtedly encouraged migration away from the trader's rendezvous to the plains where buffalo offered an abundant food resource.[11]

The fur trade, which resulted in the Tetons' mounting stock of firearms, made them a formidable power by the second half of the seventeenth century. Father Allouez wrote in the mid-1660s that the Sioux "have conducted hostilities against all their enemies, by whom they are held in extreme fear." [12] The Lakotas used this technological advantage in two ways: to keep their northern forest opponents, the Crees and Assiniboines, at bay, and to dominate the unarmed, sedentary horticultural villagers of southwestern Minnesota, the Iowas, Otoes, and Cheyennes. Such domination not only allowed the Tetons to open additional buffalo-hunting territories, but it also enabled them to procure a new commodity for the European market — slaves. When demand for furs slackened periodically, the Sioux raided their neighbors for captives. Europeans had little use for buffalo hides at this time, but would trade for slaves. Thus, according to the historian Frank Secoy, "raiding for captives became an important economic adjunct that, unlike beaver hunting, did not interfere with a progressive adaptation to Plains life." [13]

During the first half of the eighteenth century the Tetons continued to hunt, trap, raid, and trade, while journeying ever westward into the prairies east of the Missouri. They returned east each spring to gather with the eastern Dakotas in large trade fairs at the Blue Earth River. The fairs later shifted to the James River, farther west in eastern central South Dakota. Here they exchanged pelts for firearms, ammunition, knives, needles, and cloth, which the eastern Dakota had obtained from European traders. During the summer they returned to the prairies, following the buffalo. In the course of their pursuits, the Sioux encountered horses. These animals, which had come to the northern plains from the Spanish Southwest, later revolutionized the Sioux buffalo-hunting economy. Temporarily, however, an equestrian lifestyle helped establish a balance of power in the Missouri Valley.[14]

The populous horticultural peoples of the Missouri valley had obtained horses as well as metal weapons from the Southwest by the early eighteenth century. Mounted Omaha, Arikara, Mandan, and Hidatsa villagers, who also fortified their villages with moats and ramparts, defended themselves reasonably well against Teton incursions. George Hyde describes the Oglalas and Brulés in the mid-eighteenth century as "poor people afoot in the vast plains." They "came to the Missouri in a hard season," he writes, "to beg at the Arikara towns."[15] The Lakotas probably obtained their first horses from the Arikaras in peaceful trade. Unfortunately, such cordial reciprocity did not prevail. According to their winter counts, the Lakotas organized their first mounted war party in 1757–58, likely to steal horses from the Arikaras.[16] The "Teton Sioux was always a hardy beggar, with nothing humble about him; and if these people came to the Arikaras one day to beg, they returned on another day to waylay the Arikaras and kill them."[17]

The adoption of the horse improved the Lakotas' military technique and proved to be a boon to their economy. But two other factors upset the military equilibrium of the Missouri Valley: the new Missouri River trade, centered in St. Louis, and the smallpox epidemics of the late eighteenth century. French and Spanish traders in the late eighteenth century opened the Missouri to a flourishing trade in buffalo robes, deer skins, bear hides, buffalo tongues, and tallow. This market, which assured the Tetons a steady supply of guns and ammunition, gradually replaced their pelt trade through the Great Lakes and Montreal. The Sioux now prosecuted wars against their western neighbors to support their equestrian buffalo-hunting existence, securing "horses and hunting grounds sufficient to support a population that was growing rapidly."[18]

While the Lakota population increased, that of their horticultural neighbors collapsed. The Arikaras, Mandans, and Hidatsas suffered grievously from the smallpox epidemics of the 1770s and 1780s, reducing the populations of these village peoples by as much as four-fifths. The French trader Jean-Baptiste Truteau, for example, reported in 1795 that thirty-two populous Arikara villages had been reduced to two.[19] The Tetons, because of their mobility, escaped the ravages of the disease and, by the 1790s, broke the power of these village groups. Writing at the turn of

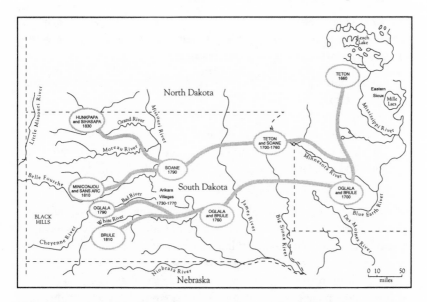

Map 3. Migrations of the Teton Sioux, c. 1600–1800. Adapted from George Hyde, *Red Cloud's Folk: A History of the Oglala Sioux Indians* (Norman: University of Oklahoma Press, 1937; revised ed., 1957), p. 319.

the nineteenth century, the French explorer Pierre-Antoine Tabeau described the Sioux as openly pillaging the plains "without anyone opposing them except by complaints and feeble reproaches." The Tetons used their military superiority to control the flow of European goods to the upper Missouri villagers and thus relegated their sedentary neighbors to a state of dependency. According to Tabeau, the Arikaras had become to the Tetons "a certain kind of serf, who cultivates for them and who, as they say, takes, for them, the place of women." [20]

By the time of the Lewis and Clark expedition in 1804–6, the Lakotas dominated the upper Missouri and contested the prairies between the Missouri and the Black Hills with the Kiowas, Arapahos, Crows, and Cheyennes.[21] President Jefferson, who recognized the "immense power" of the Tetons, urged Lewis and Clark "to make a friendly impression" on the Sioux "because we learn they are very desirous of being on the most friendly terms with us." Captains Lewis and Clark doubted Teton friendliness,[22] if not their "immense power," yet recognized that delicate diplomacy was essential in breaking the Sioux monopoly over the upper Missouri trade.[23] Following a testy confrontation with Black Buffalo's Brulé

Sioux in September 1804, the American explorers recognized clearly that their diplomacy had failed. While camped at Fort Mandan in the winter of 1804–5, Clark reflected ominously on that encounter:

> [The Tetons] are the vilest miscreants of the savage race, and must ever remain the pirates of the Missouri, until such measures are pursued, by our government, as will make them feel a dependence on its will for their supply of merchandise. Unless these people are reduced to order, by coercive measures, I am ready to pronounce that the citizens of the United States can never enjoy but partially the advantages which the Missouri presents.[24]

At the time Clark recorded his vituperative commentary on the Sioux, the northern Nguni-speaking peoples of pre-Shakan Zululand were engaged in open warfare in a conflict that eventually gave rise to the Zulu kingdom. Prior to the Zulu king Shaka kaSenzangakhona (c. 1787–1828), however, *Zulu* referred strictly to a relatively small clan of people living in the middle reaches of the White Mfolozi River. When Shaka founded the Zulu kingdom in the early nineteenth century, he extended the use of *Zulu* to the many clans he incorporated into the Zulu state. Hence, one cannot use the term *Zulu* in any rigid definitional sense, but only, as the historian Jeff Guy suggests, in "convenient descriptive terms."[25]

In the pre-Shakan era the Zulu were one of many chiefdoms bounded on the north by the Phongolo River, on the south by the Thukela River, on the west by the Drakensberg Mountains, and on the east by the Indian Ocean. A number of scholars have devised specific genealogies for the peoples who came to inhabit Zululand, yet all these accounts lack historical validity.[26] In fact, many of the ethnic divisions that represent concrete reality in Africa today did not exist before the end of the nineteenth century. According to the historian Patrick Harries, European experts who "descended on the continent" at the beginning of the colonial era attempted to classify African societies according to an evolutionist epistemology. "Homogeneity replaced heterogeneity; unity and reason replaced disunity and confusion. This belief in the modernizing rationality of science," he suggests, "was strongly to structure the way in which future generations made sense of African society."[27] In South Africa, the Department of Native Affairs launched a systematic effort to differentiate African "tribes" in 1925. Its stated purpose was to promote "the smooth and harmonious administration of tribal affairs and . . . the prevention of friction."[28]

The best that can be said on the origins of the "Zulu" people is "that the historically known African societies of the region emerged locally from long-established ancestral communities of diverse origins and of heterogeneous cultures and languages."[29] Certainly by the time of European contact in the sixteenth century, the pre-Shakan peoples were farming and herding and living in village homesteads ruled by chiefs. The Portuguese chronicler João Baptista Lavanha, of the shipwrecked *Santo Alberto*, described the region immediately south of Zululand in 1593 as heavily populated and prosperous. In Lavanha's account, the inhabitants cultivated millet, "from which cakes and wine are produced," and tended cattle that were "very fat, tender, well-flavoured, and large, the pastures being very rich." They also manufactured iron implements and valued iron and copper. "For very small pieces of either [metal]," he said, "they will barter cattle, which is what they most prize, and with cattle they drive their trade and commerce." As Lavanha put it, "cattle forms their treasure."[30] In 1589 the Portuguese chronicler Diogo do Couto described the inhabitants of pre-Shakan Zululand as having no kings, "but all is in the possession of chiefs . . . who are heads and rulers of three, four, or five villages."[31]

Between the sixteenth and nineteenth centuries the pre-Shakan peoples also traded ivory and cattle with Europeans at Delagoa Bay, and in return received brass, beads, and by the time of Shaka, macassar oil. Whereas the control of trade and acquisition of firearms played a major role in Teton expansion, trade constituted a less significant factor in the formation of the Zulu kingdom, although, in the words of Elizabeth Eldredge, "it served as a source of wealth which powerful people were able to control and manipulate to increase their own sway," hence stimulating "the emergence of socio-economic inequalities."[32] First, the goods received in the exchange contributed to the prestige of chiefly groups, though they lacked the compulsion of the gun. Second, the pre-Shakan economy pivoted around the production of cattle and crops. The option to exploit trading opportunities meant an agricultural economy capable of sustaining the increased demands placed upon it. Only those pre-Shakan chiefdoms capable of producing more crops and cattle could engage in trade.[33] Trade contributed to economic growth and political consolidation, but one must also look to the dynamics of agricultural production in understanding the origins of the Zulu kingdom.

Zululand is divided between the fertile lowlands and major river valleys (*zantsi*) and the less fertile uplands (*enhla*).[34] Unlike the uplands, the coastal plain has soils of high natural fertility. The Phongolo, Mfolozi, and Mhlatuze floodplains, extending inland for a considerable distance, contain alluvial soils and are of high natural fertility as well. The period of fallow in the pre-Shakan era corresponded to the relative fertility of each region. *Zantsi* peoples might have short or no fallow, whereas *enhla* groups might fallow their fields for up to twenty years.

Pre-Shakan farmers adjusted to these conditions by adopting cereals with different production and harvesting characteristics. Before 1700 the most important staples were millet and sorghum. Of the two, sorghum is the more drought-resistant. It matures relatively quickly and is capable of surviving short rainy seasons. Millet is capable of flourishing in infertile soils as well, matures in eight to nine months, and can survive extended periods of drought. Sorghum probably represented the most important cereal in Zululand prior to the mid-eighteenth century.[35] By the end of the century, maize, a more nutritious yet less versatile cereal, likely replaced or at least coexisted with millet and sorghum in many parts of Zululand.[36]

The homestead (*umuzi*, pl. *imizi*) served as the principal pre-Shakan production community. Any characterization of a "typical" pre-Shakan homestead belies regional, local, and social variations,[37] but such a site usually consisted of a circle of dwellings built around a cattle enclosure. A male homestead head managed the community, which included his wife or wives and their children, his younger brothers and their wives and children, his mother, and unrelated dependents. The married women and their daughters managed the cycle of crop production, from digging, planting, and weeding to harvesting, threshing, and storing. This prodigious workload convinced a European castaway that pre-Shakan women did "all the work."[38]

According to Jeff Guy, "cereal production was not only fundamental to the existence of [pre-capitalist southern African] societies, but absorbed massive amounts of labour time dominating not only the productive processes, but profoundly affecting social life generally."[39] Crop production, however, represented only part of pre-Shakan agriculture — by the early nineteenth century, cattle likely exceeded the human population of Zululand[40] and played a more vital role in the agricultural economy. Cows, tended by boys and young men, served as a vital subsistence resource. More importantly, cattle represented the "materialisation of human labour." According to Guy, "the movement of cattle . . . in exchange for women, as tribute, gifts, or to establish clients, was in fact the movement of expended labour and potential labour power."[41]

Successful cattle keeping in pre-Shakan Zululand required a variety of grassland ecologies. Sourveld predominated in the coastal regions and highlands, mixed grasses occupied most of the higher areas of the transitional zone, and sweetveld grew in the drier lowlands of the major river valleys. To successfully exploit this grazing potential, herders shifted their stock among a variety of the pastures when land was available. In the spring, herders moved cattle to the sour mountain grasslands. During the summer and fall, herds moved to the transitional areas of mixed grasses. And in the dry winter months, cattle moved to the lowlands to take advantage of the palatable yet delicate sweetveld. Fresh springs, normally plentiful throughout Zululand, enabled herdsmen to move their cattle within a twenty-mile radius in periods of normal rainfall, and slightly farther in times of drought.[42]

Cultures can accommodate a range of ecological conditions over the expectable limits of variation. If those limits are exceeded, however, significant cultural transformations can occur, as the Lakotas would find in their adaptation to an equestrian buffalo-hunting economy. The peoples of the Zululand uplands, much like the Tetons in Minnesota, experienced such limits by the late seventeenth century. The archaeologist Martin Hall argues that "the terminal Iron Age population of the [uplands] had far exceeded the capacity of the high grasslands to support livestock and . . . as a result, the independent status of the economic system in this area must have been sacrificed for the sake of a reliance on valley or coastal winter grazing."[43]

The Hlubi chiefdom represented the major upland polity in pre-Shakan Zululand—by one estimate, the Hlubi numbered 250,000 in 1800.[44] Faced with an ecological crisis, the Hlubi gained control over additional territory in the eighteenth century. However, unlike the political consolidation of the major lowland chiefdoms of this era—the Ndwandwe, Mthethwa, and Qwabe—Hlubi expansion was not accompanied by major social change. Instead, it helped *provoke* the social changes that led eventually to the Zulu kingdom. How did such a process occur?

In all likelihood, the Hlubi made a number of ecological adjustments to the difficult upland environment in the pre-Shakan era, each one postponing disaster a bit longer. By the eighteenth century the Hlubi may have sought more promising winter grazing in the eastern lowlands. To their misfortune, the strategy backfired. Instead of abating their economic vulnerability they aggravated it. In response to Hlubi incursions, lowland chiefdoms such as the Mthethwa, Qwabe, and others transformed themselves for better defense and productivity. Their response was initially defensive and therefore transformational—rather than sending herds over wider areas, *zantsi* chiefs worked human labor harder. They

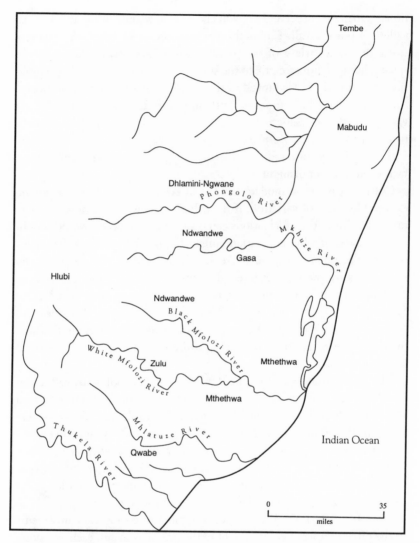

Map 4. Pre-Shakan Chiefdoms, c. 1800. Adapted from David Hedges, "Trade and Politics in Southern Mozambique and Zululand, c. 1750–1830" (D. Phil. Thesis, University of London, 1978), p. 188.

gained greater control over the productive and reproductive potential of men and women—the most significant feature, as will be seen, of the emerging *amabutho* system.[45]

Consequently, Hlubi access to adequate winter grazing eroded steadily during the eighteenth century. The Hlubi, in response, adopted an offensive strategy, expanding southward along the foothills of the Drakensberg. This process was nontransforming, in that it replicated existing strategies over wider areas.[46] The Hlubi did not significantly reorganize their circumcision sets, for example, and they paid dearly for it. The Ngwane attacked them in 1822, confiscated their cattle, and killed eighty thousand Hlubi men, women, and children.[47] In the words of the Hlubi informant Mabonsa kaSidhlayi, "the whole Hlubi tribe collapsed like the breaking of a bottle to atoms."[48]

In contrast, a number of lowland chiefdoms adopted age-set regiments during the eighteenth century.[49] Jobe organized two *amabutho* on the basis of age during his rule over the Mthethwa in the second half of the eighteenth century.[50] Informants to the Natalian civil magistrate James Stuart reported that two age-based *amabutho* existed among Khondlo's (1753–1813) Qwabe, and were used by Khondlo's son, Phakathwayo (d. 1818), who formed five of them. Magaye (d. 1829), leader of the Cele, organized five age regiments; Zwide (d. 1824) of the Ndwandwe had four; and Matiwane (d. 1828) of the Ngwane used three age-based *amabutho*.[51]

What advantage did pre-Shakan chiefs gain by forming these disciplined age sets? The *amabutho* system, above all, augmented chiefly authority over human labor. Guy argues that "the social principle upon which South African pre-capitalist societies were founded" was "the continuous acquisition, creation, control, and appropriation of labour power." Such "labour power was realised by men through the exchange of cattle for the productive and reproductive capacities of women." In effect, then, the transfer of cattle from the husband's father's homestead to the wife's father's homestead represented "a transfer of *labour power*: the labour power of the wife herself in the homestead and the land attached to the homestead, and the labour power of the children which she produced as a wife and mother."[52]

The emerging *amabutho* system derived from this principle. Upon being gathered into age-set regiments, men (and, by the Shakan era, women) labored for the chief for fifteen to twenty years, during which time they could not marry. They were responsible for managing the chief's homesteads, herds, and crops. By exercising such control over men's labor for about one-third of their productive lives,[53] a chief also expanded his authority over the reproductive potential of his chiefdom. In delaying marriage, the chief delayed "the whole process of homestead formation."[54]

To fully realize this productive and reproductive potential, pre-Shakan chiefs sought access to transitional pasturage, fertile croplands, and defensible hills. The Mthethwa, for example, progressively gained control over most of the lower Mfolozi River Valley during the second half of the eighteenth century. The royal kraal sites of Jobe were located midway between the alluvium beds of the Mfolozi and several defensible hills. Under Jobe's son Dingiswathe, the Mthethwa extended their control over the hill range between the Mfolozi and Mhlatuze rivers. Dingiswayo, who established his major kraal in even higher country, proceeded to gain control of the mid-Mfolozi Valley by the early nineteenth century. The Zulu were one of the peoples absorbed during this phase of Mthethwa expansion.[55]

In contrast to the political centralization evident in pre-Shakan state formation, Lakota hegemony in the northern central Great Plains came to exist despite the decentralization that accompanied their movement into the prairies. By 1800 the Lakotas "apparently ceased to practice any cohesive form of unitribal chieftaincy, hereditary or otherwise."[56] A number of commentators reported on the feud-ridden, factionalized band structure of the Lakotas at the turn of the century. Tabeau attributed this factionalism to "their form of hunting which does not permit of their living together in too great numbers . . . ; the spirit of unsociability and of discord which exists among the particular tribes; [and] the ambition and the jealousy of the too numerous chiefs." As he put it, "individual quarrels arise which perpetuate, in families, hatred and revenge. Thus by a just defiance, which experience sanctions, a [Teton] is always armed even in his lodge."[57] Political consolidation and institutional restructuring among the Tetons did occur, but only during the course of the nineteenth century.[58]

How, then, had the Lakotas arrived at their predominant position by the time of the Lewis and Clark expedition? Their acquisition of firearms and horses, their proficiency as hunters and warriors, and their avoidance of epidemic diseases undoubtedly propelled Teton expansion. Yet their predominance relied as well on success in adjusting to significant economic and ecological changes in the seventeenth and eighteenth centuries. The strength and flexibility of the Lakota social organization, typified by the *tiyospaye* and *akicita*, provided the key for this adaptation.

The *tiyospaye* or band, which represented the core social, kinship, residential, political, and economic unit in Lakota society, was exceptionally adaptable to a seminomadic existence. Raymond DeMallie refers to the *tiyospaye* as "the patterned way in which people related to one another in order to live."[59] An ideal *tiyospaye* consisted of five to twenty families, who might live together with other *tiyospaye* in the winter, or join others in the summer for communal buffalo hunts and the sun dance. Each *tiyospaye* had a leader, likened to a father, who received advice from an informal council of adult males. Biological relatedness did not necessarily constitute a criterion for reckoning relationships within each *tiyospaye* — rather, in DeMallie's words, "people considered themselves related to one another because they lived together and cooperated with one another." The system offered considerable flexibility in membership and residence. Such flexibility served as a political safety valve — it prevented factionalism from becoming self-destructive. "Any man who wanted to be recognized as a chief tried to set up his own *tiyospaye*; if he could gain followers, he established his position. If his followers were unhappy with him, they simply moved to another *tiyospaye*." [60]

The typical Lakota family unit consisted of a man, his wife or wives, and their children. Occasionally an unmarried sister, cousin, or widowed parent might be included in this group. Women, who set up tipis, collected wood and water, preserved corn for the winter, dug turnips, cooked, and engaged in various handicrafts, were also the principal child rearers. Mothers nursed children for two to three years and typically devoted considerable loving attention to them. Seldom physically punished, children were nonetheless taught to be responsible and self-reliant. According to the anthropologist Jeanette Mirsky, since women refrained from baby talk with their infants, a mother might address her baby in this way: "Daughter, lie still and don't cry. I am going over to —— but I will hurry right back to you. I won't be long. Don't be frightened." And when she returns: "There daughter, what did I tell you? That I would be right back. And here I am and I shall stay with you the rest of the day." [61]

The *akicita*, another integrative institution, similarly supported the transition to a plains existence, especially insofar as that existence came to depend on the communal buffalo hunt. Oglala informants in the early twentieth century defined *akicita* as

> those who see that there is general order in camp when traveling from one place to another; those who attend to the duties of overseeing the buffalo hunt so that no one may chase the buffalo singly; those who see that all can charge the buffalo at once or split up the party so that when one chases buffalo one way, the other band closes in; and those who supervise the chase to get better results. They also see that no one kills another. [62]

Lakota band leaders typically appointed one *akicita* society per season and distributed the responsibility to competing societies over the years.

Among the Oglalas, a recruit had to have been in at least one war party and could join an *akicita* as early as his sixteenth year if he had killed an enemy.[63] In enforcing the laws of the camp, a camp marshall, according to Tabeau, could kill an offender's dogs and horses, break his weapons, dismantle his lodge, and seize his possessions. This authority was not arbitrary, however, for checks and balances existed. "But as their right is only temporary, as they will in their turn be subject to the same sort of power," Tabeau wrote, "they fear as much as they are feared."[64] Clark Wissler pointed out that one could not decline *akicita* service, but could be discharged for misconduct. As he said, "appointment to the service was regarded as an honor."[65]

The Tetons' power rested in part on their proficiency in adapting traditional institutions to new economic and ecological conditions while simultaneously undergoing political decentralization. The Zulu became predominant in southeastern Africa through a similar adaptation of traditional institutions—the transformation of circumcision sets into multifunctional age-set regiments, whereby young men were required to perform service for their chief for as long as two decades. In contrast to the Tetons' decentralized band structure however, transformations in pre-Shakan Zululand resulted in a centralized kingdom by the early nineteenth century.

Pre-Shakan *amabutho*, like Sioux *akicitas*, enhanced the economic capacity of a preindustrial people. Unlike *akicitas*, however, *amabutho* also served as military "regiments" for their chiefs. In this respect, age-set regiments are more akin to Sioux war societies.[66] The military potential of pre-Shakan *amabutho* took on particular significance by the early nineteenth century. Drought, known to pre-Shakan peoples as the Madhlathule famine, struck Zululand in the early 1800s. Lunguza told James Stuart that his people ate grass during this famine, and, as he recalls, "dogs were also killed and eaten."[67] The Madhlathule famine sharpened the conflict among the most expansionist chiefdoms—most notably the Mthethwa, Qwabe, Ndwandwe, and Ngwane—and bitter warfare ensued. During the course of these wars the relatively insignificant Zulu ruling house emerged triumphant. The results were twofold: (1) the emergence of a powerful, centralized state ruled by Shaka, and (2) a period of unprecedented suffering in southern and central Africa, known as the Mfecane. Whereas demographic contraction boosted the expansion of Teton bands in the North American plains, depopulation followed in the wake of the Zulu triumph.

C H A P T E R 3

Indigenous Empires

Y the early nineteenth century, the Sioux and Zulu social
formations had generated an internal dynamic for aggressive expansion. Sioux economic prosperity depended on
acquiring additional buffalo-hunting territories, pilfering
horses, and dominating sedentary agricultural villagers.
Pre-Shakan chieftains prospered by controlling pastures and fertile croplands, accumulating cattle, and controlling the productive and reproductive processes of their people. All of this added up to competition and
conflict with their indigenous rivals. The Lakotas prevailed—they swept
across the northern central plains during the first half of the nineteenth
century, crushing their opponents in deadly warfare. The Zulu royal
house succeeded as well—under Shaka kaSenzangakhona, the Zulu absorbed hundreds of chiefdoms inhabiting the region between the Thukela
and Phongolo rivers and rooted out resistance with ruthless abandon. In
effect, the Sioux and the Zulu built their own empires in the first half of
the nineteenth century by dominating and subjugating indigenous com-
petitors. Since their ambitions complemented, more or less, those of the
United States and Great Britain, the Zulu and Sioux still awaited confrontations with their major imperial rivals.

The Oglalas and Brulés, the most populous of the seven Lakota bands,
spearheaded the Sioux advance into the plains southwest of the Missouri
River. By the mid-nineteenth century these bands migrated in a region
encompassing the Black Hills in western South Dakota, the headwaters
of the White and Niobrara rivers in northwestern Nebraska, and the
Laramie plains in eastern Wyoming. The Saones, a collection of Teton
peoples including the Miniconjous, Two Kettles, Hunkpapas, Sihasapas,
and Sans Arcs,[1] followed in the wake of their Oglala and Brulé kinsmen.
They pursued buffalo herds in a territory bounded on the north by the

Heart River in southwestern North Dakota, and on the south the Cheyenne River in southwestern South Dakota.[2]

Sioux expansion on the high plains, a region characterized by relatively
low rainfall, cold, harsh winters, and relentlessly hot summers, occurred
for three major reasons. First, unlike most of the indigenous peoples of the
Great Plains during this era, the Lakotas experienced population growth.
A growing population intensified the demand for buffalo products and the
trade items those products could command. Second, buffaloes, the heart
of the Teton economy, proved increasingly fickle beasts. Not only did
the herds continue to migrate toward the western mountains, but their
numbers progressively thinned as well. Finally, to maintain an equestrian
buffalo-hunting economy in light of these constraints, the Lakota needed
horses and supplementary food resources. As a result, wars of conquest
against their neighbors, especially the Pawnees and Crows, intensified.

The disastrous epidemics of the first half of the nineteenth century,
which more than halved the Plains Indian population, had relatively little
effect on the Lakotas. Based on the inexact censuses of the period, one
can estimate that the Teton population doubled during the first quarter
of the century, then doubled again between 1825 and 1850, an era replete with smallpox and cholera. The Lakotas probably numbered at least
twenty thousand by 1850.[3]

The Tetons did not fully escape the effects of these deadly diseases. The
fur trader Edwin Denig claimed that the Brulés suffered more than any
other Sioux band. No Brulé, he suggested, would "lift his voice in favor of
the white people or the government, who, as they say, sends diseases to cut
them off."[4] But compared to such sedentary horticultural peoples as the
Mandans, Hidatsas, and Arikaras, the seminomadic Brulés fared reasonably well. They, along with the Oglalas, moved progressively away from
the Missouri River, the major epidemic corridor. Government physicians
vaccinated a number of their Saone kinsmen in 1832, in time for these
Lakota bands to avoid the catastrophic smallpox epidemic of 1838.[5] Avoidance of disease, along with a birthrate capable of doubling the population
every twenty-five years, provided the Lakotas considerable incentive to
intensify their search for buffalo.

An increased demand for buffalo products by American traders along
the Missouri and Platte compounded this demographic situation. The
twenty years between 1820 and 1840 represented the most propitious
period for the fur trade in the Great Plains, and perhaps the greatest era
of prosperity for the Lakotas. The American Fur Company, which controlled the upper Missouri trade, operated over one hundred stations de-

pendent on Sioux trade in furs. The most important trading post for the Tetons was Fort Pierre, near the present city of Pierre, South Dakota.[6] Hiram Martin Chittenden, a company trader who is a major authority on trading conditions at that time, rated the Sioux as the most important people in the buffalo trade. Teton "country was one continuous range for the buffalo," he wrote in his classic *American Fur Trade of the Far West*, and "as a result the traffic in buffalo robes was exceedingly heavy, and the quantities of these peltries that were shipped from the Sioux country were very great."[7]

Traffic down the Missouri River in robes, hides, and tongues increased dramatically between 1830 and the late 1840s. In 1830, for example, traders shipped 2,600 robes from their upper Missouri posts to St. Louis. By 1833 this figure jumped to over 40,000, and increased to an average of 90,000 annually between 1835 and 1843. In 1848, 110,000 buffalo robes were shipped downriver.[8] The Lakotas received in exchange firearms, cooking utensils, tools, and liquor—despite the federal government's banning of spirit traffic in 1823. According to Edwin Denig, the introduction of Anglo-American products gave the Sioux "a greater reliance on their own powers, increased their hunting operations, and [improved] their domestic comfort."[9]

This cornucopia in fur traffic, so vital to Sioux prosperity, reached its limits by the late 1840s. Two factors converged to reduce the supply of buffaloes on the Great Plains. First, Sioux hunters disposed of their game resourcefully when herds were scarce, since the buffalo served their subsistence needs so effectively. But the Sioux exercised less care in times of plenty, especially when provided incentives by white traders. For example, the artist George Catlin, who visited Fort Pierre in May 1832, reported that a Sioux hunting party killed fourteen hundred bison, extracted the tongues, and abandoned the carcasses. In return for these delicacies, which traders salted and shipped downriver to St. Louis, the Indians received "but a few gallons of whiskey."[10] Second, the slaughter of buffaloes by white hunters for pleasure as well as profit, an activity that increased dramatically after midcentury, played an equally significant role in the decline of the bison population. From 1841 to 1852, 157,717 immigrants passed over the Platte River trail on their way to Oregon, California, and Utah. Their presence wrought havoc on the buffalo and pushed the surviving herds farther west and north.[11]

A diminishing and migratory resource, combined with an expanding Lakota population, heightened competition in the Great Plains for horses, food, and profitable hunting grounds. The Tetons responded by waging war on the Crows, Pawnees, Kiowas, Arikaras, Mandans, and Hidatsas, allying briefly with the United States in 1823, and joining more permanently with Cheyennes and Arapahos around 1825. The pact with the Americans proved fragile. Colonel Henry Leavenworth enlisted the support of fifteen hundred Tetons to punish the Arikaras for their assault on General William Ashley's trading party earlier in 1823. Leavenworth's decision to sack an Arikara village but allow the inhabitants to escape filled the Lakotas with contempt for whites, a feeling that would persist for years.[12] On the other hand, the Sioux-Cheyenne-Arapaho alliance "would dominate the north and central plains for the next half century."[13]

Sioux ascendancy in the Great Plains corresponded chronologically with the rise of the Zulu in southeastern Africa. Like the Lakotas, the Zulu came to dominate an extensive region as well as inspire terror and hatred among their foes. Unlike the Sioux, however, the Zulu formed a centralized state. How does one explain the difference? The Lakotas, more centralized in theory prior to their migrations into the Great Plains, adopted political structures in keeping with an equestrian, seminomadic, buffalo-hunting economy. In other words, a shifting, migratory resource required a flexible, decentralized political structure. Zulu state formation occurred in the context of the struggle for dominance and survival among northern Nguni farmers, ongoing since the eighteenth century, but especially desperate in the first two decades of the nineteenth. A major feature of this competition was the emergence of strong chiefdoms made that way by consolidating their control over land, resources, and people. The Zulu state represented the end product of this centralizing process.

That the Zulu came to dominate the northern Nguni seems inevitable only in retrospect. One can readily imagine a centralized state emerging in Zululand in the nineteenth century under the leadership of the Mthethwa, Ndwandwe, Qwabe, or Dhlamini-Ngwane, who all possessed disciplined age-set regiments by the end of the eighteenth century. The Zulu advantage rests in the person of Shaka. Shaka kaSenzangakhona formed a centralized kingdom by (1) exploiting the military potential of reformed *amabutho*, and (2) devising effective political structures and ideological integrative devices that linked the health of the Zulu ruling house with its regiments.

Shaka, born in the late eighteenth century, was the illegitimate son of the Zulu chieftain Senzangakhona and Nandi, a young woman from the Langeni people. During Nandi's pregnancy Senzangakhona sought to disclaim his paternity by assuring "the other women that Nandi was not pregnant, but suffered from a complaint called itshaka or looseness of the intestines, which was the cause of the swelling." [14] The boy's birth shattered the king's alibi. Shortly thereafter Nandi fell into disfavor with Senzangakhona and returned to the Langeni with her son.

During his childhood Shaka apparently felt himself to be an outcast — of royal birth yet a refugee — and consequently developed a spirit of vindictiveness combined with a marked indifference toward the sufferings of others. Shaka joined one of Dingiswayo's regiments at age twenty-two, and soon became recognized by the Mthethwa chieftain as a capable warrior and leader. Following his father's death in 1816, Shaka plotted the execution of his half brother Sigujana, the legitimate Zulu heir, and seized the Zulu throne. Two years later, in the wake of Dingiswayo's death, Shaka absorbed the Mthethwa confederacy. Between 1816 and 1818 Shaka formed three age regiments and housed them in permanent residences (*amakhanda*). He revolutionized warfare by teaching his men to use the short stabbing spear, discard their sandals, and fight at close range.[15]

By the mid-1820s the greatly enlarged Zulu chiefdom held supreme authority between the Thukela and Phongolo rivers, principally through the defeat of the Ndwandwe, the neutralization of the Qwabe, and the absorption of the Mthethwa. In 1819 the Zulu defeated Zwide's Ndwandwe, a victory, in the words of John Omer-Cooper, that represents "a turning point in Shaka's career and in the whole history of the Mfecane." [16] Zwide's people had been the Mthethwa confederacy's major rival. The battle in 1819 severely weakened the Ndwandwe's position in the north. In 1826 a revitalized Ndwandwe chiefdom led by Zwide's son, Sikunyane, mounted an unsuccessful assault on the Zulu kingdom. By this time the Zulu had achieved supreme mastery in the region.[17]

In 1818 Shaka led all of his regiments southward in an assault on Phakathwayo's Qwabe. Phakathwayo mobilized five *amabutho* and confronted the Zulu in a stalemate at the Mhlatuze River. Early in the confrontation Shaka's regiments captured Phakathwayo's ekuDabukeni kraal a few miles west of Eshowe. Shaka's success demoralized the Qwabe *amabutho*, incapacitated the Qwabe leader, and opened the Qwabe chiefdom to total destruction. The Zulu confiscated the royal cattle herds and left the Qwabe chiefdom intact, thus neutralizing the most powerful chiefdom in Zululand next to the Ndwandwe.[18]

Shaka's conquests contributed to the famine, migration, and human suffering that affected a large portion of southeastern Africa in the early nineteenth century. In the twentieth century scholars have characterized this era as the Mfecane, a term that probably derives from the Xhosa word *ukufaca*, which means "to be weak; emaciated from hunger." [19] The chaotic movement of refugees [20] compounded the violence that afflicted the Sotho-Tswana peoples of the highveld interior during this era as well. The human conflict on the highveld in the 1820s and 1830s is conventionally described as the Difaqane, a Sotho variant of Mfecane.

In a series of recent papers, [21] the historian Julian Cobbing has characterized the Mfecane as a myth, fabricated by whites to cover up their contributions to the depopulation of the interior of South Africa in the nineteenth century. A significant feature of this myth, in Cobbing's view, is the image of Shaka as a bloodthirsty monster as well as the instigator of the Mfecane: by blaming the catastrophe on Zulu military aggression, apartheid apologists in the twentieth century have found a convenient excuse for the continuation of white supremacy. [22] Cobbings's characterization of the Mfecane as an "alibi," "invented" to disguise external white agency, does not square with the sources. As the historian Leonard Thompson puts it, "there is . . . a plethora of evidence from African as well as white sources that the [Mfecane] wars were essentially internal African affairs." [23]

Furthermore, the emergence of Shaka's Zulu kingdom is rather more than systematic genocide. The Zulu's ability to control people, like the Tetons' success in dominating sedentary horticulturists, was as important as their capacity to terminate them. The Zulu absorbed the Mthethwa confederacy, Khumalo, Cube, Mbo, Thembu, Langeni, Cele, and Ngcobo, incorporated their young men into Zulu *amabutho*, and captured young women as potential wives. In some instances Shaka executed the existing ruler, but more often he grafted a chief into his territorial hierarchy. A good example is Shaka's conquest of the Dube. According to Stuart's informant Jantshi, the Dube chief Kutshwayo "like many others, was attacked merely to make him pay tribute, i.e., reduce him to become a subject and then instate him as an *induna*." [24]

Subdued and independent chieftains from all parts of Zululand paid regular visits to Shaka's royal kraal at Bulawayo to confirm their allegiance to the Zulu state. According to the trader Nathaniel Isaacs, Shaka "knew at all times the condition and strength of every tribe around him, both independent and tributary," [25] so it became prudent for chiefs to maintain cordial relations with the king. As Dr. Andrew Smith observed, "chiefs who keep much at home and who rarely go on visits to the king are looked upon by him with suspicion." [26] Isolation in turn attracted espionage and possibly retaliation.

The Zulu kept their enemies at bay by creating buffer zones. The trader

Henry Francis Fynn estimated that the Zulu "ravaged and depopulated the country to a distance of 300 miles to the westward, 200 miles to the northward and 500 miles to the southward."[27] An especially large stretch of territory between the Thukela and Mzimvubu rivers, once the most densely populated region of Natal, was virtually devoid of population by the mid-1820s according to Stuart's informant Maziyana.[28] By 1826 Shaka had accomplished his geopolitical objectives: the neutralization or destruction of rival centers of power and the creation of protective buffers on his northern and southern borders. Like the Lakotas of the 1840s, the Zulu held unprecedented power in their respective region.

Zulu hegemony rested on the strength of the versatile *amabutho* system. Between 1816 and 1828 Shaka made use of at least fifteen male age regiments, and by the mid-1820s could mobilize forty thousand men in service to the kingdom.[29] Initially, male recruits tended cattle and carried shields for male warriors. They were eventually collected into an age set and either remained in an established *ibutho* or separated into their own royal homestead.[30] In addition to serving as an external army, Zulu *amabutho* tended the king's crops, repaired royal homesteads, and policed the kingdom. When Shaka's *amabutho* did fight, they did so to appropriate cattle from neighboring communities, much as the Lakotas raided for horses, not to display their martial virtuosity.[31]

Shaka also formed three female age sets of eight thousand to ten thousand women each, who supplied their male counterparts with agricultural produce. These women also served as potential wives for male warriors. Shaka forbade sex between unmarried initiates, except for a type of external intercourse known as *ukuhlobonga*, and bestowed permission to marry only to his veterans. Illicit sex among unmarrieds was a capital offense.[32] Restrictions on marriage gave Shaka control over the reproductive processes of his kingdom. Women produced crops as well as children, and children formed new homesteads. By exercising such authority, Shaka controlled the "reproduction of production communities."[33]

Shaka's control over production extended down to the average homestead, where homestead heads still extracted surplus production and where workers of the next generation emanated. Economic organization at this level, however, showed real continuities with the pre-Shakan past. Probably one half of the population of the Zulu kingdom maintained a relatively traditional existence even at the height of Shakan power. Certainly the *amabutho* system deprived the homestead of most of its young men and some of its women; yet female elders and children continued to replicate a subsistence existence characteristic of the pre-Shakan era. If, for example, all homestead males lived away temporarily at an *ikhanda*, the eldest or first-married wife took charge of local subsistence production. If the eldest surviving son returned from *amabutho* service he became the family heir. He acquired all of his father's property, goods left by his deceased brothers and sisters, and the authority to determine whether his mother should remarry. Should the homestead head return to his homestead, he would resume his local leadership responsibilities and eventually retire within his local chiefdom.[34] In short, the basic Zulu kinship structure, much like the Sioux *tiyospaye*, remained formally intact even during the most dramatic centralizing and expansionary phases of the Shakan era. The European intrusion beginning in the 1830s strained this kinship system far more profoundly.

What *had* changed from the pre-Shakan to the Shakan era? Social inequality, political centralization, and ideological integration reached unprecedented dimensions: men intensified their exploitation of women, elders successfully constrained youth, and rulers more effectively dominated their subordinates. In the words of the historian Peter Colenbrander:

> in the pre-*Mfecane* period men and women worked for the most part to sustain the immediate community in which they resided. Furthermore, the homestead head . . . had limited power to delay the distribution of bridewealth among his young adult sons, and so to prevent them from establishing their own households free from his control. After the Shakan revolution, the labour power of both sexes was utilised for considerable lengths of time by a dominant and largely exclusive elite for purposes of its own, namely the maintenance of the state which was the source of its wealth and power. The homestead now formed part of the productive base of the state to which it had become politically subordinated.[35]

Politically, authority devolved in relation to the Zulu ruling house. At the highest level was the king, the senior member of the Zulu ruling lineage, and the royal family. The closest advisers to the Zulu king were territorial chiefs known as *izikhulu*. Typically they represented the dominant lineages in the kingdom and advised the king on important matters of state. Under Shaka the power of the territorial chiefs was "merely nominal," according to Fynn, "as no chief would dare to propose anything in opposition to the King, as such conduct would be detrimental to his future safety."[36] Beneath the *izikhulu* were appointed state officials of varying ranks and status known as *izinduna*. They supervised *amabutho* as bureaucrats and military commanders. Their loyalty and efficiency proved vital to Shaka's political success. According to Omer-Cooper, *izinduna* "constituted a nascent appointive bureaucracy which could be used to increase centralization and liberate the ruler from dependence on his potentially rebellious relatives."[37]

Shaka nurtured the loyalty of his subordinates by apportioning his vast cattle herds. According to A. T. Bryant, "the cattle of the Zulu king, amassed by conquest or raid, amounted to tens of thousands."[38] Fynn reckoned that "the whole country, as far as our sight could reach, was covered with . . . droves of cattle."[39] Shaka in turn redistributed this vast store of wealth with great liberality. "Cattle were given to the captains and highest in rank by the king," recorded the American missionary George Champion, "some tens perhaps to the highest, while the lowest must be satisfied with two, four, or six."[40]

Socially, authority in the Zulu kingdom was circumscribed by gender as well as by age. For example, when the Zulu king granted Zulu males permission to marry, they signified the privilege by wearing a headring. The headringed or "white" Zulu served as veterans and only as reserves in major battles. The nonheadringed or "black" Zulu formed the frontal assault in the crescent formation, and experienced limited contact with females who had been gathered into age-set regiments. The putting on of headrings, according to Stuart's informant Madikane, had become customary in the pre-Shakan era[41] and probably replaced circumcision.

Ideologically, Shaka reinforced his authority through rituals linking the health of the Zulu ruling house with the vitality of his *amabutho*. For example, chanting praises to the living and departed royalty and sacrificing to the ancestral spirits of the Zulu ruling house occurred frequently at individual *ikhanda*. Periodically, *amabutho* delivered praises in mass gatherings at emaKhosini, the Zulu royal burial ground. Rituals at emaKhosini, according to Stuart's informant Mtshapi, brought about great excitement: "as soon as the great national chant [was] sung the whole army [was] knit together . . . and infused with courage."[42]

The creation of the *inkatha*, a thick coiled mat and symbol of Zulu unity, represented one of the most important state rituals. Each Zulu king created his own mat and assembled his regiments for this purpose in similar ways. Zulu doctors (*izinyanga*) directed the ceremony by administering an emetic to assembled *amabutho*. Each man then vomited into a straw-filled pit. The doctors worked the affected straw into a thick coiled mat, adding to it bits of material drawn from the regimental huts. This ritual, according to Stuart's informant Ndukwana, "would take place in time of peace though when there was some reason for supposing a war might come about." [43] The *inkatha*, kept in a special hut under permanent guard, visibly expressed Zulu corporate unity. In the words of Stuart's informant Sivivi, "people were said to be bound up into it." [44] To Baleni, "the binding round and round symbolizes the binding together of the people." [45]

The Lakotas did not form a centralized state, but like the Zulu, they maintained a certain degree of ideological unity during the nineteenth century through the annual sun dance. In addition, the Sioux intensified social inequality throughout the Great Plains, but unlike the Zulu, not within their own polity. Rather, they succeeded in subjugating their neighbors through economic warfare.

By the 1840s, for example, raiding became the principal method of obtaining horses for the Sioux, and the Crow stock, at least for the Oglalas, served as the major source. As Edwin Denig explained, "before the influx of strangers into the Platte and Arkansas country [the Oglalas] could procure wild horses which, with those purchased from the traders, were enough to serve their hunting purposes. But since the means of supply has been cut off they are obliged to draw upon the Crow for animals absolutely needed for their existence." [46] The Saones concentrated their assault on the horticultural peoples of the upper Missouri, stealing horses and, in lean times, trading for corn and beans. [47]

Competition for lucrative hunting zones in eastern Wyoming and southeastern Montana led to bitter conflict between the Tetons and Crows. The Crows, hit hard by smallpox and cholera between 1838 and 1849, also found themselves literally surrounded by enemies — Blackfeet and Assiniboine-Crees to the north, Shoshonis on the west, Cheyennes to the south, and especially, Lakotas in the east. [48] Skirmishes between Tetons and Crows intensified throughout the first half of the nineteenth century, [49] reaching a crescendo in the Laramie plains by the 1840s. By the 1850s, the Lakotas had driven the Crows out of Wyoming and were pushing them up the Yellowstone in southeastern Montana. [50] "Situated as they now are," Denig observed at midcentury, "the Crows cannot exist as a nation. . . . warred against by the Blackfeet on one side and most bands of the Sioux on the other, [and] straying along the Platte trail where they contracted rapid and deadly diseases, will soon lead to their entire extinction." [51]

In the 1830s the Oglalas and Brulés contested the Pawnees for the South Platte and Republican river valleys in southern Nebraska. The Pawnees, a powerful sedentary people numbering about twelve thousand at the beginning of the decade, suffered grievously from smallpox in 1838. One year later, Bull Bear's band of Oglalas overwhelmed the Skidi Pawnees to capture the Platte River hunting grounds.[52] The Pawnees persisted in efforts to hunt buffalo in the western plains, and the Sioux continued to harass them. The Brulés made frequent horse-raiding expeditions on Pawnee villages in the 1850s and 1860s, killing indiscriminately.[53] Pawnee women farmed in compact groups, according to the anthropologist Gene Weltfish, because "the Sioux made a particular point of attacking and scalping them as they were going into the fields or coming home. This was presumably to exert sufficient pressure to chase the Pawnees from their territory and induce them to abandon it entirely."[54] The Sioux strategy succeeded—in 1873, following a Lakota attack which left over one hundred Pawnees dead, the Pawnee people decided to abandon Nebraska and move to Indian Territory. A census in 1879 put the Pawnee population at 1,440.[55]

What impact did this dramatic expansionary success have on Sioux political organization? The evidence for the period from about 1804 to 1850 suggests little of the institutional elaboration and political checks and balances described by the anthropologist Clark Wissler in his classic work *Societies and Ceremonial Associations in the Oglala Division of the Teton Dakota*, published in 1912. Rather, one continues to find an accelerating trend away from hereditary chieftainship and toward the self-made band chief, as well as the factionalism that persisted from the eighteenth century. The institutions described by Wissler did not likely become "traditional" until the post-1850 era, when the United States government pressured the Lakotas to act as a single legal and political entity.

Wissler's sophisticated study relied heavily on the ethnographic fieldwork of James Walker, an agency physician at Pine Ridge Reservation from 1896 to 1914. Walker's informants described a complex, hierarchical political structure among the Oglalas, in which authority devolved democratically from an elderly chief's society to a band council, known as the *wicasa itancan*. The band council, consisting of seven lifetime members whose positions were often hereditary, delegated its authority to four headmen or "shirt wearers," supreme councilors charged with the general welfare of the group, and four *wakicunze*, responsible for selecting camp sites and deciding when hunting would be permitted. The decisions of the *wakicunze* were enforced by the *akicita*. This political organization applied only to large camps, like those characteristic of the Oglala, and to temporary periods, like the communal buffalo hunt and the annual sun dance.[56]

Wissler's idealized picture of Oglala political organization, in which power devolved formally from a hereditary band council to a hierarchical cast of headmen, *wakicunze*, and soldiers, seems inconsistent with Lakota ecological constraints and does not square with the evidence. The Teton buffalo-hunting economy, which forced people to disperse in winter and concentrate in summer, required more fluidity and flexibility in social organization than Wissler's model allows.[57] Furthermore, charismatic, self-made band leaders like Bull Bear, Red Cloud, and Crazy Horse, not hereditary chiefs, seem to have exercised the most significant authority in Oglala camps during much of the nineteenth century. The historian Francis Parkman, who visited the Oglala in 1846, observed that a chief was "honored and obeyed only so far as his personal qualities . . . command[ed] respect and fear."[58] If an Oglala chief possessed such characteristics, according to Denig, his *akicita* proved "prompt and efficient [in] carrying out with vigor any laws decided upon by [him]."[59]

The career of Bull Bear illustrates the significance of a strong-willed *tiyospaye* leader in the Teton political structure. Four Oglala band chiefs and four "head warriors" signed their first treaty with the United States in 1825. Bull Bear is listed in the treaty as head warrior of the Kiyuksa band of Oglalas, and Crazy Bear as chief. By 1834 the four bands identified in the treaty of 1825 were known as the Bear People—the followers of Bull Bear—and had migrated from the Black Hills southward to the forks of the Platte River. George Hyde describes Bull Bear as "a great chief but something of a tyrant, holding his turbulent followers in check by roaring at them and promptly putting a knife into any man who did not heed his orders."[60] He may have employed headmen and *wakicunze*, but Bull Bear's authority seems to have rested on his personality and the loyalty of his *akicita*.[61]

Bull Bear's career also points to the instability of the Lakota political system. In 1841 Red Cloud murdered Bull Bear after a lingering quarrel between the Kiyuksas and the Bad Faces, Smoke's band of Oglalas. The event split the Oglalas into two major factions, a division that persisted into the reservation period. The Kiyuksa continued to move into Pawnee hunting grounds on the Platte and Smoky Hill rivers, and the Bad Faces, led later by Red Cloud, migrated north and west.[62]

The rift in Lakota politics occurred at precisely the time of another migration, in which white emigrants began following the Platte River road toward destinations in the west. The Oglalas expressed puzzlement over this movement at first, but gradually realized that these whites "were spoiling the Platte valley, destroying the grass and timber, driving off the game, and turning the valley into a white man's country where the

Indian was only tolerated as an unwelcome intruder."[63] At this historical moment, however, the Tetons represented the predominant power in the northern central plains.

Shaka fulfilled his territorial ambitions by 1828, but all was not well in the Zulu polity. A climate of fear and paranoia pervaded the kingdom, based in large part on Shaka's casual disposal of his subjects. Not only European observers, who purposely exaggerated Shaka's "bloodthirsty" nature after the king's death,[64] but Zulu informants as well, commented on this phenomenon. On the flimsiest pretexts, according to Fynn, Shaka "had men seized and their eyes taken out of their sockets; and then they were allowed to move about and be ridiculed by all who met them."[65] Shaka put to death the sick and aged on the grounds that they detracted from the greatness of the Zulu kingdom. He held dancing competitions and would kill those who willfully danced out of step with the others. He once casually ordered a childbearing woman split open as to observe the position of her fetus. Shaka had no children because he feared them as potential rivals. Since he never married, he executed mistresses found to be pregnant or ordered the fetus aborted.[66] Lunguza kaMpukane captured succinctly the tension pervading Zululand: "The Zulu country was like a pit, or a snuffbox, for you did not know where to run to; that is, if a man had to be killed it was inevitable that he would be killed, for there was nowhere else to run to."[67]

Perhaps the most outrageous atrocity under Shaka's rule occurred during the hysteria accompanying the death of his mother, Nandi, in 1827. According to Fynn and Isaacs, Shaka encouraged the murder of thousands of innocent Zulu mourners who allegedly expressed unconvincing sorrow for the deceased.[68] Due to the ease with which Shaka eliminated his enemies, real and imagined, dissension remained underground. Yet it likely flourished by the final year of his rule. One unsuccessful effort on the king's life occurred as early as 1824. By 1828 potential assassins were better organized. With the majority of his warriors away fighting the Gasa kingdom in the north, an *induna* named Mbopha stabbed the king to death. The plot had been devised by Mkabayi, the sister of Senzangakhona, and Shaka's half brothers Dingane and Mhlangana.[69] Dingane succeeded Shaka as king of the Zulu.

Political discord in the Zulu kingdom peaked on the eve of an event that figures prominently in Afrikaner nationalist historiography. In the mid-1830s Afrikaner emigrants trekked north from the Cape frontier in quest of productive farmlands in Transorangia, the Transvaal, and Natal.

This exodus became known as the Great Trek, and was used afterward by Afrikaner patriots to forge a sense of ethnic unity.[70] Since many of these whites regarded Africans as either enemies or fit only for servile labor, the Zulu people faced an unprecedented military challenge. But the Zulu dominated the region between the Phongolo and Thukela rivers in southeastern Africa—they, like the Lakotas, engaged their potential foe from a position of strength.

CHAPTER 4

Collaborators of a Kind

HE open frontier for the Sioux and Zulu reached its limits by the mid-nineteenth century. Each people, who had accumulated unprecedented power and prosperity in their respective regions, now faced an ongoing struggle with white settlers imbued with a sense of racial destiny and driven by capitalist incentives. These settlers were restrained somewhat by governments professing humanitarian aims toward the indigenes. Therefore, arbiters courted both the Zulu and Sioux, seeking a peaceful transition to political stability and economic prosperity. The Lakotas and Zulu demonstrated some willingness to collaborate with these officials in the name of self-preservation. For the Sioux, leaders such as Conquering Bear, Little Thunder, and Red Cloud, and for the Zulu, Mpande and his son Cetshwayo, served as major mediators with the United States and Great Britain in the mid-nineteenth century. At the time, these powerful rulers usually acted in good faith, and in some cases gained significant concessions for their people. As these leaders were to find, however, the closing frontier made it progressively difficult to distinguish negotiators from enemies.

Francis Parkman observed in 1846 that "until within a year or two, when the emigrants began to pass through [Teton] country on the way to Oregon, they had seen no whites, except the few employed about the Fur Company's posts. They thought them a wise people, inferior only to themselves. . . . But when the swarm of *Meneaska*, with their oxen and wagons, began to invade them, their astonishment was unbounded. They could scarcely believe that the earth contained such a multitude of white men. Their wonder is now giving way to indignation; and the result, unless vigilantly guarded against, may be lamentable in the extreme."[1] Parkman could not have been more prophetic—tensions between the Sioux and United States mounted during the next two decades, at times erupting into open warfare, as emigrant traffic to the west intensified. George Hyde writes that "from 1855 to 1868 the one thing that might be termed the policy of the Teton chiefs was this almost universal determination to oppose any further white encroachments on their lands."[2] Despite the reality of white encroachment into Lakota hunting grounds, the Sioux continued to expend considerable energy against indigenous foes in a series of offensives against them in Powder River country during the 1850s and 1860s.[3]

For example, the winter count of the Miniconjou White Bull, nephew of Sitting Bull, alludes to skirmishes with whites only twice between 1854 and 1876. In contrast, he cites conflicts between Sioux and Crows or Assiniboines fifteen out of these twenty-two years.[4] Battiste Good, a Brulé Sioux, records seven conflicts with other Indians, principally Crows, during this same period, and only one with whites.[5] The Oglala winter counts of No Ears, Short Man, and Iron Crow reflect a similar preoccupation with indigenous foes, especially the Crows and Pawnees.[6]

In fact, the Sioux assault on the Crows, Pawnees, and Assiniboines became a sideshow in the 1850s and 1860s — the real crisis was boiling down to a contest over land rights in the central prairies between the Lakotas and the *wasichus*, white people. But the United States government did not seek to annihilate the Tetons, despite the aggressive urgings of settlers, stage coach companies, mining conglomerates, and some military analysts. Instead, the government sought Sioux mediators to negotiate some alternative to extermination.[7]

In 1849 the United States government transferred responsibility for Indian affairs from the War Department to a new executive unit, the Department of the Interior. During the next two decades leading military officials sought to recoup Indian responsibilities from Interior, but to no avail. As political appointees, most of the commissioners of the Indian Bureau had no previous knowledge of Indians, but did subscribe to a set of consistent principles: (1) as humans, Indians were fully capable of being uplifted from barbarism, and should be convinced, and if necessary, compelled, to accept the government's benevolent intentions to "civilize" them; (2) to facilitate "civilization," Indians should be concentrated on reservations removed as far away as possible from whites.[8] From its inception, therefore, the Indian Bureau embraced principles riddled with contradictions. Indians were to be compelled to accept an approved white cultural model, thereby liberating them from their "barbaric" condition. In all likelihood, their liberation would require their subjugation, the destruction of their society in order to save it. In other words, policies designed to offer an "alternative to extinction" might well result in the military annihilation of aggressive Indian societies like the Sioux.

Furthermore, native Americans should be dispatched to distant reserves, separating them as far as possible from the white society they were to emulate. Consequently, Indians were to be segregated in order to be integrated into the American mainstream, a paradoxical scenario at best.

In 1850 President Zachary Taylor appointed Luke Lea as the first commissioner of the Indian Bureau. Lea, a novice in Indian matters, sought a federal appointment following his defeat in the Mississippi gubernatorial contest. Despite his unfamiliarity with Indian issues, Lea wasted little time rationalizing the government's policy of concentration and civilization:

> When civilization and barbarism are brought in such relation that they cannot coexist together, it is right that the superiority of the former should be asserted and the latter compelled to give way. It is, therefore, no matter of regret or reproach that so large a portion of our territory has been wrested from the aboriginal inhabitants and made the happy abodes of an enlightened and Christian people.

In his first annual report, Lea continues:

> It is indispensably necessary that [our wilder tribes] be placed in positions where they can be controlled and finally compelled by sheer necessity to resort to agricultural labor or starve. . . . In the meantime, the government should . . . secure them the means and facilities of education, intellectual, moral, and religious.[9]

The Indian Bureau, at least in the beginning, preferred moral suasion to outright force. But if the government was to coax the Sioux to embrace Christian enlightenment and agricultural prosperity, it needed to find collaborators. Otherwise, the United States might as well hand Indian affairs back to the military.

During the reign of Dingane (1828–40), the Zulu, like the Sioux, remained preoccupied with indigenous foes, launching assaults on the Ndwandwe, Qwabe, Swazi, Mpondo, Bhaca, and Ndebele. Dingane shared Shaka's anxiety over the European presence in Natal, however. In 1828, for example, Shaka sought an alliance with George IV to protect the Zulu kingdom from future British aggression, but the Zulu king was not sanguine. According to Shaka's closest European associate, Henry Fynn,

> [Shaka] saw clearly that as soon as he died the country would be overrun, i.e., conquered by the white man—the makers of muskets,

gunpowder and ships. This then was the substance of his prophecy: "As soon as I go, this country of ours will be overrun in every direction by the white man. Mark my words." [10]

Dingane sought outside protection as well, but his plan backfired. In 1830 the civil commissioner from Albany district in the eastern Cape Colony informed the Cape governor that a deputation representing Dingane's government brought "a message to the effect that the chief wished to live at peace with neighbouring natives, to enter into trade with the Colony, and to receive a missionary who might instruct his people." [11] The Cape governor dispatched Dr. Andrew Smith to Natal to determine more precisely the nature of Dingane's request as well as the suitability of the region for European settlement. Smith's return to the Cape in 1834 and favorable report of the Natal journey encouraged 150 Cape merchants to petition the British government to annex Port Natal and its hinterland, form a government there, and establish a military garrison to protect the Natalian trade. [12]

The British government rejected this petition, but its rejection did not stop the European intrusion. By 1835 approximately thirty European traders lived at Port Natal, and by 1837 eight American and British missionaries resided in Natal and Zululand. Dingane invited Francis Owen of London's Anglican Church Missionary Society to establish a mission at the Zulu king's capital, Mgungundhlovu, despite the objections of Dingane's principal *induna*, Ndlela. [13]

The mounting European presence led to friction between the Zulu and whites at Port Natal. In 1833, following their retreat from unsuccessful campaigns against the Bhaca and Mpondo in the south, the Zulu skirmished near present-day Durban with Europeans and Africans following a shooting incident in which Zulu captured and killed several Khoi hunters. According to the trader Allen Gardiner, Dingane subsequently "ordered all his people then inhabiting the district between the Port and the [Thukela] to withdraw," as the traders evacuated their base temporarily, "naturally apprehensive of retaliation on the part of" the Zulu chieftain. [14]

The British and American influence in Natal and Zululand anticipated a larger European influx into the region, one that would hamstring Zulu expansionism much more seriously. By 1837 pioneer Afrikaner families from the Cape Colony began crossing the Drakensberg into upper Natal. Like the African peoples they encountered during their journeys, the so-called voortrekkers were farmers and herders, and they brought with them large flocks of sheep and herds of cattle. In addition, the trekkers brought servants of Khoi descent, wagons, horses, and muskets, all of which gave them the military capacity to hold their own against any hostile African group. Four principal voortrekkers led their respective parties: Andries Hendrik Potgieter, an experienced commando leader; Gert Maritz, a wainwright; Piet Uys, a farmer; and Piet Retief, an experienced field commandant.[15]

The trekking parties, unified in their desire to escape the confines of Cape administration, degenerated quickly into factions. In 1837 Potgieter, supported temporarily by Maritz and Uys, led a commando against Mzilikazi's Ndebele in the Transvaal. The Ndebele, weakened from recent attacks by the Zulu and Griqua, were wrenched from their principal settlements and driven north. Earlier that same year Retief guided his party eastward into Natal. Seeking a territorial cession there from the Zulu king, he met with Dingane at Mgungundhlovu. Dingane approved Retief's request on condition that the Afrikaners return the cattle they allegedly pilfered from the Zulu during the Boer trek into Natal. Retief complied and sent word to his anxious companions on the western slopes of the Drakensberg that Natalia awaited them. By the end of 1837 hundreds of Afrikaner families poured through the mountain passes and settled along the headwaters of the Thukela River.[16]

In the aftermath of his euphoric meeting with Dingane, Retief's gravest tactical error was his demeaning advice to the Zulu king on the consequences of Zulu expansionism. In a letter from Port Natal addressed to Dingane in November 1837, Retief wrote: "The great Book of God teaches us that kings who conduct themselves as [Mzilikazi] does are severely punished, and that it is not granted to them to live or reign long; and if you desire to learn at greater length how God deals with such bad kings, you may enquire concerning it from the missionaries who are in your country."[17]

Dingane's major faux pas, on the other hand, was his decision to execute Retief, seventy other Afrikaners, and thirty Coloured servants at Mgungundhlovu in February 1838. Dingane invited Retief's party to the Zulu capital under the pretense that the Zulu would officially cede "Port Natal, together with all the land annexed, that is to say from the [Thukela] to the [Mzimvubu] River westward and from the Sea to the North" to the trekboers. On the third day of festivities, however, Dingane ordered his men to carry their guests off to a nearby hill to torture, execute, and leave them "to be devoured by vultures and hyenas."[18] Dingane followed this action with a punitive strike against the Afrikaner families living in western Natal, killing nearly five hundred men, women, and children, and capturing about thirty-five thousand cattle and sheep.[19] What motivated Dingane to take this drastic step? Perhaps he saw it as a preemptive strike to thwart the European intrusion into Natal. In all likelihood, Dingane had been contemplating the attack for some time.[20]

Retief's foolish bravado found its parallel in the Great Plains in 1854 in the person of Lieutenant John L. Grattan. Grattan, born in Vermont and a graduate of West Point in 1853, was posted at Fort Laramie the next year. Observers described Grattan as bold, daring, and enthusiastic, "but rash and impulsive almost beyond belief." Charles Page, an assistant surgeon in the army, wrote that "it was Mr. Grattan's opinion, as expressed often and in earnest, that, with thirty men, he could whip the combined force of all the Indians of the prairie."[21] When Sioux began congregating near the fort for their annual annuity goods in the summer of 1854, a tragedy was waiting to happen.

According to the Treaty of 1851, signed at Horse Creek near Fort Laramie, the government promised to make annual annuity payments to the Sioux for fifty years in return for Teton cooperation in allowing emigrant travel along the Platte Road. The treaty placed the Brulé headman Conquering Bear in charge of enforcing its provisions. As usual, the Sioux began assembling near the fort in late July, awaiting the dispensation of supplies. On August 18 a sickly cow wandered away from a Mormon wagon train passing nearby on its way to Utah, and High Forehead, a Miniconjou visiting the Brulé camp, shot the beast, roasted it, and shared it with his friends. The Mormon, a recently converted Danish immigrant, filed a complaint with the commander at Fort Laramie, Lieutenant Hugh Fleming. Fleming was indecisive. He held a skeletal garrison and was justifiably fearful of provoking a conflict with the Sioux. Grattan, second in command, predictably recommended a swift resolution of the matter. The next day Fleming capitulated and dispatched Grattan to the Sioux encampment to arrest the culprit. "There is no doubt that Lieutenant Grattan left this post with a desire to have a fight with the Indians," Major William Hoffman wrote in November 1854, "and that he had determined to take the man at all hazards."[22]

Grattan led a detachment of thirty men, including his abusive, drunken interpreter, Auguste Lucien. Lucien braced himself during the journey to the Brulé camp with several pints of whiskey. When Grattan arrived, Conquering Bear, along with several other prominent Lakota leaders, tried to dissuade the soldiers from arresting High Forehead and offered to give the Mormons a mule in place of the cow. Meanwhile, Lucien was riding back and forth in front of the apprehensive assembly of Sioux, hurling belittling epithets and howling war whoops at them. Grattan would settle for nothing less than the Miniconjous' surrender and, following a forty-five-minute standoff, ordered his troops to fire. Conquering Bear, who exerted considerable leadership in trying to mediate the dispute, fell, mortally wounded. In response, Brulé warriors reinforced by Oglala sympathizers descended on Grattan and his men with a vengeance. Only one trooper made it back to the fort, and he died several days later. Grattan, one of the first soldiers to fall, died at the age of twenty-four—exactly the number of arrows found in his corpse. According to the official military report, "he could be identified only with his pocket watch." [23]

Reaction to the Grattan debacle was mixed—regional newspapers called for revenge, whereas the Indian Bureau and a number of military officials regarded the incident as Grattan's blunder. But Secretary of War Jefferson Davis, viewing Grattan's demise as "the result of a deliberately formed plan" by the Sioux, recalled vacationing Colonel William S. Harney from Paris, France, to retaliate. [24]

Harney, known to many Lakotas as "Wasp" and "The Butcher," organized a command at Fort Kearny in Nebraska and led his column out on August 24, 1855. He told Sioux leaders the following year he was "very mad" during his march up the Platte, determined to subject hostiles to a sound licking. In contrast, the Indian Bureau's agent at Fort Laramie, Thomas Twiss, wished to avoid a major conflict and sent runners out to coax "friendlies" to move south of the Platte. Twiss's message failed to move Little Thunder's Brulé camp near Ash Hollow. Little Thunder, who replaced Conquering Bear as principal mediator for the 1851 Treaty, had been working diligently to restrain his aggressive warriors and expected some appreciation for his efforts. Instead, the proximity of Little Thunder's camp to the Platte Road put him squarely in the path of the Wasp's whirlwind. [25]

Monday, September 3, 1855, was "a busy and exciting day for us," wrote Captain John Todd of the Sixth Infantry, "but a bloody and disasterous [sic] one to the Sioux." On the previous evening Harney's forces descended into Ash Hollow, positioning themselves for an attack on the Brulé camp on the morning of the third. At daybreak Little Thunder, carrying a white flag, came out to plead with Harney not to fight. "How far this peaceable and friendly disposition was begotten by the presence of the troops before him, burning to avenge their murdered comrades, cannot be known, but a smaller party, doubtless, would have met with a different reception," Todd reasoned. Harney told the Brulé leader to go back to camp and prepare his warriors for battle, and if Little Thunder wanted to escape death, "to get out of the way as quickly as possible." [26]

The Butcher's troops struck the village in a hammer-and-anvil maneuver, putting the inhabitants to flight. A large mass of warriors sought escape up a ravine, but the infantry "poured a plunging fire upon them with our long range rifles, knocking them out of their saddles, right and left." [27] The cavalry pursued fugitives for over five miles, slaughtering fleeing villagers with fierce resolution. Altogether, eighty-five Sioux were killed, and seventy women and children taken as prisoners.

Todd boasted that there had seldom "been such an utter rout and disorganization of a band of Indians." [28] Hyde views Little Thunder's whipping as problematic. The chief was friendly, but some of his villagers had been responsible for waylaying a Salt Lake stage the previous November. Harney's troops found papers stolen from the Salt Lake mail, as well as the clothes of some of Grattan's men and two female scalps.[29] Perhaps these were the discoveries that motivated some of Harney's troopers to hack the pubic hair from dead Brulé women.[30]

The disaster that befell Little Thunder's village, which heartened Captain Todd and perplexed George Hyde, raised the ire of the historian Doane Robinson: "Though hailed as a great victory and an additional plume in Harney's crest of fame, the battle of Ash Hollow was a shameful affair, unworthy of American arms and a disgrace to the officer who planned and executed it. The Indians were trapped and knew it and would have surrendered at discretion had an opportunity been afforded them." [31] More significantly, the battle radicalized a generation of Sioux who would truck no future settlements with whites. A fourteen-year-old Oglala boy named Curly, later known as Crazy Horse, witnessed the aftermath of Ash Hollow. At first the sight of dead men, women, and children probably sickened him. But, one can imagine, when he saw the young sister of Long Spear, with her dress pulled up exposing her mutilated genitals, "all the sickness in the boy was past, and the heat of anger too, leaving him cold, as a man is cold when planning a fight years ahead, waiting, thinking how he would make it come out." [32]

Following his victory at Ash Hollow, Harney moved his troops north and wintered them at Fort Pierre on the Missouri River. In early March 1856 he parleyed with representatives from every Teton band, obtaining their signatures on a treaty penned by the Wasp. The signatories agreed to cease hostilities and accept the decisions made by chiefs and subchiefs appointed by Harney. In addition, each Lakota camp would be policed by soldiers uniformed and maintained by the government. Harney's treaty, drafted without the consent of the Indian Bureau, was killed in the Senate. Regardless, Teton leaders began passing around the war pipe as soon as Harney departed Fort Pierre. During an unprecedented council in the Black Hills in the summer of 1857, the Lakotas "pledged themselves to resist any further encroachments on Teton lands."[33]

Just as Harney had avenged Grattan, Andries Pretorius, a seasoned Afrikaner commando leader, sought to punish Dingane for his massacre of Retief and party in 1837. In late November 1838 Pretorius set off from Natal for Mgungundhlovu with about five hundred well-armed men, nearly sixty supply wagons, and two cannons. On Sunday, December 9, Pretorius's secretary Jan Bantjes recorded that chaplain Sarel Cilliers led the commando in vowing "that should the Lord be pleased to grant us the victory, we [will] raise a house to the memory of His great name."[34]

Whether Cilliers's vow was made in the literal terms Bantjes suggests, or represents a retrospective rationalization for Pretorius's mission, is open to historical debate. In any case, Afrikaner intellectuals in the late nineteenth century resurrected and embellished the event to unite the *volk* against the British imperial threat. In more recent times the Day of the Vow—formerly known as Dingaan's Day and the Day of the Covenant—has constituted a significant pillar of Afrikaner nationalism as well as a South African public holiday. The date celebrated, however, is the sixteenth, not the ninth, because the former represents the day Zulu warriors stained the Ncome River red with their blood.[35]

On the Saturday following the alleged vow, the commando laagered its wagons at a prominent bank on the Ncome River. Shortly after the camp arose on the hot, still morning of December 16, it came under attack by ten thousand Zulu warriors, running toward the Boer wagons en masse. "Their approach, although frightful on account of the great number . . . presented a beautiful appearance," Bantjes observed.[36] From their defensively advantageous position, the Afrikaners poured cannon and musket fire into the Zulu soldiers, most of whom lacked firearms. The fight turned quickly into a rout. Around three thousand Zulus died in what became known as the Blood River battle, whereas no whites were killed and only three wounded. Blood River, in the words of the historian Leonard Thompson, "was a classic example of the devastating superiority of controlled fire, by resolute men from a defensive position, over Africans armed with assegais and spears, however numerous and however brave."[37]

Pretorius's Victory Commando proceeded to Mgungundhlovu, but found it abandoned and in flames. Less than a mile from Dingane's kraal they discovered the remains of Retief and his men. Among the rotting corpses, Pretorius's commando came across a leather bag containing the treaty ceding Natal to the voortrekkers. The Republic of Natalia was theirs, or so it seemed. When Pretorius returned to his base camp on the Thukela River, he learned that a detachment of British soldiers had occupied Port Natal on December 4. The historians Edgar Brookes and Colin Webb point out that the object of this mission, "so far as the changing and hesitating instructions of the Colonial Office might be said to have an object, was to restore peace between the Trekkers and Dingane."[38] The Boers feared it presaged a more permanent British presence. For the moment, however, the voortrekkers were less interested in the dangers of British encroachment in Natal than in taking advantage of the fractures in the Zulu polity.

Following the catastrophe at Blood River, a number of powerful men in Zululand shifted their support from Dingane to the king's brother, Mpande. Mpande was a savvy survivor in the Machiavellian world of Zulu politics. In all likelihood, he avoided the fratricidal temptations of both Shaka and Dingane by remaining submissive and docile. Because of his relative passivity, scholars ordinarily depict Mpande as a simpleton, "the fool of the family."[39] If so, this alleged dolt survived to rule the Zulu kingdom for thirty-two years, longer than the combined reigns of Shaka, Dingane, and Mpande's son Cetshwayo. In addition, unlike his brothers and perhaps even his son, Mpande died a natural death.

In September 1839 Mpande defied his brother for the first time. Rather than supporting Dingane's war against the Swazi, Mpande split the kingdom by leading thousands of Zulu supporters southward across the Thukela River into the republic of Natalia. The Volksraad, the trekker government at their new capital of Pietermaritzburg, seeing a chance to intervene in Zulu politics, allied with Mpande in a northern campaign against Dingane. The alliance prevailed—Dingane's army was crushed, and the king himself eventually captured and executed by the Swazi. Pretorius, commandant general of the new South African Republic (later the Transvaal), bestowed the Zulu kingship on Mpande in return for the new king's vassalage to Natalia. With Mpande set up as their puppet in the north, the Afrikaners returned to Natal with a booty of more than thirty-six thousand cattle.[40]

The Zulu people still remember Mpande's secession and alliance with the Boers as "the breaking of the rope that held the nation together."[41] Indeed, Mpande's rule reverted to the centrifugation characteristic of

2. *Umpande the King of the Amazulu* [Mpande]. Drawn and lithographed by George French Angas. In Angas's *The Kafirs Illustrated* (London: Hogarth, 1849), Plate 11.

pre-Shakan politics, which in turn fashioned a tempered despotism. Consequently, the relaxation of tensions in the Zulu kingdom convinced thousands of Mfecane refugees to return to Natal. Between 1840 and 1843 Natalia's African population quintupled to fifty thousand, vastly outnumbering the resident Boers. The trekkers, who kidnapped African children to remedy their labor shortages, viewed this migration with mixed emotions. Facing a dilemma that would recur again and again, "a white minority was faced with the problem of reconciling its need for security with its dependence on the labor of conquered peoples." [42]

The influx of Africans sealed the fate of the trekker republic. When the Volksraad sought to relocate "surplus" Africans to the south of the colony, thereby threatening the territories claimed by Faku's Mpondo, British colonial authorities scrambled to forestall the impending demographic disaster. The British did not want to annex Natal, but they wanted stability in the eastern Cape. In addition, the acquisition of Natal would mollify outspoken evangelicals as well as commercial enthusiasts. Therefore, "with manifest reluctance" according to the historian John S. Galbraith, the Colonial Office authorized the annexation of Natal in December 1842.[43] Too feeble to resist, the fledgling republic capitulated, but not happily. By the end of the 1840s, the majority of emigrants had abandoned Natal for the highveld.

In October 1843 British commissioner Henry Cloete worked out a treaty with Mpande that set the boundary dividing Natal and Zululand at the Thukela and Mzinyathi rivers. No longer a vassal in the eyes of the British, Mpande opened a dialogue with the highveld Boers. In 1847, for example, he ceded the Klip River triangle in northern Natal to a group of Afrikaners in violation of the aforementioned treaty. The British convinced Mpande to repudiate the cession and then dispatched a garrison to prevent the Boers from occupying their Klip River "republic." Thereafter, Mpande avoided confrontations with the British but continued to court the Boers. Caught between two expansive forces, the king needed to keep every diplomatic option available.[44]

Internally, Mpande blunted potential sibling rivalries early on in his reign. In 1843, sensing an assassination plot directed against him, Mpande ordered the death of his brother Gqugqu, along with Gqugqu's wives and children. These killings sent thousands of refugees into Natal, whose safety was guaranteed in the Cloete Treaty. Boasting of his ruthlessness, perhaps to dispel his pusillanimous image, Mpande once told J. W. Shepstone that "the only way to govern a Zulu is to kill him." [45] By the mid-

1850s, however, as Mpande's ambitious sons Cetshwayo and Mbuyazi reached manhood, the king's power began to decline.

Mpande favored Mbuyazi, his second-eldest son, to succeed him as Zulu king. Most of the territorial chiefs and *izinduna* preferred Mpande's eldest son, Cetshwayo. Born in 1832, Cetshwayo was recruited into the Thulwana regiment in his late teens. As he matured he attracted supporters calling themselves Usuthu, a drinking boast derived from the corpulent Suthu cattle breed.[46] Cetshwayo impressed others with his political savvy, sagacity, and commanding presence. When John William Colenso, bishop of Natal, met Mpande's son in 1859, he was struck by Cetshwayo's "air of dignity" and referred to him as this "fine, handsome young fellow . . . with a very pleasant smile and good-humoured face, and strong deep voice."[47] In the early 1870s Natal's secretary for native affairs, Theophilus Shepstone, regarded Cetshwayo as "a man of considerable ability," with great "force of character," and "remarkably frank and straightforward."[48]

In 1856 Cetshwayo found it necessary to exercise his leadership skills in a deadly civil conflict with his brother, Mbuyazi. As tensions mounted, iziGqoza, Mbuyazi's faction, took up residence near the Thukela River in a tract of country ceded them by Mpande. In December, Cetshwayo's Usuthu followers attacked iziGqoza at Ndondakusuka, massacring thousands of men, women, and children, and killing Mbuyazi along with five of Mpande's other sons. The corpses of victims who drowned in the Thukela washed up on Durban beaches days after the battle.[49]

His power circumscribed, Mpande continued to reign if not rule. Without fail, the king formed new age regiments, regulated marriage, and managed state rituals. Cetshwayo elected not to usurp these kingly functions, but did not hesitate to lay the groundwork for his own regime. In 1861, for example, he negotiated separate, far-reaching agreements with the Transvaal Boers and the British. In return for the Transvaalers' support for his succession, Cetshwayo ceded the Boers an indeterminate tract of western Zululand. The British countered by sending Theophilus Shepstone to Zululand to conclude a separate treaty with Cetshwayo. Shepstone acknowledged Cetshwayo as Mpande's successor during a tense meeting in April. He also befriended the Zulu prince, a friendship that proved to be a fatal mistake for the Zulu kingdom.[50]

Red Cloud's fatal miscalculation was to trust the federal government in 1868. At issue were the Black Hills, sacred territory to the Sioux, and the Powder River country, which the Lakotas had wrested from the Crows during the previous two decades. The government clearly recognized the Sioux's attachment to the Black Hills. During Lieutenant Gouverneur K. Warren's topographical expedition there in the summer of 1856, Warren's party encountered an angry Teton assemblage. Though the Sioux did not attack, "the grounds of their objection to our traversing their region were very sensible," Warren recorded, "and of sufficient weight . . . to have justified them, in their own minds, in resisting us."[51] As for Powder River territory, the development of gold mines in Idaho and Montana necessitated a new passageway to this western El Dorado. On March 1, 1865, Congress authorized construction of a road from Fort Laramie to Bozeman, Montana. The proposed Bozeman Trail, which bisected the last major Teton buffalo range, placed the United States and the Sioux people on a collision course.[52]

Ironically, as one hostility ended at Appomattox Court House on April 9, 1865, another was peaking on the plains. Incensed by the American attack on Black Kettle at Sand Creek,[53] the mounting emigrant traffic on the Platte road, and the prospects for more traffic on the Bozeman Trail, Brulés and Oglalas assaulted wagon trains, ranches, stage stations, and telegraph offices. Also that spring Red Cloud raised a large force of Oglalas and Cheyennes to harass James Sawyer's road-building party, surrounding it for fifteen days on the Powder River. Although the Red Cloud coalition retreated, their leader exercised considerable authority in restraining hotheads aching for an attack.[54]

Red Cloud's power in 1865 was informal yet substantial. He was not a chief, and may not have been a head warrior.[55] Regardless, the Oglalas recognized Red Cloud as a significant leader at this time, in part because of his military successes against the Crows, Pawnees, and Shoshonis, as well as his growing defiance toward the white intrusion.[56] Many in the United States government thought highly of Red Cloud as well. In March 1866, for example, Colonel Henry E. Maynadier, commander of Fort Laramie, wrote that Red Cloud and the Brulé leader Spotted Tail "rule the [Sioux] nation."[57]

Unlike Spotted Tail, whose people lived south of the Platte, Red Cloud cared deeply about the fate of Powder River country, where the Oglalas hunted frequently. Therefore, given the government's interest in opening the Montana road, Red Cloud was a pivotal figure in every government peace initiative between 1866 and 1868. In June 1866, for example, the treaty commissioner E. B. Taylor convinced Spotted Tail and other friendly chiefs to sign a peace treaty at Fort Laramie granting whites a right-of-way through Powder River country. Red Cloud, present at the

3. *Red Cloud.* Oil painting by Henry Raschen, collection of Lee and David Blumberg.

council, heaped scorn on the agreement, refused to sign, and withdrew. His defiance scuttled the talks, but soon thereafter Taylor, exercising either self-deception or guile, wired the Indian commissioner that a "satisfactory treaty" had been concluded with the Sioux. "Most cordial feeling prevails," Taylor conjectured.[58]

Colonel Henry B. Carrington was not as sanguine as Taylor. Carrington, charged with constructing fortifications along the Bozeman Trail, set out with some trepidation from Fort Laramie in the summer of 1866 with an inexperienced infantry battalion and inadequate supplies of ammunition. Dutifully, Carrington went about constructing post headquarters, named Fort Phil Kearny, meanwhile badgering his department commander in Omaha for troop reinforcements. Carrington had good reason to be wary. Red Cloud's warriors, revitalized by a sun dance in July, harassed Carrington's fort day and night, all summer and fall, absolutely determined to rid the country of whites.

Their opportunity to strike a devastating blow against Carrington's troopers came on December 21, 1866. Early that morning Carrington sent Captain William J. Fetterman and eighty men to relieve a wood train under attack. Fetterman, who had once boasted that he could "take eighty men and ride through the whole Sioux nation," got suckered by an age-old Teton decoy tactic and charged rashly into an ambush. By the time the support column arrived, Fetterman's entire contingent had perished. Corpses, mutilated beyond recognition, lay strewn amid the snow-dusted slopes above Big Piney Creek.[59]

"Of course, this massacre should be treated as an act of war and should be punished with vindictive earnestness, until at least ten Indians are killed for each white life lost," divisional commander William T. Sherman wrote in response to the Fetterman debacle.[60] Much to Sherman's chagrin,[61] however, Congress responded by forming commissions to prosecute peace with the Sioux. The Sanborn Commission recommended abandonment of the Bozeman Trail forts and the establishment of an eighty-thousand-square-mile reservation between the Missouri and Yellowstone rivers. Congress endorsed the Sanborn proposals and created a peace commission in July 1867 "to identify and remove the causes of hostility and attempt to consolidate all the Plains Indians on reservations."[62]

The Taylor Peace Commission, which included disgruntled warriors such as Sherman and Harney, was at first dominated by its pacifistic chair, Nathaniel G. Taylor. Taylor had been appointed Indian commissioner by President Andrew Johnson in March 1867. A Princeton graduate and Methodist minister, Taylor served as a congressman before and after the Civil War. He was representative of a group of eastern humanitarians unsettled by the warfare engulfing the plains in the 1860s. The millions of whites advancing upon the Indians "will soon crush them out from the face of the earth," he wrote in July 1867, "unless the humanity and Christian philanthropy of our enlightened statesmen shall interfere and rescue them."[63] Taylor, convinced he must persuade warring Indians to move to reservations as quickly as possible, believed it his divine duty to transform them into Christian farmers. He did not question the validity of his assumptions, nor did Taylor see that his "humanitarianism" was as misguided as Sherman's bellicosity. The Sioux were fighting to preserve their lands as well as their way of life. In essence, they were struggling to *prevent* being subordinated to another culture's worldview.

The commissioners journeyed to Fort Laramie in November 1867 to parley with Red Cloud. When the Oglala leader spurned them by not showing, Harney called for a military offensive, but Taylor's approach prevailed. The commission returned to the fort the following spring, this time carrying a treaty seemingly guaranteed to bring Red Cloud to council and a lasting peace to the plains. The Treaty of 1868 called for the Sioux to relinquish their right to occupy permanently all nonreservation lands; abandonment of the Bozeman Trail forts; the establishment of the Great Sioux Reservation (South Dakota west of the Missouri River, including the Black Hills), on which unauthorized whites would never be permitted "to pass over, settle upon, or reside"; and the reservation of land north of the North Platte River and east of the Bighorn Mountains as unceded Indian territory, off limits to all whites.[64]

Eventually, 159 Sioux chiefs signed the treaty, but what did they accept? As John Gray points out, the Treaty of 1868 is filled with "gross contradictions," ceding "territory admittedly unceded" and confining the Sioux "to a reservation while allowing [them] to roam elsewhere. . . . The mass of Indians must have remained largely ignorant of its contents," Gray suggests, "and it is inconceivable that any Indian was truthfully informed of all its provisions."[65] A number of Sioux signatories were skeptical as well. American Horse told generals Harney and John Sanborn at Fort Laramie that "I will sign, and if there is anything wrong afterwards I will watch the commissioners, and they will be the first one[s] that I will whip."[66] The whole Indian-white treaty-making process, according to Raymond DeMallie, was inherently flawed:

> Perhaps the single most frustrating aspect of the entire history of treaty making was the inability of the two sides to communicate with one another meaningfully. Both whites and Indians used the councils to deliver speeches composed in advance. Specific objections or questions by Indians were rarely answered when they were raised, but were answered a day or more later in the course of lengthy speeches. Many questions went unanswered, and many objections were simply ignored.[67]

Despite much uncertainty, Red Cloud finally signed the treaty in November 1868, long after the commission had departed Fort Laramie. The commissioners had assembled in Chicago a month earlier to deliberate on the mounting Indian-white violence on the southern plains, precipitated in large part by General Winfield Hancock's untimely military expedition through Kansas in 1867. The absence of Senator John Henderson, a Taylor supporter, gave the hawks on the commission a majority of votes. Led by Sherman, the commissioners resolved to end all treaty negotiations with Indians, legitimated the use of force in moving Indians to reservations, and recommended that the Indian Bureau be transferred to the War Department. Ulysses S. Grant, who sat in on the meeting, told a reporter afterward "that the settlers and emigrants had to be protected even if it meant the extermination of every Indian tribe."[68]

The sentiments of the next president of the United States did not bode well for Red Cloud's folk. Like the Zulu, the Lakotas were approaching the vortex of an expansionist whirlwind, trying to steady themselves for the ordeal. They had resisted as well as negotiated, and now entrusted the fate of their people to the seemingly benevolent agents of imperialism. Unfortunately, both the Sioux and Zulu discovered in the 1870s that they had positioned themselves for a colossal betrayal.

C H A P T E R 5

Agents of Empire

 HE 1870s marked a decisive turning point for the Sioux and Zulu. Both peoples, plagued with internal economic woes and destabilized by endemic political factionalism, had become barriers to an advancing white frontier. The Great Sioux Reservation and unceded territory blocked the exploitation of the Black Hills, hindered the development of the Northern Pacific Railroad, and foiled the Indian Bureau's schemes to concentrate and civilize the Lakotas. Zululand, one of the last independent African states in southern Africa, posed an obstacle to Britain's confederation plans in the region, bottled up labor supplies for the mining industries, and harnessed spacious tracts of land fancied by Natalian sugar farmers. In these circumstances, the intercultural bonds forged in the 1860s began to unravel. Formerly sympathetic white administrators, responding to political expediencies in the 1870s, came to view total war against the Zulu and Sioux as an inescapable necessity. Obsessed with manufacturing a *casus belli*, these agents of empire paved the roads to the Little Bighorn and Isandhlwana.

According to the Treaty of 1868, the Sioux retained the right to live outside government reservations as long as a sufficient number of buffaloes existed to justify the hunt. Some herds continued to roam the northern central plains throughout the 1870s, but their ranks were thinning. Under siege by professional buffalo hunters, the North American bison population faced extinction. "Hide hunters" who arrived on the plains by means of the Union Pacific Railroad slaughtered entire herds, killing up to three million beasts per year in the early 1870s.[1] Pleased by this carnage, Philip H. Sheridan, commander of the Great Plains during the Grant administration, wrote, "If I could learn that every buffalo in the northern herd were killed I would be glad. The destruction of this herd would do more to keep Indians quiet than anything else that could happen."[2]

The diminution of their most important subsistence resource forced thousands of Tetons into government agencies during the early 1870s. Some camped permanently and were regarded as "friendly" by the government. A great many others, however oscillated between the unceded territory and the camps. General D. S. Stanley referred to the latter as "violent and troublesome fellows" who spent half their time at the agencies "and the other half at the hostile camps." Stanley alleged that these "hostiles" would "abuse the agents, threaten their lives, kill their cattle at night, and do anything they can to oppose the civilizing movement, but eat all the provisions they can get." [3]

The competing attractions of security and freedom polarized Sioux politics, galvanizing new leadership. The government continued to court Red Cloud and Spotted Tail, each of whom collaborated to gain the greatest possible advantage for his followers. [4] For example, both leaders held out for government agencies outside the Great Sioux Reservation, ones closer to their traditional hunting territories. After years of haggling, the government relented in 1873, establishing the Red Cloud and Spotted Tail agencies in northwestern Nebraska. [5] But even though Red Cloud and Spotted Tail continued to speak on behalf of great numbers of Oglalas and Brulés, they did not speak for all the Lakota people. New leaders such as the Hunkpapa Sitting Bull and Crazy Horse of the Oglalas, who advocated armed resistance to all whites, began to attract many followers to the Powder River country.

In the aftermath of the 1868 treaty, Sitting Bull in particular came to personify the spirit of uncompromising, ethnocentric hostility to white encroachment found among many Sioux at the time. A deeply religious man, convinced that his visionary powers derived from a harmonious convergence with universal spiritual forces, Sitting Bull believed that contact with whites would weaken and eventually destroy Teton culture. Those who shared his concern looked to the Hunkpapa holy man as their last best hope in defending the Sioux way of life. Consequently, by the early 1870s Sioux recalcitrants came to regard Sitting Bull as head chief of all the Lakotas. [6]

Sitting Bull's obstinacy spawned a fair number of detractors, but his compassion gained him a multitude of admirers. Fanny Kelly, a white captive who spent the better part of five months living with Sitting Bull and his family, described the Hunkpapa leader as "a true nobleman, and great man. He was uniformly gentle, and kind to his wife and children and courteous and considerate in his intercourse w. others." During Kelly's captivity in 1864, the Sioux experienced disastrous food shortages. Sitting

Bull "and his wife," Kelly reported, "often suffered w. hunger to supply me w. food."[7] The interpreter Frank Grouard said the "name Sitting Bull was a 'tipi word' for all that was generous and great. The bucks admired him, the squaws respected him highly, and the children loved him."[8]

But many Sitting Bull enthusiasts admired him for his unqualified hatred of white civilization, Fanny Kelly notwithstanding. Mrs. C. Weldon, a missionary to the Hunkpapas, reported that Sitting Bull "distrusted the innovations sought to be forced upon the Indians. . . . white civilization," with its hypocrisy and avarice, "did not impress him," she said. "He never signed a treaty to sell any portion of his people's inheritance, and he refused to acknowledge the right of other Indians to sell his undivided share of the tribal lands."[9] In the words of Evan Connell, Sitting Bull "was about as consistent and inflexible as a man could be."[10]

The swelling ranks of Sitting Bull enthusiasts gravely concerned military authorities. In the winter of 1873–74, for example, Sioux dissidents from the north entered Red Cloud and Spotted Tail agencies, plundered stores, and killed several whites, including a Lieutenant Levi Robinson. In response, General Sherman ordered up cavalry and infantry from Fort Laramie under the command of Colonel John E. Smith to quell the unrest. By the time the troops arrived, however, following a harrowing winter trek, the crisis had passed. Nevertheless, Smith established a military post near Red Cloud Agency in case of future trouble. He named it Fort Robinson, in honor of the fallen lieutenant.[11]

In response to the Sioux provocation at the agencies, Sherman wrote Sheridan in March 1874 that many people "even [Interior Secretary Columbus] Delano, would be happy if the troops should kill a goodly proportion of those Sioux, but they want to keep the record to prove that they didn't do it. We can afford to be frank and honest," Sherman continued, "for sooner or later these Sioux have to be wiped out or made to stay just where they are put."[12] Sherman's vow came true sooner rather than later, hastened along by events at the periphery of empire.

Like the Sioux, the Zulu faced a severe subsistence crisis during the 1870s. Analogous to the diminishing buffalo population in the Great Plains, the Zulu kingdom was plagued by cattle shortages. Several factors underlay the problem. First, new diseases such as lung sickness, introduced by white traders from Natal, ravaged Zululand herds between the late 1850s and early 1870s. Second, pasture degeneration, a product of severe overgrazing during the reigns of Dingane and Mpande, an indirect precipitant of pre-Shakan state formation, contributed to the depletion of stock.

Compounding ecological degradation, the Zulu population had increased significantly during the early years of Mpande's rule. By the early 1870s it stood at 300,000, a threefold increase since 1840. Finally, drought, a periodic bane to Zululand farmers, returned with a vengeance during the 1860s and 1870s, with 1878–79 representing an especially dry season.[13]

Since cattle were used for patronage and paying fines, diminished livestock reserves also affected the power of the Zulu monarch.[14] But Cetshwayo, who became king at Mpande's death in 1872, faced even more troubling issues of authority. Namely, the king had to combat the persistent decentralizing forces in his kingdom, especially the problem of divided loyalties among some of his more powerful white advisers and territorial chiefs. The most notable examples, John Dunn and Hamu, both defected to the British side at the outset of the Anglo-Zulu War.

John Dunn, born in Natal and orphaned at an early age by his English parents, took up transport riding and hunting in his teens. He first visited the Zulu kingdom in 1853, and in 1856 joined forces with Mbuyazi during his struggle with Cetshwayo's Usuthu. Regardless, Cetshwayo befriended Dunn, viewing the white man's bilingualism a useful skill in Zulu relations with Natal. The future king invited Dunn to settle in Zululand in 1858 and granted him a substantial territory in the south of the kingdom. From this base, Dunn amassed considerable wealth and power by the 1870s. While serving as Cetshwayo's major adviser to the white colonies, Dunn married forty northern Nguni women, accumulated over three thousand head of cattle, hired a private army of 250 African hunters, and recruited Tsonga laborers for Natal at an annual salary of three hundred pounds. Dunn also imported the lion's share of the twenty thousand antiquated, muzzle-loading firearms that reportedly entered Zululand during the 1870s. Yet Dunn's extensive ties to the colonial world rendered his loyalty suspect. Indeed, Dunn joined the British soon after Isandhlwana and profited by Cetshwayo's demise.[15]

Even more troubling for Cetshwayo was the disposition of his elder brother, Hamu. Unlike Dunn, Hamu supported Usuthu in 1856, and since that time had built up a strong personal following in northwestern Zululand. In addition, Hamu developed extensive trading interests outside the Zulu kingdom through the advice of Herbert Nunn, a white trader whom the Zulu chief allowed to reside in his northwestern district. Abutting the Transvaal in the Blood River frontier, Hamu's northwestern boundary with the Boers had been a source of contention for years. During the 1870s Hamu grew increasingly critical of Cetshwayo's handling of the border controversy, with tensions exploding at the *umkhosi* in 1878. At this first-fruits festival, Hamu's Thulwana regiment assaulted Ngobomakhosi, Cetshwayo's favorite *ibutho*, leaving scores dead. Hamu's wider loyalties with the colonial world, combined with a festering sibling rivalry, led him to negotiate with the British for postwar concessions on the eve of the Anglo-Zulu War itself.[16]

Similar schisms emerged among the southern Nguni-speaking Xhosa in the 1850s. Following a half century of military subjugation, expropriation, missionary enterprise, and commercial temptation, the Xhosa lost over 100,000 cattle to a lung sickness epidemic that struck in 1854. This devastating epidemic, combined with the experience of defeat, resulted in Xhosa prophecies predicting that the dead would rise and the British driven into the sea if only the Xhosa people killed the rest of their cattle. The majority of Xhosa complied. By the end of 1857 they had destroyed 400,000 head of cattle, and in the ensuing famine, over 40,000 Xhosa died of starvation. The Xhosa cattle-killing experience divided the people into two parties, the "soft" believers and the "hard" unbelievers. The majority "soft" faction regarded itself as the loyal defender of the traditional Xhosa values of mutual aid and communal solidarity. The "hard" party, composed principally of men like Hamu who benefited from the economic and social opportunities of the colonial presence, considered the killing senseless.[17]

To combat the centrifugal forces in his kingdom, as well as to cement his alliance with Natal in order to gain diplomatic advantage in the Transvaal-Zululand border dispute, Cetshwayo invited Theophilus Shepstone to the king's "coronation" in 1873. What seemed like prudent diplomacy at the time later proved to be a major miscalculation. Shepstone possessed an agenda quite distinct from Cetshwayo's, one that placed Zulu interests in a most precarious position.

Shepstone, the son of a Methodist missionary, was raised on the eastern Cape frontier. Before taking up the post of Natal's secretary for native affairs in 1853, a position he would hold for the next twenty-two years, Shepstone served as an agent for the African refugees of the Shakan wars and diplomatic agent for the African peoples of Natal. Shepstone's experience with dispossessed Africans fashioned a paternalistic temperament, as well as a conviction that he retained an intimate understanding of the "native mind." As secretary for native affairs, Shepstone believed that Africans should be governed separately and not allowed to settle permanently in "white" areas. He also felt that "divide and rule" represented an effective means of preventing a "native combination" that might challenge white supremacy. As he said, "tribal distinctions that obtain among [Africans] are highly useful in managing them in detail."[18]

In effect, Shepstone exercised an early form of indirect rule—Nguni chiefs enjoyed semi-independence in their respective territories under the paternal guidance of Natalian officials. Such stable African communities could be taxed, serving two significant functions. First, tax revenues paid the costs of colonial administration, saving the European taxpayer unnecessary expense; and second, taxes nudged the African from subsistence production into the colonial economy, a necessary preliminary for the indigene's civilizational "uplift." Shepstone possessed supreme confidence that his system of African administration assured all Natalians peace, prosperity, and racial harmony.[19]

African leaders who deviated from Shepstone's paternalistic utopia found themselves at risk. In 1873, for example, the Hlubi leader Langalibalele, whose people had been "located" in the Drakensberg foothills following their departure from Zululand to Natal in 1848, ran afoul of the Shepstonian system. His offense was failing to see to it that all the guns in his reserve were registered. In theory, all Africans possessing guns in South African colonies were required to register them with colonial magistrates. By the early 1870s a number of Langalibalele's young men had purchased guns while away working at the diamond mines, raising fears among Natalian authorities of a conspiratorial "combination." When Langalibalele failed to appear before the court in Pietermaritzburg after repeated summons, Shepstone and Lieutenant Governor Benjamin Pine planned, organized, and accompanied a punitive mission.[20]

On October 29, 1873, sixty-five hundred troopers invaded the Hlubi reserve. Although Langalibalele had escaped into Basutoland, the British force attacked the location, killing two hundred resisters. Eventually the Hlubi chief was captured and, in early 1874, tried before a court that included Shepstone and Pine. Denied defense counsel, Langalibalele was banished from his location for life and conveyed to Robben Island, outside Cape Town, in August 1874. In addition, Natal confiscated the livestock and expropriated the lands of the chief's subjects. Shepstone later characterized his own motives in the Langalibalele affair as originating from an "ardent love of justice."[21]

As a colonial agent Shepstone was motivated by a number of concerns, perhaps none more important than his grandiose vision of British imperial expansion. For years, Shepstone had dreamed of using the Blood

River territory under dispute between the Zulu and Boers as part of a "safety valve" for "surplus" and potentially volatile Africans in Natal, as a passage for migrant laborers from the north, and most importantly, as a road for British expansion up to the Zambesi frontier.[22] That ultimately this safety valve "will also be occupied by Europeans cannot be doubted," Shepstone argued,

> but if the land can be acquired, and put to the purpose I have suggested, the present tension in Natal will be relieved, and time be gained to admit of the introduction of a larger population of white colonists. . . . But it will be a mistake to suppose that the relief afforded by this measure would be but temporary or that the difficulty it is proposed to abate could ever again reach its present dimensions; because the outlet being to the North, the abatement admits of permanent extension towards a climate unsuited to Europeans but not so to natives.[23]

For these reasons, Shepstone regarded the "coronation" as an opportunity to gain special political leverage in the Zulu kingdom, using the occasion to cast a decisive shadow over Zulu sovereignty.

In fact, the so-called coronation of September 1, 1873 was a farce. Shepstone later argued that he installed Cetshwayo as king, when in reality the Zulu had held a separate ceremony a month before Shepstone's celebrated "installation."[24] Moreover, Shepstone promulgated certain laws restricting the implementation of capital punishment within the Zulu kingdom, and he argued that these regulations had been accepted as binding by Cetshwayo himself. Later in the 1870s Shepstone and High Commissioner Bartle Frere would cite violations of these laws as a pretext for declaring war on the Zulu kingdom. In truth, the laws were worded ambiguously and could be interpreted as restricting the activities of Cetshwayo's territorial chiefs rather than the king.[25] Cetshwayo found it extraordinary that he had supposedly accepted laws from Natal whose "breaking" might serve as an excuse for war. As he said in 1876, "I do not agree to give my people over to be governed by laws sent to me by [Natal]. . . . Mr. Shepstone . . . deceived the white men, saying I had agreed to his laws."[26]

Nonetheless, the "coronation" is significant in that it marks the first, albeit farcical, attempt by the British to subject the Zulu to imperial overrule in the 1870s. Britain's attempt to combine its South African territories into a white-dominated confederation during the remainder of the 1870s made future overtures toward the Zulu much more deadly serious.

As in South Africa, the activities of "men on the spot" played a considerable role in bringing on war with the Sioux. Sherman's brusque sentiments toward nonreservation Sioux remained consistent throughout the 1860s and 1870s. As he wrote in 1873, the Sioux "must be made to know that when the Government commands they must obey, and until that state of mind is reached, through persuasion or fear, we can not hope for peace."[27] But after Sherman moved his headquarters from Washington to St. Louis in May 1874, the result of a dispute with Secretary of War William Belknap, the general distanced himself from the decision-making loop. As far as the Sioux were concerned, two other individuals played more significant roles in enforcing Grant's peace policy: Lieutenant Colonel George Custer, the Seventh Cavalry commander, and Major General Philip Sheridan, commander of the Division of the Missouri.

Custer, the "Boy General" of Civil War fame, regarded himself an expert on the subject of the Great Plains, especially when it came to understanding the "Indian problem." In an essay written in 1868 entitled "The Red Man," Custer judged the Sioux and other Indians as noble savages yet doomed to extinction. In sententious prose, Custer argued that Indians "once stood in their native strength and beauty, stamped with the proud majesty of free born men, whose souls never knew fear or whose eyes never quailed beneath the fierce glance of man. But . . . now," he wrote, "they are like withered leaves of their own native forest, scattered in every direction by the fury of the tempest." Custer predicted that the Indian was perched "on the verge of extinction, standing on his last foothold, clutching his bloodstained rifle, resolved to die amidst the horrors of slaughter." Soon, Custer concluded, the Indian would "be talked of as a noble race who once existed but have now passed away."[28]

In the same year as his "Red Man" essay, Custer sought to fulfill his dire predictions at Black Kettle's Cheyenne village on the Washita River, in present-day Oklahoma. Black Kettle, a consistent peace advocate, had been victimized by Colonel John M. Chivington's volunteers at Sand Creek, Colorado, four years earlier. The chief's encampment now lay within range of Sheridan's winter campaign in the southern plains. Sheridan's orders to Custer were simple and direct: "To proceed south, in the direction of the Antelope hills, thence towards the Washita River, the supposed winter seat of the hostile tribes; to destroy their villages and ponies; to kill or hang all warriors, and bring back all women and children."[29]

As dawn broke on November 27, Custer divided his command and prepared for an attack. He had yet to ascertain the size of the village or the nature of the surrounding terrain, an omission for which he was later criticized. Nevertheless, to the accompaniment of his regimental band's rendition of "Garry Owen," Custer led the charge across the river into the village. For the startled inhabitants, the ensuing melee was deadly— Black Kettle, his wife, and nearly three hundred villagers, including many women and children, perished in the onslaught. And as per Sheridan's instructions, Custer ordered the Cheyenne pony herd slaughtered as well.[30]

"We have cleaned Black Kettle and his band out so thoroughly that they can neither fight, dress, sleep, eat or ride without sponging upon their friends," Custer boasted in a letter to Sheridan the day following the Washita battle. Although Washita established Custer's reputation as the preeminent plains Indian fighter of the era, it nevertheless served to tarnish his image as well. Specifically, Custer deserted a missing unit under the command of Major Joel Elliot at Washita, only to find the mutilated remains of Elliot and his men some ten days later. The episode strained Custer's relations with a number of his fellow officers and men, including his Little Bighorn cohort, Frederick Benteen.[31] In addition, Custer, whose wife, Libbie, remained in Monroe, Michigan, in 1868, may have taken on a teenage mistress named Monahsetah from the Cheyenne captives at Washita. According to Cheyenne oral tradition, Monahsetah bore a child fathered by the "Boy General."[32]

Custer, tainted victor at Washita, played a central role in two major provocations leading directly to the outbreak of the U.S.-Sioux War of 1876–77: the Yellowstone expedition of 1873 and, the following year, the reconnaissance of the Black Hills. The Yellowstone expedition occurred in conjunction with the proposed extension of the Northern Pacific Railroad, which had proceeded from Minnesota to the Missouri River between 1870 and 1872. In 1873 the Northern Pacific proposed to advance up the Yellowstone Valley, arguably part of the unceded territory from the 1868 treaty. As far as the Sioux were concerned, the northern boundary of this "unceded" cession was irrelevant. The advance of the railroad promised to bring hunters, soldiers, and immigrants, guaranteeing the destruction of the last great buffalo herd on the plains. For Sitting Bull's people, the only alternative was war. In stark contrast to the Lakota view, Custer, like his superiors Sherman and Sheridan, regarded railway development as the supreme pacifier:

> The experience of the past, particularly that of recent years, has shown too that no one measure so quickly and effectually frees a country from the horrors and devastations of Indian wars and Indian depredations generally as the building and successful operation of a

4. George Armstrong
Custer. Woodcut in
Leslie's Illustrated,
26 March 1864.

railroad through the region overrun. . . . So earnest is my belief in
the civilizing and peace-giving influence of railroads [that their ex-
tension] through an Indian country . . . would for ever after have preserved peace with the vast number of tribes infesting the [plains].[33]

Custer, who represented mainstream thinking on the "Indian question"
by the 1870s, reflects the contradictory impulses in the formulation of
United States Indian policy. In the words of the historian Richard Slotkin,
"the makers of the Indian policy wanted both to subjugate the Indians—
which implied making war—and to establish a regime characterized by
peace; they wanted to protect Indian rights, while at the same time extinguishing Indian title to the land to facilitate the building of railroads."[34]

The army provided munificent escorts for each Northern Pacific survey. In 1873, for example, fifteen hundred soldiers, including ten troops
of the Seventh Cavalry under Custer's command, accompanied the sur-
veyors. Looking to "subdue and intimidate" any hostile Sioux, Custer
engaged Lakota warriors on two occasions in early August. In the first
engagement, near the mouth of the Tongue River, Custer ordered his

cavalry to charge about three hundred Sioux combatants. He later exulted that "despite their superiority in numbers [the Sioux] cowardly prepared for flight." One week later, on the Yellowstone, Custer's troops encountered around five hundred Teton warriors, who, despite giving significant resistance, once again broke and fled. Custer believed the Sioux coalition to have been organized by Sitting Bull. The Hunkpapa leader, Custer concluded, had for once "been taught a lesson he will not soon forget." [35]

Custer's confidence as an Indian fighter without equal carried over into an even riskier venture the following year: a survey of the Black Hills. The Black Hills expedition of 1874, like the Washita campaign, was conceived by General Sheridan. "Little Phil" Sheridan, whom Sherman compared to a "persevering terrier dog," [36] sympathized with the plight of the Sioux but did not allow sentimentality to dictate military policy. "I have the interest of the Indian at heart as much as anyone," he wrote in 1872, "but many years of experiences have taught me that to civilize and Christianize the wild Indian it is not only necessary to put him on Reservations but it is also necessary to exercise some strong authority over him." [37] More explicitly, Sheridan wrote Adjutant General E. D. Townsend in 1869 that the

> Indian is a lazy, idle vagabond; he never labors, and has no profession except that of arms, to which he is raised from a child; a scalp is constantly dangled before his eyes, and the highest honor he can aspire to is, to possess one taken by himself. It is not to be wondered at, therefore, if he aims for this honor when he grows up; especially in there is no punishment to follow the barbarous act. The Government has always been very liberal to Indians, especially whenever they have settled on reservations; the lands allotted to them have been of the very best character, making them perhaps by far the richest communities in the country.[38]

As for nonreservation Tetons, Sheridan saw "no other way to save the lives and property of our people, than to punish [the Sioux] until peace becomes a desirable object." [39] Toward this end, Sheridan obtained permission from the Interior Department in 1873 to conduct a reconnaissance of the Black Hills for the stated purpose of establishing a major fort.[40] This region, part of the Great Sioux Reservation guaranteed to the Sioux in the Treaty of 1868, was the most sacred of Lakota territories.

Sheridan appointed Custer to lead the expedition. Custer's coterie in the summer of 1874 included two companies of infantry, several reporters to immortalize the adventure, and two miners Custer hired at his own expense to scout the region for gold. The miners found what Custer later reported as "paying quantities" of the precious metal, precipitating an invasion of the region by thousands of gold seekers in 1874 and 1875. Sheridan ordered his officers to deter the influx if possible, but added that "should Congress open up the country to settlement by extinguishing the treaty rights of the Indians, [I] will give cordial support to the settlement of the Black Hills."[41] Even before the expedition Custer had expressed a preference for the occupation of the region by white farmers and stockmen. Prior to his departure, Custer wrote General Terry that "the country to be visited is so new and believed to be so interesting that it will be a pity not to improve to the fullest extent the opportunity to determine all that is possible of its character, scientific and otherwise." Should the Sioux resist this effort, Custer recommended "a sound drubbing."[42]

In his report on the Black Hills expedition, Custer offered lavish descriptions of the terrain and its resources. For example, on one occasion he ascended Harney Peak and was struck by the contrast between "the bright, green verdure of these lovely parks with the sunburned and dried yellow herbage to be seen in the outer plains." Custer compared the soil to that of a rich garden, sprouting hundreds of acres of delicious raspberries. "Nowhere in the States have I tasted cultivated raspberries of equal flavor to those growing here," he wrote.[43] Custer's enthusiasm for the agricultural potential of the Black Hills validated the claims of contemporary railroad brochures that spoke of "parks" and "Edenic verdure" to promote the agrarian development of the West.[44]

Custer's expedition to the Black Hills, which did much to advertise the mineral and agricultural potential of the region, precipitated the crisis that resulted in his own demise. Outraged by white trespassers, Sioux recalcitrants attacked miners, settlers, and emigrants throughout 1875. The acting interior secretary, B. R. Cowan, pointed out emphatically to the governor of Dakota Territory that the Treaty of 1868 guaranteed no one but the Sioux were "permitted to *pass over, settle upon,* or *reside*" in the Black Hills. "The only power to alter this provision," Cowan pointed out, "is that which made the treaty and then it must be done with the consent of the Indians."[45] General Terry, in contrast to Sheridan and Custer, strongly upheld Cowan's position: "I submit that it is of the greatest importance that any attempt to defy the law and to trample on the rights secured to the Sioux by the Treaty of 1868 should be met in the most rigorous manner *at the very outset.*"[46]

At first, the government sought to quell the unrest by purchasing the Black Hills from the Sioux. A commission headed by Senator William B. Allison traveled to Red Cloud Agency in September 1875 and parleyed

with Red Cloud, Spotted Tail, and several other Lakota chiefs. The negotiations went nowhere—the government offered six million dollars, but
Red Cloud insisted on six hundred times that amount to take care of
"seven generations ahead." Insulted by what he regarded as penurious
commissioners, the Oglala chief opted to watch an Arapaho sun dance
rather than attend the final meeting.[47]

Unable to halt white trespassers and unsuccessful in purchasing the
Black Hills outright, the government then turned to the final solution to
the Sioux "problem." In a meeting in Washington on November 3, 1875,
President Grant, Secretary of War Belknap, Interior Secretary Chandler,
Commissioner of Indian Affairs Edward Smith, and generals Sheridan
and Crook decided to stop the army's Black Hills anti-miner campaign
and to punish nonreservation Sioux. Six days after the Washington conference, Indian Bureau Inspector Erwin C. Watkins filed an angry report
replete with Frereian echoes that met with the full approval of Watkins's
superiors. Watkins argued that the Sioux held United States troops "in
contempt, and, surrounded by their native mountains, relying on their
knowledge of the country and powers of endurance, they laugh at the
futile efforts that have thus far been made to subjugate them." The Sioux,
Watkins continued, were "lofty and independent in their attitude and
language to Government officials, as well as the whites generally," and
furthermore, he pointed out, they "claim to be the sovereign rulers of the
land." Watkins then proceeded to issue his draconian recommendation:

> In my judgment, one thousand men, under the command of an ex-
> perienced officer, sent into their country in the winter, when the
> Indians are nearly always in camp, and at which season of the year
> they are most helpless, would be amply sufficient for their capture
> or punishment. The Government has done everything that can be
> done, peacefully to get control of these Indians, or to induce them to
> respect its authority. Every effort has been made, but all to no pur-
> pose. They are still as wild and untamable, as uncivilized and savage,
> as when Lewis and Clark first passed through their country. . . . The
> true policy, in my judgment, is to send troops against them in the
> winter—the sooner the better—and whip them into subjection.[48]

Heretofore, the policy of Interior had been to protect Indian title,
negotiate with indigenous mediators, and keep the military at bay. In
November 1875, however, the agency reversed nearly three decades of
tradition. Interior Secretary Zacharia Chandler, "a blustering ex-Senator
and Michigan political hack,"[49] literally handed the disposition of Sioux

affairs to General Sheridan. The general issued an ultimatum to non-reservation Sioux to report to their agencies by January 31, 1876, or face military reprisals. Sheridan, who believed the Sioux would regard the ultimatum as "a good joke," worried that "unless they are caught before early spring they cannot be caught at all." [50]

The irony of Sheridan's concern expressed itself poignantly on the afternoon of June 25, 1876. In the end, however, the general's troops prevailed. The Americans believed in the destiny of white settlement and capitalist expansion, demanded its indigenous foe to comply, and precipitated crises at the periphery of empire that ensured a military showdown. That Custer and Sheridan bear significant responsibility for the war against the Sioux seems clear; but their actions make sense only in relation to the broader policy objectives formulated by bureaucrats in Washington. As will be seen, similar circumstances prevailed in the events leading to the outbreak of the Anglo-Zulu War.

The conflict against the Zulu kingdom arose in the context of Britain's attempt to unite its South African possessions into a white-dominated confederation during the 1870s. Confederation became the orthodoxy of Lord Carnarvon, colonial secretary from 1874 to 1878. The fastidious Carnarvon, nicknamed "Twitters" by Disraeli, viewed confederation as a logical extension of Britain's strategic and economic interests in the region. As he wrote to Bartle Frere in 1876, the British "must be prepared to apply a sort of Munro [*sic*] doctrine to much of Africa." [51] "But the most immediately urgent reason for general union," Carnarvon reasoned in the same year, "is the formidable character of the native question, and the importance of a uniform, wise and stern policy in dealing with it." [52]

The Zulu kingdom, wedged between Natal and the Transvaal, represented the heart of the so-called native question. In the broadest sense, the Colonial Office regarded a strong, independent Zulu kingdom as a dangerous example for other Africans in the region, who might wish likewise to achieve equality with whites. The very existence of an independent Zululand fueled conspiracy theories among colonial officials throughout the 1870s of a Zulu-led "native combination" to rid the region of Europeans. Sir Garnet Wolseley put the issue bluntly in 1875: "[I do] not believe it to be possible for the two races to live together on perfect terms; one or the other must be the predominant power in the State, and if the very small minority of white men is to be that power, the great native majority must be taught not only to confide in its justice, but to realise and acknowledge its superiority." [53] In addition to their concern over

Zululand's independent existence, the British anguished over two other problems. First, the ongoing conflict between the Zulu kingdom and the Transvaal over disputed territory in the Blood River frontier posed a security threat for the region. Second, an independent Zululand bottled up potential laborers for white farmers[54] and harnessed vast tracts of fertile farmland, coveted by Transvaal Boers and Natalian sugar planters.

Carnarvon selected apostles who shared his imperial vision and seemed likely to execute the confederation scheme successfully, especially with regard to the "native question." In 1876 he dispatched Theophilus Shepstone to the Transvaal with vague instructions authorizing the native secretary to annex the Boer republic to the British Crown. Shepstone had consistently backed Cetshwayo's position in the Zulu-Boer boundary dispute since the "coronation" of 1873. In that year Shepstone wrote that Cetshwayo was "a man of considerable ability, much force of character," dignified, frank, and sagacious. Shepstone thought Cetshwayo to be not "very warlike," yet nonetheless "proud of the military traditions of his family, especially the policy and deeds of his uncle and predecessor, Chaka."[55]

In 1877 political expedience dictated a shift in Shepstone's thinking. Having annexed the Transvaal on behalf of Great Britain in April, Shepstone, the newly appointed administrator there, openly supported Boer claims in the boundary dispute. To justify his switch, Shepstone claimed to have found new evidence favorable to the Boers. Since he failed to ever reveal the location of such evidence, a more likely explanation for Shepstone's policy adjustment related to his expansionist goals. Mocking Shepstone's change of heart, John Sanderson wrote in the *Fortnightly Review* that "it is—as the Zulus have not been slow to observe—at least remarkable that it is only since Sir T. Shepstone became Administrator of the Transvaal country, that he has become convinced of the justice of the Transvaal claims."[56] Cetshwayo likened Shepstone to a woman with twins—"he has given one the breast, and now he gives it to the other."[57] Arguably, however, by annexing the disputed territory to the Transvaal, now a British dependency, Shepstone could proceed to carry out his grand vision of a "safety valve" and road to the north.[58]

At a meeting with Zulu notables on the western boundary of the Blood River on October 18, 1877, Shepstone tried to rationalize his change of heart in soothing, paternalistic rhetoric. Unconvinced, the Zulu delegation berated Shepstone and accused the former secretary of betraying them. "Their bearing was haughty," Shepstone wrote of the Zulu leaders, "and it seemed difficult for them to treat me with the respect that they had usually paid me." It was evident, Shepstone concluded, "that our meeting was not to be a very cordial or pleasant one."[59]

Spurned at the Blood River encounter, Shepstone's memoranda to the Colonial Office assumed a decided bellicosity. For example, he informed Carnarvon in December 1877 "that if hostilities should occur with Cetywayo, which I shall endeavor by all means in my power to avoid, . . . nothing short of the complete breaking up of the Zulu power will afford any guarantee of quiet in the future."[60] Perhaps Shepstone revealed his hand even more clearly in a memorandum dispatched to Carnarvon a fortnight later: "Had Cetywayo's thirty thousand warriors been in time changed to labourers working for wages, Zululand would have been a prosperous peaceful country instead of what it now is, a source of perpetual danger to itself and its neighbours."[61]

In June 1878 the bishop of Natal, John William Colenso, told F. W. Chesson, secretary of the Aborigines Protection Society, that "I have lost all faith in [Shepstone's] sense of justice & truthfulness." Colenso, who had once been a close friend of Sir Theophilus, believed that Shepstone would "never forget or forgive the rebuff he got from the Zulus at the Blood River" and might now engage in "crafty under-scheming." Colenso expressed fear "that something will be done to provoke a war with [Cetshwayo], a war which would be most unjustifiable and wicked."[62]

Colenso, bishop of Natal between 1852 and his death in 1883, established Bishopstowe, near Pietermaritzburg, and founded the mission Ekukhunyeni. The bishop spent his career in South Africa defending free religious inquiry against the theological obscurantism of the Anglican Church hierarchy and, throughout the last decade of his life, championing the rights of Africans in Natal and Zululand. For his "heretical" pursuits the settler community ostracized him, and colonial officials branded Colenso a "meddler." Colenso, as Jeff Guy puts it, was not "a twentieth-century liberal who somehow wandered into the wrong century."[63] He was a product of his times — Colenso, much like the "humanitarian" Indian commissioner Nathaniel Taylor, assumed the superiority of his culture and believed it his duty to subordinate Africans to his world vision. Appropriately, Africans knew him as the paternalist Sobantu, "the father of the people." A courageous and principled man, Colenso was nonetheless unable to see that injustice was the essence of imperialism. Thus, when Bishop Colenso witnessed British officials maneuvering for a showdown with the Zulu kingdom in the late 1870s, he was pushed to the limits of his faith. That Britain initiated such unjustifiable aggression

5. Bartle Frere (engraved from a drawing by Sir George Reid), in Sonia Clarke, ed., *Zululand at War, 1879* (Johannesburg: Brenthurst Press, 1984), p. 54. Courtesy of Brenthurst Press and the Bodleian Library. Bodleian shelf mark 621.16S.7.

"negated the basic principles upon which his political, moral and religious existence was founded." [64]

As Colenso surmised, Shepstone had been prejudiced by the Blood River encounter. Furthermore, Shepstone's opinions carried significant weight with Carnarvon as well as with the colonial secretary's second major missionary for confederation, Bartle Frere. Frere arrived in Cape Town in March 1877 as Britain's new high commissioner to South Africa. As a former president of the Royal Geographical Society and fervent evangelical Christian, Frere lobbied enthusiastically in the 1870s for the extension of British civilization to the Zambesi and beyond.[65] Frere's previous administrative experience in India[66] instilled a commanding self-confidence and convinced him that "a native and comparatively uncivilised power [could] co-exist alongside a European power, and . . . be gradually raised by it to a higher civilisation." Frere believed, however, that "it is undoubtedly necessary that the two powers should settle from the first which is to be the superior, and which is to be subordinate." [67]

Following such logic, Frere's task in South Africa became clear. In his mind, a defensible, self-governing white dominion could exist only if all potential black resistance was eliminated. He perceived the Zulu kingdom, revitalized under Cetshwayo and seemingly as powerful as ever, as the principal African obstacle. Therefore, the Zulu must be subjugated.

Frere grounded his bellicosity on a number of considerations. First, he believed that subjugation would bear significant economic fruits. He wrote that the Zulu were not "the wolf-like savages one might suppose from their mode of attack." Indeed, he posited, "the Zulu military organization is an excrescence quite alien to the natural habit of the people." Their training "develops every animal power and instinct," he argued, "till they become parts of a frightfully efficient man-slaying war-machine." If Cetshwayo's "iron rule" could be completely broken down, Frere reasoned, the Zulu might be transformed into a menial labor force: "They belong to the same race which furnishes the good-humoured volatile labourers and servants who abound in Natal, men very capable of being moulded in the ways of civilization and, when not actually trained to manslaughter, not naturally blood-thirsty, nor incurably barbarous." [68]

In addition, Frere believed Cetshwayo was working behind the scenes to promote a black "combination" to rid Natal of all Europeans, a view shared and inspired by Shepstone.[69] "I need not observe that in this Colony the existence of a very great mass of natives within it, who are often supposed to be under very imperfect control," Frere wrote in September 1878 to Michael Hicks Beach, Lord Carnarvon's replacement as colonial secretary, "and to be liable to follow the lead of their former fellow subjects across the border, has been always regarded as a cause for anxiety." Although "the Colonial natives are said to be, at present, unusually quiet and free from excitement," Frere warned, "I have heard this variously accounted for, sometimes as an evidence of their complicity with the warlike intentions of the Zulu nation." [70] In a similar vein, Frere wrote R. W. Herbert in the same year "that Shepstone and others of experience in the country, were right as to the existence of a wish among the great chiefs to make this war a general and simultaneous rising of Kaffirdom against white civilization." [71]

Furthermore, Frere as well as Shepstone made extensive use of missionary reports from Zululand, especially those of the Anglican Robert Robertson, to justify aggression toward Cetshwayo. Robertson, who enjoyed little success in attracting African converts, had grown frustrated and embittered by the late 1870s. A notorious drunk, and vulnerable to the sexual attractions of young women on his station, Robertson blamed his personal misery on Cetshwayo and those "thousands of wild Zulus" who had only "learned the name of the Evil one" from the white man. By late 1877 Robertson lamented that as tragic as a conflict with the Zulu might be, "there are worse things than war sometimes."[72]

Frere had reached similar conclusions. Working feverishly during 1878 to lay the groundwork for confederation, Frere prepared the Colonial Office for war against the Zulu kingdom. In September, for example, he wrote that "the preservation of peace in Natal depends simply on the sufferance of the Zulu Chief, that while he professes a desire for peace every act is indicative of an intention to bring about war, and that this intention is shared . . . by the majority of his people."[73] In manufacturing a *casus belli*, Frere exaggerated the significance of various incidents, including the exodus of missionaries from Zululand in mid-1878. Frere informed the colonial secretary that virtually every missionary had been "terrified out of the country." Although Cetshwayo disliked most Christian missionaries, he had never persecuted them. According to Colonel Anthony Durnford, the mission stations in Zululand had converted only a handful of Africans, "as the king considers that the moment a man becomes a Christian he is *no use*. Indeed he is right in his own point of view, as the few *supposed* Christians are an idle useless lot."[74] In all likelihood, the missionaries decided to quit Zululand on the advice of Shepstone, who warned them of an impending "political crisis."

Alarmed at the unremitting enmity toward the Zulu reflected in Frere's memoranda to the Colonial Office during the latter months of 1878, Michael Hicks Beach, the new colonial secretary, cautioned Frere to avoid an expensive and unnecessary colonial conflict. The somber Hicks Beach, known to his political enemies as "Black Michael," advised Frere in October "that by the exercise of prudence, and by meeting the Zulus in a spirit of forebearance and reasonable compromise, it will be possible to avert the very serious evil of a war with Cetywayo."[75] In November Hicks Beach added that with mounting problems in Eastern Europe and Afghanistan, "we cannot now have a Zulu war."[76] But a certain fatalism regarding hostilities with Zululand had overtaken the Colonial Office by late 1878. For example, in October Hicks Beach asked the Foreign Office to seek Portuguese consent to land British troops at Delagoa Bay in case of war.[77] The government's failure to restrain Frere prompted Sir William Harcourt, during parliamentary debate, to portray an imaginary letter from Hicks Beach to the High Commissioner:

6. *Cetewayo, the Zulu King* [Cetshwayo]. In *The Illustrated London News*, vol. 74, 22 February 1879, p. 165. N. 2288 b. 6. Courtesy the Bodleian Library, University of Oxford.

My dear Sir Bartle Frere,
I cannot think you are right. Indeed I think you are very wrong but after all, I feel you know a great deal better than I do. I hope you won't do what you're going to do; but if you do I hope it will turn out well.[78]

On December 10, 1878, the day before Frere's commissioners delivered to a Zulu delegation an ultimatum sure to bring war,[79] the high commissioner wrote Hicks Beach that "after the most anxious consideration I can arrive at no other conclusion than that it is impossible to evade the necessity for now settling this Zulu question thoroughly and finally."[80] In fashioning the ultimatum, Frere dismissed a boundary commissioners' report submitted in July 1878 that awarded the bulk of the disputed Blood River territory to the Zulu kingdom.[81] Shortly after the ultimatum lapsed and British forces invaded in January, Frere expressed puzzlement to the colonial secretary over the Zulu's "innate tendency to suspicion of the motives and acts of everyone. It is, perhaps," Frere speculated, "to a great extent the result of their present system of government." [82]

Alternatively, the Zulu had grown cynical by Shepstone's duplicity, Frere's manufactured *casus belli*, and the Colonial Office's acquiescence. As in the United States, "men on the spot" engineered a crisis at the periphery of empire that made war inevitable. Their decisions, despite the handwringing one might find at the metropolis, complemented the broader policy objectives of imperial expansion. The carnage at Isandhlwana and Rorke's Drift, as well as the Little Bighorn, was the immediate price for this unglamorous adventure in empire building. The Zulu and Sioux people sustained the long-range costs.

OLLOWING the outbreak of war, the British military exercised a decisive influence in the destruction of the Zulu kingdom, whereas in North America, the army's conquest of the Sioux must be understood in relation to the demise of the buffalo herds, the influx of settlers, and the expansion of railways across the Great Plains. In both cases, however, the war's aftermath encompassed unprecedented suffering for the indigenous peoples, culminating in Wounded Knee and the partition of Zululand. In part, this tragic denouement resulted from the schismatic proclivities in the Zulu and Sioux polities. But the tensions that set Lakota against Lakota and Zulu against Zulu did not occur in a vacuum. In fact, the settlement policies adopted by the United States and Great Britain encouraged such factionalism and played a substantial role in the dissolution of each reserve by the end of the 1880s.

In the wake of Custer's defeat, the army prosecuted war against the Sioux with new forts on the Yellowstone River, an additional twenty-five hundred cavalry privates, and control over the Sioux agencies. Determined to avenge Custer, officers such as Terry and Crook were also wary of a foe that had annihilated the seasoned troops of the Seventh Cavalry. But the large conventional columns they organized to prevent a similar catastrophe proved to be relatively useless against their unconventional enemy. Their futility reflected a larger problem — the U.S. military's failure to formulate a consistently effective doctrine in fighting such an unorthodox foe.[1] Sheridan sympathized with his subordinates. As he told Sherman, "the operations of Generals Terry and Crook will not bear criticism. . . . I approved what was done, for the sake of the troops, but in doing so, I was not approving much, as you know."[2]

Less attached to the conventional military wisdom, Colonel Nelson A. Miles scored numerous successes throughout the winter of 1876–77 by pursuing the Sioux doggedly in the most miserable of conditions. Elated by his own achievements, Miles wrote Sherman, his wife's uncle, that in contrast to Crook, "enough has been done to demonstrate what can be accomplished by a perfect spy system, a properly organized command, and such energy & management used as enables us to *find, follow,* and *defeat* large bodies of these Indians every time and under all circumstances." Miles's self-serving bombast rankled Sherman as well as Sheridan, but given positive results, they tolerated his excesses.[3]

Miles's achievements did not include the capture of Sitting Bull, who led his followers to sanctuary in Canada in early 1877. Yet the relentless pressure of Miles and his rival Crook convinced the other major Sioux "hostile" to quit the armed struggle. On May 6, 1877, Crazy Horse, with over eleven hundred followers, twenty-five hundred ponies, and one hundred firearms, surrendered at Red Cloud Agency. "Crazy Horse did not surrender with the humility of a defeated, broken-spirited chief," according to Jesse Lee, a military agent at Spotted Tail Agency in 1877. "He was an unsubdued warrior—a great soldier chief," in the words of Lee, "and had come in to make such terms as would bring peace and rest to his people, who had scarcely known defeat under his valiant leadership."[4]

Widely regarded as one of the greatest Lakota warriors, Crazy Horse lost his "shirt-wearer" status in 1870 following an adulterous affair with Black Buffalo Woman. In compensation, band elders selected Crazy Horse war leader of the Oglalas. A quiet man who seldom attended tribal councils, Crazy Horse spoke through his actions. According to his companion, He Dog, "Crazy Horse always led his men himself when they went into battle, and he kept well in front of them." Rather than charging recklessly into the face of the enemy, however, Crazy Horse "used judgment and played safe." The Oglala leader did not "like to start a battle unless he had it all planned out in his head and knew he was going to win."[5] Captain John Bourke attributed the Oglala chief's general popularity among the Lakotas to Crazy Horse's generosity. According to Bourke, Crazy Horse "made hundreds of friends by his charity towards the poor, as it was a point of honor with him never to keep anything for himself, excepting weapons of war." Bourke had "never heard an Indian mention [Crazy Horse's] name save in terms of respect."[6]

The goodwill surrounding the surrender of Crazy Horse degenerated into open hostility by the summer of 1877. At issue was the government's proposal to move the Sioux agencies to the Missouri River. Crazy Horse believed Crook had promised his people an agency in Powder River coun-

7. *Custer vs. Crazy Horse* by Kills Two. In Hartley Burr Alexander, ed., *Sioux Indian Painting*, part I (Nice, France: C. Szwedizicki, 1938).

try as well as an opportunity to hunt buffalo in that region. His overt indignation over the "Great Father's" apparent betrayal convinced the agent at Red Cloud that Crazy Horse was an "incorrigible wild man." Compounding the tension, the government sought to recruit Sioux scouts in a campaign against the Nez Perces, resulting in a fatal misunderstanding. Asked if he would join the campaign, Crazy Horse responded that he would fight until there were no Nez Perces left. Frank Grouard, the interpreter, misinterpreted the chief's response, deliberately or not, to suggest that Crazy Horse would fight until no *white* men were left. Fearing that great trouble was brewing, Crook ordered the commander at Camp Robinson to arrest and detain the Oglala leader. Following his capture, both Indians and soldiers tried to disarm Crazy Horse on September 7, 1877. In the ensuing scuffle, a young infantryman mortally wounded the Oglala with a sharp bayonet thrust.[7]

Crazy Horse's ignominious death may have spared him life imprisonment at Dry Tortugas, Florida.[8] In contrast, the rest of the Lakota people faced confinement on a much-reduced Great Sioux Reservation by the summer of 1877. The previous autumn, the government dispatched yet another Black Hills commission to the Sioux agencies to serve the Tetons a Hobson's choice. In the annual Indian appropriations act, Congress decreed that until the Sioux surrendered all rights to the Black Hills and unceded territory, they would receive no subsistence. The commission, headed by former Indian commissioner George Manypenny, obtained some signatures on the agreement—far fewer, however, than the three-fourths of all adult males required in the Treaty of 1868. Nevertheless, since the ultimatum in effect represented a fait accompli, the commission dispensed with legalities and settled for an acceptance.[9] The dissolution of the Great Sioux Reserve had begun.

Following their successful defense at Rorke's Drift, the British soldiers remained confident of avenging their slain comrades at Isandhlwana. Lord Chelmsford, chastened by the Isandhlwana disaster, chose to withdraw the central column into Natal for a number of weeks, temporarily leaving the brunt of the avenging to Colonel Evelyn Wood's northern force. At Kambula, early on the morning of March 29, 1879, a Zulu named Mbangulana told Wood of an approaching Zulu army under the command of Cetshwayo's chief minister, Mnyamana. This information, which represented a monumental betrayal to the Zulu army and a godsend to Wood's, enabled the British to prepare an effective defense. As at Isandhlwana, nearly twenty thousand Zulu warriors advanced on the British camp at Kambula in the early afternoon of the twenty-ninth. The fighting continued all afternoon, with Wood's troops pouring repeated volleys into the charging *amabutho*, and ended at nightfall with a resounding British victory. The British lost eighteen soldiers, compared to the Zulu figure of two thousand. This staggering loss convinced a number of Zulu to quit the struggle, opting instead to return to the safety of their homesteads. Kambula "was by far the most important and decisive battle of the Zulu War," according to the historian C. T. Binns, "for after this action the Zulu armies realized that they could not hope for any future success against the superiority of British arms."[10]

Regardless of mounting successes in the Anglo-Zulu War, Chelmsford could not escape the Isandhlwana nightmare. Denounced by the press at home, Chelmsford came to be regarded by government officials as an obstacle to progress in South Africa. Sir Garnet Wolseley, selected to replace Chelmsford as field commander on May 28, 1879, wrote that "*Chelmsford's folly* has seriously postponed the accomplishment of [confederation]."[11] *Punch*, which castigated the general with a satirical broadsword, adorned

Wolseley's pending arrival in South Africa with the poem "Two W's of War," associating Wolseley with the hero of Waterloo:

> When Wolseley's mentioned, Wellesley's brought to mind;
> Two men, two names, of answerable kind.
> Called to the front like Wellesley, good at need,
> Go, Wolseley, and like Wellesley, greatly speed! [12]

Wolseley did not arrive in the field until July 7. In the meantime, Chelmsford suffered another humiliation, followed by a partial vindication. On June 1 the prince imperial of France, while serving on the general's staff, was killed during a Zulu ambush. The prince's death extinguished the flickering hopes of the Bonaparte dynasty and raised a major furor in Europe. On the fourth of July, however, Chelmsford's forces defeated the last Zulu army, killing fifteen hundred and setting fire to the royal capital of Ulundi. Chelmsford, awarded a Knight Grand Cross of the Bath in August 1879, largely as a result of the Ulundi victory, never served in the field again. [13]

During the course of the war, Chelmsford rejected a series of peace overtures from Cetshwayo, the last arriving one week before the battle of Ulundi. The general, determined to resuscitate his image in the wake of Isandhlwana, ignored these efforts. Cetshwayo, more concerned with survival than self-esteem, escaped to Mnyamana's kraal following the Ulundi battle, and from there attempted to negotiate the terms of peace. In the second week of August, Cetshwayo dispatched three of his chiefs, including Mnyamana, as well as the Dutch trader Cornelius Vijn, to meet with Wolseley. Sir Garnet had occupied Ulundi following Chelmsford's departure from South Africa in early July. Upon their arrival at Wolseley's camp, the general convinced the Zulu delegation to surrender as prisoners of war. Vijn, a trader who knew a good economic opportunity when he saw one, offered to bring Cetshwayo to the British for two hundred pounds. Meanwhile, Cetshwayo had moved to his brother Ziwedu's kraal and turned Vijn away with the message that the king refused to surrender. [14]

Wolseley sent a cavalry to arrest the Zulu king on August 13. Cetshwayo eluded his pursuers for two weeks, relying on the loyalty of his subjects to keep their king at bay. A member of the British posse described the pursuit:

> We could get nothing from the Zulus. We were treated the same at
> every kraal. I had been a long time in Zululand. I knew the people

8. *Lieutenant-General Lord Chelmsford.* In *The Illustrated London News*, vol. 74, 1 March 1879, p. 192. N. 2288 b. 6. Courtesy the Bodleian Library, University of Oxford.

9. *Ulundi in Flames.* In *The Illustrated London News*, vol. 75, 23 August 1879. N. 2288 b. 6. Courtesy the Bodleian Library, University of Oxford.

and their habits and although I believed they would be true to their King, I never expected such devotion. Nothing would move them. Neither the loss of their cattle, the fear of death, or the offering of large bribes would make them false to their King.[15]

Finally, on August 28, 1879, the British force found and arrested Cetshwayo at a kraal deep in the Ngome Forest. Martin Oftebro, whose father had run a mission station in Zululand since the rule of Mpande, accompanied the British contingent as an interpreter. When they encountered the king, Oftebro wrote, "it was pitiful to see this once great man [so] utterly exhausted." Cetshwayo recognized the young Oftebro immediately and asked, "Was your father a friend of mine for so long that you should do this to me?" Ashamed, Oftebro tried to convince the king that it was a matter of duty, to which Cetshwayo did not respond.[16]

Under escort, Cetshwayo arrived at Ulundi on August 31. The king proceeded to Wolseley's tent through an assembly of officers with drawn swords, Dragoon Guards, and files of soldiers from the Third/Sixtieth

THE ILLUSTRATED
LONDON NEWS.

REGISTERED AT THE GENERAL POST-OFFICE FOR TRANSMISSION ABROAD.

No. 2097.—VOL. LXXV.   SATURDAY, AUGUST 23, 1879.   WITH SUPPLEMENT AND COLOURED VIEWS OF THE SEPOYS   SIXPENCE

Rifles standing at attention with fixed bayonets. Wolseley greeted Cetshwayo with startling news: Her Majesty's government had decided to depose the king, divide his kingdom among his chiefs, and subject him to imprisonment. On the afternoon of the thirty-first the British carted Cetshwayo to Port Durnford, where he was conveyed to Cape Town on the ship *Natal*. Cetshwayo remained imprisoned for the next three years. When he returned to Zululand in 1883, the Zulu king entered a murderous cauldron. "As for Zululand being *settled* by Sir Garnet Wolseley it is no such thing," the bishop of Natal wrote prophetically to a friend in May 1880. "There will be trouble there yet." [17]

In the aftermath of military conquest, Britain and the United States adopted similar settlement strategies toward their indigenous rivals. For example, both powers relied on indigenous collaborators, found it expedient to diminish the power of the traditional leadership, and promoted factionalism to keep the reserves amenable to white authority. Furthermore, in each settlement local agents, pursuing their own agendas, contributed significantly to the dissolution of each reserve by 1890. The key difference between these experiences goes to the heart of the American and British imperial "missions." The United States sought to replace the Sioux's traditional culture with a white Protestant Anglo-Saxon model for the purpose of integrating them into American society. The Lakotas, like many other Indian societies in the nineteenth century, had to be subjugated in order to be liberated from their communal "bondage," segregated in order to be integrated into the American mainstream. The patent contradictions in American Indian policy contrast with the British, whose objectives were more focused and attainable. The British imperial mission required the denationalization of the Zulu so that their labor might be exploited for the economic development of a confederated, white South Africa. To a large extent, the Zulu had been subjugated and segregated for this purpose. The search for plentiful supplies of cheap African labor drove British imperialism in South Africa. United States Indian policy was driven by the contradictory impulses of greed, compassion, guilt, and self-righteousness, but not the desire for Indian labor.

The British government assigned Sir Garnet Wolseley the task of settling Zululand in the wake of the British victory. Wolseley's instructions, vague in most respects, were quite clear on one point: he was to avoid annexation at all costs. The Anglo-Zulu War had been an expensive political embarrassment, and Her Majesty's government did not wish to incur further expenses from its South African quagmire.[18] Wolseley, always effi-

10. *The Man Who Won't Stop* [Sir Garnet Wolseley] by "Ape." In *Vanity Fair*, vol. 11, 18 April 1874. Per. 2288 b. 46. Courtesy the Bodleian Library, University of Oxford.

cient, ambitious, and self-seeking,[19] proceeded swiftly to banish Cetshwayo to Cape Town, dethrone the traditional Zulu leadership, and divide Zululand into thirteen districts. He placed a cooperative chief in each district in a system that parodied the pre-Shakan status quo. In drawing up a system that Leonard Thompson has described as "Divide and Refrain from Ruling,"[20] Wolseley relied heavily on the advice of Shepstone. He told Hicks Beach that "I had intended to divide Zululand into only about five or six territories, but Sir Theophilus Shepstone, remarking upon that, said it would be much better and safer for the country, which would be more manageable also, if these districts would be smaller and more numerous. To meet Shepstone's views on this point," Wolseley observed, "I finally decided to increase the number of chieftainships to thirteen."[21]

Wolseley broke up the kingdom's cohesion, he said, to "preclude for the future all, or almost all, possibility of any reunion of its inhabitants under one rule."[22] One of the most important "chiefs" in Wolseley's scheme was John Dunn. "My idea is to increase [Dunn's] powers by making him paramount Chief over the District of Zululand lying along the Tugela & Buffalo Rivers frontiers of Natal," Wolseley wrote. "I shall thus secure the civilizing influence of a White man over the district of Zululand nearest to us, and he and his people will be a buffer between us and the barbarous districts of Zululand beyond."[23] In addition, Wolseley recommended the appointment of a British Resident, who, in his words, was "to have no executive or administrative functions whatever."[24]

The senior official assigned to Zululand was Melmoth Osborn, a colleague and close friend of Shepstone. Osborn chafed under his limited authority, especially as tensions mounted in northern Zululand by the end of 1880. The northern districts were assigned to Hamu, Cetshwayo's half brother who had defected to the British early in the war, and Zibhebhu, a descendant of Shaka's uncle. Most of the royal family lived in these two districts. Each man, but especially Zibhebhu, abused his power by expropriating cattle and property from royal homesteads. Zibhebhu wanted "to set himself up as practically king in place of Cetshwayo," in the words of one Zulu informant.[25] By 1881 the division of Zululand was expressing itself in a civil conflict, with the royalist faction Usuthu on one side, and Zibhebhu and Hamu on the other. From prison, Cetshwayo pleaded with the British authorities:

> What crime have I committed? I have never done wrong! Why am I a prisoner? My wives and daughters—the women of the Great House—have been taken and distributed amongst my enemies in Zululand. Sibebhu has taken five of the women of the Great House as wives, and has given the others to his chiefs and headmen. The thought of this is eating into my heart. It will kill me.[26]

Prodded by humanitarian sympathizers[27] of the Zulu and wishing to restore order, the British government decided to place Cetshwayo into this maelstrom. Prior to the king's return, the Colonial Office brought Cetshwayo to England in August 1882. His celebrated visit included an audience with Queen Victoria, a tour of the Royal Arsenal at Woolwich, and a series of three interviews with Colonial Secretary Lord Kimberley. Kimberley informed Cetshwayo that a small portion of the king's country, to be defined later, would be reserved for Zulu not wishing to be subjected to his royal tutelage. Cetshwayo expressed concern over such a territorial loss, but Kimberley assured the king that "no more would be reserved than was, in the opinion of the Government, absolutely necessary."[28]

Why had the British gambled? Faced with the alternative of "assuming the responsibility of government or restoring Cetywayo," a Colonial Office under secretary later wrote, "[we] chose the latter course as an experiment, and not, it may be remarked, for the sentimental reasons to which the step has been generally attributed."[29] The gamble might have worked if a semblance of Cetshwayo's sovereignty had been restored as well, but "men on the spot" engineered another scenario. Shepstone, who continued to play a major role in Zululand affairs, opposed the return of the former king on the grounds that Cetshwayo represented all "that is opposed to civilization, Christianity, and progress"—in other words, Cetshwayo would not be amenable to white overrule. When it became clear that Cetshwayo was returning, Shepstone devised a scheme in which a substantial Zulu Native Reserve, paid for by a hut tax and available to opponents of Usuthu, would be established in southern Zululand. Osborn supported the Shepstone plan, and also insisted that Zibhebhu rule independently of Cetshwayo in the north. The Colonial Office acquiesced in the Shepstone-Osborn program and delivered the Zulu king to a partitioned Zululand in January 1883.[30]

When Cetshwayo learned of these plans from Cape governor Sir Hercules Robinson, the king expressed outrage and a sense of betrayal: "Whence these laws? They were never given in London. You say you will take all my south lands; you will also give Sibebhu lands in the north. Where then is the country I am being returned to? You elevate Sibebhu and give him my once subject lands. Why is he singled out from the thirteen and all the others debarred?"[31] Cetshwayo suspected his old nemesis Shepstone of plotting to undermine the king's authority.[32] The Zulu king arrived at Port Durnford on January 10, 1883, amid no fanfare and no friendly faces. He was greeted instead by a white contingent led by Shepstone. The former Native Affairs secretary kept the king's arrival a secret, he wrote, "in order to prevent any large gathering of Zulus, whose excitement might have reached such a pitch that they would have become uncontrollable."[33]

Shepstone succeeded only in postponing the "excitement." Civil war, virtually guaranteed by the conditions of Cetshwayo's restoration, ensued. In March 1883 Zibhebhu's forces crushed Usuthu, killing more people than in any battle in Zulu history.[34] By July the king had been driven into hiding, and he died early the next year under mysterious cir-

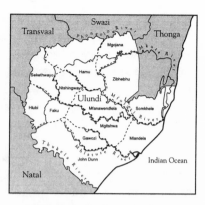

Map 5. Dissolution of Zululand, 1879–1887. Adapted from Jeff Guy, *The Destruction of the Zulu Kingdom: The Civil War in Zululand, 1879–1884* (London: Longman, 1979; reprint, Johannesburg: Ravan Press, 1982), pp. 172, 173, 236.

Wolseley's Settlement of 1879

cumstances. Cetshwayo's son and heir Dinuzulu enlisted the support of Boer farmers and defeated Zibhebhu in June 1884. The Afrikaners exacted a heavy price for their assistance. By occupying four thousand square miles of northern Zululand, the Boers prompted the Colonial Office to intervene in Zululand for the first time since 1879. "It is clear that the power of the Zulus is utterly broken," the governor of Natal reported to the colonial secretary in April 1886. "Unless they receive support from [Britain] they must eventually submit to any terms the Boers may think fit to impose."[35] The Colonial Office asked Osborn to demarcate a new Transvaal-Zululand boundary, and his final decision left much of the Boer occupation intact. When Usuthu protested Osborn's recommendation, he annexed Zululand on behalf of Britain in February 1887 to quell the unrest. "The old trust is badly shaken," Shepstone informed the Colonial Office in defense of Osborn's action.[36]

Great Britain had maintained the right to intervene in Zululand throughout the 1880s, but refrained from exercising central authority there until 1887 to avoid the costs of interference.[37] The United States assumed similar rights over the Sioux, but felt obliged to win their hearts and minds from the outset of the decade. By the end of the 1880s, however, the same cynicism of imperial motives that Shepstone detected throughout Zululand pervaded the Great Sioux Reservation.

In the 1880s the United States made a concerted effort to assimilate the Sioux and other Indians to a uniform "Americanism."[38] The Indian Rights Association, founded by William Welsh following his visit to the Great Sioux Reservation in 1881, spearheaded the drive. Welsh's father, William, had been one of the principal architects of Grant's Peace Policy.

Partition of Zululand, 1883

Partition of Zululand, 1887

According to Welsh, the Indian had to be "taught to labor, to live in civilized ways, and to serve God."[39] Specifically, the Sioux needed to rid their society of communal values, clear their minds of "pagan" beliefs, and embrace a culture based on rugged individualism. Through its forceful lobbying efforts, the Indian Rights Association played a key role in shaping federal Indian policy in the 1880s.

The historian Frederick Hoxie views Welsh's assimilation program within the broader context of America's growing cultural diversity after the Civil War. In this line of argument, the influx of ethnic and religious minorities into the United States in the latter third of the century threatened to subvert the predominance of white Protestant majority values. Indian acculturation offered one important step in the remediation of this apparent problem. Principally, success in assimilating the Indian would validate the preeminence of Protestant Anglo-Saxon culture as the preferred "American" model.[40]

To facilitate Sioux acculturation, the Indian Rights Association also favored the reduction and division of the Great Sioux Reserve. Such a measure, according to rights activists, would force the Sioux to accept Anglo-Saxon values, provide "for the inevitable advance of white civilization, and, at the same time, [secure] to the Indian an adequate and wise compensation for lands."[41] These white reformers believed, along the lines of the social theorist Lewis Henry Morgan,[42] that private ownership of property represented the key to advanced civilization. Unwittingly, by advocating the reduction of the Sioux Reservation, rights activists became strange bedfellows with land speculators, railroad magnates, and militant whites who had been espousing exterminationist rhetoric since the 1860s.

Whether humanitarian or expedient, the assimilation program was, at the very least, a revolutionary endeavor, with government agents constituting the vanguard. Success in implementing the government's far-reaching agenda depended to a great extent on finding effective collaborators. No collaborative device proved more significant than Indian police forces.[43] Indian police, responsible to each agent, served to undermine the power of uncooperative chiefs as well as produce schismatic tensions at virtually every agency. Events at the Rosebud and Pine Ridge agencies in the 1880s manifest the upheaval.

The government threatened Red Cloud and Spotted Tail with starvation in the winter of 1877–78 if they refused to move from their camps in northwestern Nebraska to new agencies located farther north along the Missouri River. In what was becoming a periodic ritual, each chief traveled to Washington in September 1877 to negotiate with the new president, Rutherford B. Hayes, and Hayes's Interior secretary, Carl Schurz. During these meetings the Great Father compromised—a winter on the Missouri, and then Red Cloud and Spotted Tail could select other sites in the Great Sioux Reserve. In the spring, the Oglalas and Brulés chose agencies south of the White River in southwestern South Dakota, known respectively as Pine Ridge and Rosebud. Farther north along the Missouri from north to south stretched Standing Rock, Cheyenne River, Lower Brulé, and Crow Creek agencies. By 1880 nearly sixteen thousand Lakotas inhabited these six agencies.[44]

Spotted Tail stood at the pinnacle of his power in 1878. He had assisted the government in negotiating with "hostiles" in 1876–77, persuading hundreds of Sioux to surrender at the agencies. Gratified by the Brulé leader's assistance, some government officials talked of designating him an "honorary officer" in the army with a lifetime salary. Born in 1823, Spotted Tail gained a reputation early on as a skilled hunter and warrior. He became a "shirt wearer" around the age of twenty-six, and by 1866 was regarded as head chief of the Brulés. Spotted Tail believed strongly that his people could not be converted to God-fearing Christian farmers, at least any time soon, and opposed any accelerated program of forced acculturation. His attitude put him on a collision course with Interior Secretary Schurz, who was determined to transform the Sioux into self-sufficient agriculturists, one way or the other.[45]

Spotted Tail dominated the agent at Rosebud in 1879–80, Cicero Newell. Newell, who had served as a Civil War officer and town marshal in Ypsilanti, Michigan, capitulated to the Brulé chief on virtually every score. The agent's only initiatives, the construction of a bakery and sawmill, amounted to embarrassing fiascoes. Miffed by Spotted Tail's insubordination, the Interior Department forced the Rosebud Sioux to organize an Indian police force in the autumn of 1879. Crow Dog was appointed police chief. Although Crow Dog felt little loyalty to Newell, he regarded his new position as a chance to build a power base rivaling that of Spotted Tail. When Newell was dismissed in the spring of 1880 for accepting bribes from his employees, Crow Dog found his opportunity.[46]

Spotted Tail disliked the new agent, John Cook, whom the Brulé leader regarded as effeminate, and relations between the two soured immediately. Crow Dog took advantage of the rift by befriending Cook, hoping to enlist an important ally in the agency power struggle. In this poisoned atmosphere, Spotted Tail ignited a controversy in the summer of 1880 that ended in his death one year later. Following a scathing denunciation of the government's Indian education policy before an assembly of white reformers in Carlisle, Pennsylvania, Spotted Tail withdrew thirty-four Brulé children attending the Carlisle Indian School.[47] Carlisle, founded in 1879, was regarded by the Indian Bureau as one of the government's best weapons in the campaign to eradicate Indian culture. Spotted Tail's repudiation of the project was unforgivable. Under pressure by Interior, Cook dismissed the Indian police at Rosebud, viewed as beholden to Spotted Tail, and selected a new force more amenable to the agent's commands. Crow Dog lost his position as police chief as well, and instead of blaming Cook, directed his wrath at Spotted Tail. An assassination plot unfolded. On August 5, 1881, Crow Dog succeeded in murdering Spotted Tail near the chief's government residence. The death of the Brulé leader left Rosebud in disarray for many years to come.[48]

A power struggle between the agent and traditional leaders on the one hand, and among indigenous factions on the other, ensued at Pine Ridge as well. Unlike Newell or Cook, the agent at Pine Ridge between 1879 and 1888 was a fearless, domineering figure, determined to have his way. Valentine T. McGillycuddy, a former post surgeon at Fort Robinson, arrived at Pine Ridge on March 10, 1879. Soon thereafter, McGillycuddy called a conference of the principal chiefs and urged them to take up the plow, warning of a time when the Great Father might hold back annuities. Red Cloud retorted that the Great Spirit had made the Indian to hunt and fish, not to work. "The white man," the Oglala chief remarked, "owes us a living for the lands he has taken from us." Flustered, McGillycuddy switched subjects, informing the Sioux leadership that he intended to organize a police force under the agent's supervision.[49]

Red Cloud concluded that McGillycuddy must go. Along with twenty-one other chiefs, including Man Afraid of His Horse, Young Man Afraid, and Little Wound, the Oglala leader signed a letter to President Hayes requesting McGillycuddy's recall. A special supervisor at Pine Ridge, James O'Beirne, concluded that the chiefs had been put up to this mischief by the previous agent, James Irwin, whom the Sioux wished restored. Therefore, O'Beirne suppressed the letter. When Interior Secretary Schurz visited Pine Ridge in early September, Red Cloud repeated his demand, but the Washington bureaucrat dismissed the complaint as an infantile paroxysm. McGillycuddy was less amused, and he fixed his attention on breaking the power of uncooperative chiefs such as Red Cloud. In his first report to Interior, McGillycuddy rationalized his plan in language reminiscent of Wolseley, Shepstone, and Frere:

> An Indian can no more serve two masters than a white man. He cannot serve his chief and the agent at the same time. The chiefs are men who have as a rule risen to their position by their superior judgment and acuteness, whether on the war path or elsewhere, and they certainly appreciate the fact that they are more important personages, as controlling, without question, a large band of savages, ready for war or peace at their command, than in the, to them, uninteresting position of a quasi-chief over a civilized community, the individuals of which will consult their own interests before they obey orders.[50]

Thereafter, McGillycuddy referred to Red Cloud as "the former chief" or "the deposed chief" in his correspondence to Washington, despite the widespread support Red Cloud continued to command among the Oglala rank and file. Nonetheless, political fissures appeared. For example, American Horse told a reporter in 1879 that Red Cloud and Spotted Tail were not cut out to be agency chiefs. Young Man Afraid and Little Wound, concerned that Red Cloud's obstinance checked Oglala progress, also began to express doubts about the head chief's leadership as early as 1880. In addition, McGillycuddy had organized a disciplined, fiercely loyal Indian police force, captained by George Sword. Sword believed the government should depose the old chiefs and appoint new ones, and he advised the Indian commissioner in August 1882 to jail troublesome Red Cloud supporters.[51]

The struggle between the obdurate head chief and the inexorable agent persisted unabated until 1888, when the Interior Department deposed McGillycuddy. The agent fell victim to partisan politics—the incoming Cleveland administration turned Interior over to southern Democrats, making Republicans such as McGillycuddy dispensable. The former agent at Pine Ridge gained appointment as head of the Dakota

Insane Asylum, prompting Red Cloud to express pity "for the poor mad people."[52]

The assault on traditional authority at Pine Ridge and elsewhere had factionalized the agencies into what whites called progressives and non-progressives. A simultaneous attack on traditional Lakota belief widened the schism even further. Wishing to rid the agencies of "demoralizing and barbarous" customs, in 1883 Interior Secretary Henry M. Teller ordered agents to suppress feasts and dances, including the sun dance. Historically, the annual sun dance served as the cornerstone of Lakota belief by reinforcing traditional values, promoting corporate unity, and releasing intense personal emotions.[53] Its proscription constituted a devastating blow to Lakota culture, but the assimilation drive had yet to run its course.

In the Sioux Act of 1889 Congress partitioned the Great Sioux Reservation into separate reserves. As part of a decade-long effort to reduce the size of Indian reservations and open "surplus" lands to white homesteaders, the Sioux Act provided for the allotment of 320 acres per Sioux family head and the opening up of about half the reserve for white purchase. The bill, put to the Sioux in the summer of 1889 as an all-or-nothing arrangement, led a number of nonprogressives to suspect that the government would take advantage of the cession by cutting agency rations. Assured by commissioners that acceptance of the agreement bore no relation to agency allocations, the requisite number of Sioux assented to its passage. Two weeks after the commission left South Dakota, Congress, in its infinite wisdom, slashed appropriations for Indian subsistence, cutting the beef issue at Pine Ridge, for example, by one million pounds. By winter the death rate at Pine Ridge rose to forty-five a month out of a population of 5,550. Then, in February 1890, President Benjamin Harrison, in violation of the agreement, threw open the ceded territory to white settlement before the Sioux inhabitants of those lands had taken out allotments.[54]

Convinced that they had been bamboozled by the federal government once again, many Sioux turned on progressives, calling them "fools and dupes" for capitulating to the land settlement.[55] By early 1890 disgruntled Lakotas also began turning to the Ghost Dance religion. The Ghost Dance, based on the teachings of Wovoka,[56] promised followers a new millennium in which Sioux hegemony would be resurrected in the northern central plains. Lakota converts danced, sang, and prayed around poles, adapting Wovoka's teachings to their sun dance ceremony.[57] "We did not think we were doing any harm by dancing our religious dances and praying to the Great Spirit to send the deliverer to us quickly," re-

Map 6. Dissolution of the Great Sioux Reservation, 1868–1889. Adapted from Robert M. Utley, *The Last Days of the Sioux Nation* (New Haven, Conn.: Yale University Press, 1963), p. 43.

Treaty of 1868

ported the Brulé Two Strike. "We had no thought of going on the war path against the Govt. or our white neighbors."[58]

Nevertheless, agents interpreted the movement as a sinister plot to overthrow white authority and sought to suppress it. In response, the Ghost Dancers grew increasingly militant. At Standing Rock, for example, the agent, James McLaughlin, who regarded Sitting Bull as the "high priest and leading apostle of this latest Indian absurdity," believed that the movement could be smothered by arresting the Hunkpapa leader and a few of his ilk.[59] Under McLaughlin's orders, police lieutenant Afraid of Bear led a posse of forty-three to arrest Sitting Bull on the night of December 15, 1890. A fight erupted. During the melee, Afraid of Bear's sergeant shot Sitting Bull in the chest and head, killing the famous Sioux holy man instantly.[60]

At Pine Ridge the new agent, Daniel Royer, an inept druggist and banker whom the Sioux nicknamed "Young Man Afraid of Indians,"[61] dispatched a hysterical telegram to the Indian commissioner on November 15, 1890:

> Indians are dancing in the snow and are wild and crazy. I have fully informed you that employes [*sic*] and Government property at this agency have no protection and are at the mercy of these dancers. Why delay by further investigation? We need protection and we need it now.[62]

As in 1876, Interior handed the matter to the War Department. Major General Nelson A. Miles, the seasoned champion of the previous war with the Sioux, commanded the operation.

Miles, like his fellow officers George Crook, John Gibbon, and John Bourke, felt compassion and anger regarding the conquest of the Native Americans in the late nineteenth century. In this respect, they shared

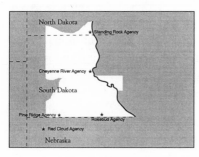

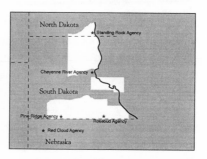

Agreement of 1876   Act of 1889

much in common with such officers as Anthony Durnford, the fallen British colonel at Isandhlwana. On the one hand, Miles admired the Indians' purer form of existence before the coming of the white man and extolled the "courage, skill, sagacity, endurance, fortitude, and self-sacrifice" of the Native American. On the other hand, Miles chafed under the military's limited decision-making capacity in the "pacification" of "hostiles" and deeply resented civilian criticism of the army's Sisyphean task. The historian Thomas Leonard characterizes the hostility felt by Miles and others in the military: "The government broke treaties and yet expected the Army to keep the peace through trust. Western settlers clamored for protection at the same time their land grabs provoked Indian retaliation. 'Friends' of the Indians . . . damned the Army when blood was shed at the same time that they demanded a forced acculturation."[63]

In the Ghost Dance crisis, Miles believed that military control of the Sioux agencies would keep the Lakotas "under absolute control and beyond the possibility of doing harm."[64] The technological capacity of his culture buoyed Miles's confidence. In contrast to 1876, a network of forts, railways, and telegraph lines ringed the Sioux homeland, making it possible to dispatch troops to the seat of conflict within hours. The major trouble spots by December 1890 seemed to be Pine Ridge Agency, where Oglala and Brulé dancers had occupied a remote "Stronghold" in the northwestern corner of the reservation, and Cheyenne River Agency, where Big Foot's Miniconjou Ghost Dance followers had taken in thirty-eight Hunkpapa refugees in the wake of Sitting Bull's murder at Standing Rock. Miles ordered the arrest of Big Foot, assigning the task to Lieutenant Colonel Edwin V. Sumner.[65]

Sumner had parleyed with the Miniconjou chief in early December, concluding at the time "that Big Foot was making an extraordinary effort to keep his followers quiet."[66] Sumner therefore expressed reluctance to arrest Big Foot and preferred instead to keep the Miniconjou camp under surveillance. Big Foot's younger followers grew wary of the military presence, however, and convinced the reluctant chief to accept an invitation by Oglala leaders to come and restore harmony in Pine Ridge. On the night of December 23 the Miniconjou camp slipped away undetected.[67]

Outraged by Sumner's folly, Miles assigned Custer's old regiment the task of intercepting the Miniconjous. On December 28 the Seventh Cavalry, under the command of Colonel James W. Forsyth, encountered Big Foot and his followers and escorted them toward the agency at Pine Ridge. On the night of the twenty-eighth the assembly of soldiers and Sioux camped in the valley of Wounded Knee Creek, twenty miles east of the agency. The officers provided Big Foot with an army tent equipped with a stove, due to the old chief's bout with pneumonia. Forsyth, ordered to disarm Big Foot's camp and transport his people by rail to Omaha, proceeded to surround Big Foot's camp with five hundred troops and four Hotchkiss cannon at dawn on the twenty-ninth.[68]

"There was a great uneasiness among the Indians all night," an eyewitness, Dewey Beard, recalled, for the Sioux "were fearful that they were to be killed."[69] Big Foot's men sensed a trap. During a troop search for Sioux weapons, Black Coyote, a deaf "crazy man," according to the eyewitness Turning Hawk,[70] fired at the soldiers. Within seconds, troops of the Seventh replied with a volley directly into the crowd of warriors, followed by desperate hand-to-hand combat. Meanwhile, the Hotchkiss guns poured a murderous fire of fifty two-pound shells per minute on the Sioux camp, killing and wounding men, women, and children indiscriminately.[71]

Sioux survivors, including a number of women carrying infants, fled southward toward the safety of a nearby ravine. Troops of the Seventh pursued them up the gully and into the open countryside, firing at the fleeing Sioux over a distance of two to three miles. "There can be no question," in the opinion of the anthropologist James Mooney, "that the pursuit was simply a massacre, where fleeing women, with infants in their arms, were shot down after resistance had ceased and when almost every warrior was stretched dead or dying on the ground."[72] When the smoke cleared, the battlefield was littered with the corpses of Big Foot and most of his followers, including forty-four women and eighteen children. Miles, outraged by the killing of noncombatants, relieved Forsyth of his command, although the colonel was quickly reinstated by the secretary of war.[73]

The last of the Ghost Dancers did not surrender until January 15, 1891, but the Wounded Knee disaster symbolizes the denouement in Sioux efforts to resurrect the open frontier. Whether the killings at Wounded Knee Creek represent the "most regrettable of frontier encounters" [74] or a deliberate massacre by the remnants of Custer's Seventh [75] depends to some extent on one's point of view. At the very least, Wounded Knee to the Lakota people conveys the ultimate indignity. On New Year's Day 1891 a troop detachment returned to the Wounded Knee battlefield. The soldiers found four babies still alive, bundled in shawls close to their dead mothers. Only one survived. The bloodied corpses of Big Foot's folk, frozen into grotesque contortions, were collected and tossed into a mass grave. After the winter passed, the Sioux put a wire fence around the site and painted the posts red, a modest attempt to dignify the victims at Wounded Knee.

Following their annexation of Zululand in 1887, the British allowed Zibhebhu and his armed followers to return to their original district. Within months, civil war with Usuthu erupted again. Britain intervened, arresting Dinuzulu and exiling him to Saint Helena in 1888. [76] In less than ten years, Zululand, like the Great Sioux Reservation, witnessed the collapse of its traditional leadership, surrendered much of its original territory, lost a significant portion of its population to war and famine, and was reduced from self-sufficiency to economic dependency. And in each case, local agents played significant roles in shaping the ultimate disposition of each reserve, albeit within a climate of opinion that sanctioned the inevitability of white expansionism. In one respect, however, the experiences of the Zulu and Sioux differ sharply. American efforts to assimilate the Lakotas had failed. As the Episcopalian missionary James Cross wrote from Rosebud in 1891, "if my work during the year were measured by the baptisms and the number received into the church it would be but a poor showing of what I believe has been the real missionary work." [77] By way of contrast, in South Africa Shepstone's wish of converting Cetshwayo's warriors to wage laborers had been fulfilled. Zululand became one of the major sources of African labor on the Rand goldfields by the early 1890s. [78] But whether as unassimilated dependents or unskilled laborers, both the Sioux and Zulu had paid more than their fair share of the cost of Anglo-American empire building in the late nineteenth century.

CHAPTER 7
Images of Empire

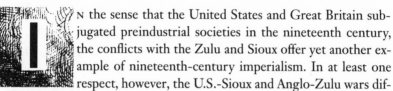 N the sense that the United States and Great Britain sub-
jugated preindustrial societies in the nineteenth century,
the conflicts with the Zulu and Sioux offer yet another example of nineteenth-century imperialism. In at least one
respect, however, the U.S.-Sioux and Anglo-Zulu wars dif-
fered significantly from a number of other imperial encounters with indigenous rivals during this era. Specifically, each western power experienced a calamitous setback—the Little Bighorn and Isandhlwana, defeats
that shocked and confounded contemporaries. Consequently, the wars
against the Zulu and Sioux attracted considerable attention from contemporary scribes, pundits, and artists, whose representations of those battles
transformed each into a myth. A myth, according to the American studies
scholar Richard Slotkin, "performs its cultural function by generalizing
particular and contingent experiences into the bases of universal rules of
understanding and conduct; and it does this by transforming secular history into a body of sacred and sanctifying legends." [1]

Why were Isandhlwana and the Little Bighorn converted into legends?
This chapter suggests several reasons. First, the battles took the press
by surprise, and when it rushed to compensate for its inattention, it did
so, in the words of the historian Carl Becker, without fear and without research. Second, each event became mired in partisan politics and
was manipulated enthusiastically by the political opposition to bash the
governments in power. In these circumstances, scapegoating assumed a
higher priority than truth seeking. Finally, popular attitudes toward the
Zulu and Sioux—already conditioned by the racist ideologies of the late
nineteenth century; the guilt, compassion, and anger associated with empire building; and the romantic conceptions of the American frontier—
congealed. [2] By scoring such unlikely victories, the Zulu and Sioux passed
into popular culture as quintessential "noble savages."

The battles at Isandhlwana and the Little Bighorn came as a shock to nations conditioned by a sense of Anglo-Saxon cultural superiority, and therefore found the press taken by surprise. In Britain, for example, "accurate information was at a premium, little was known about Zululand and proper names were largely guesswork." [3] Initially, the British press rendered "Isandhlwana" as "Isandula." At the time of the battle only one correspondent, Charles Norris-Newman of the Tory London *Standard*, was on the scene. Norris-Newman, a careful and competent former imperial officer, accompanied the central column in its invasion of Zululand. [4]

When news of the battle broke, however, a host of "special" correspondents steamed southward to the Cape. The *Times*, which had distinguished itself in the nineteenth century for its prompt coverage of foreign news, [5] sent its correspondent Francis Francis. The *Daily News* sent Archibald Forbes, a man who fraternized "with half the general staffs of Europe." [6] The *Illustrated London News*, the finest illustrated news magazine of the time, [7] sent its gifted artist Melton Prior. A number of other periodicals relied on private letters and official memoranda for their coverage of the war. [8]

In its coverage of the Little Bighorn, the U.S. press was at least as ill prepared as its British counterpart, focusing instead on the Centennial Exposition in Philadelphia, celebrating the centenary of national independence, and on the worst economic depression in the nation's history. [9] As in Chelmsford's invasion of the Zulu kingdom, only one correspondent, Mark Kellogg, accompanied Terry's column. Kellogg, the assistant editor of the *Bismarck Tribune*, sent reports of the expedition to Bismarck, North Dakota, which were then relayed to the *New York Herald*. Unlike Norris-Newman, who survived the Anglo-Zulu War, Kellogg was killed at Little Bighorn. Colonel Gibbon found Kellogg's body in a ravine four days after the battle. [10]

News of the Little Bighorn battle, following a series of slapstick adventures, arrived in Bismarck on July 5. The editor of the *Tribune*, Clement Lounsberry, telegraphed information hastily to the *Herald*, then fashioned his own special edition, which was distributed in Bismarck the next morning. The *Herald*, edited by James Gordon Bennett, Jr., embellished Lounsberry's account, keeping the essentials intact. Each story portrayed the battle as a "massacre" and offered vivid details of savage barbarity. Lounsberry's headline told of squaws mutilating the dead and "victims captured alive and tortured in the most fiendish manner." "What will Congress do about it," Lounsberry asked. "Shall this be the beginning of the end?" [11]

Bennett's *Herald*, a consistent purveyor of exterminationist rhetoric, followed its Bighorn histrionics with a series of stories in which Sitting Bull is transformed into a symbol of predatory savagery. "It adds a pang to the deaths of Custer and his heroic command," Bennett lamented, "that they fell at the hands of such a savage," a pronouncement justifying Bennett's recommendation for draconian punishment.[12] In a similar vein, Britain's *Saturday Review* converted Cetshwayo into a "bloodthirsty barbarian," whose actions placed him outside the confines of international legal considerations. The *Review*, like the *Herald*, chided philanthropists for romanticizing the deeds of these alleged savages and called upon British troops "to inflict a crushing defeat on the Zulus."[13]

Howls for revenge poured forth from much of the rest of the British press as well, even among publications that questioned the wisdom of the Anglo-Zulu War. The *Times* argued for "swift and terrible retributions" against the "black Napoleons" of Zululand.[14] The *Daily Telegraph* counseled the British army to "cool the warlike ardour of the savage warriors" and to make the Zulus "pay dearly for their triumph of a day."[15] Alexander Allardyce, writing in the conservative *Blackwood's Edinburgh Magazine*, thought it useless "to urge prudential considerations on savages," and wished to "avenge the slaughter" of his countrymen as "speedily and effectually" as possible. "Exemplary punishment for the king who has dared to defy British power, to break the peace of South Africa, and to drag his wretched vassals into a contest where they must necessarily be the losers, is an object that supercedes all other considerations," Allardyce counseled.[16] Even *Punch*, which ridiculed the British high command mercilessly during the war, carried a print depicting a Zulu warrior standing before a stern schoolmaster and writing repetitively on a blackboard, "Despise Not Your Enemy" (illus. 12).[17]

In both Great Britain and the United States, the press, mired in partisan politics, targeted scapegoats. The *New York Herald*, for example, which offered frequent, vivid exposés of corruption in the Grant administration, wrote on July 16, 1876, that Custer had been killed by "the celebrated policy of General Grant, which feeds, clothes and takes care of [the Indians'] noncombatant force while the men are killing our troops," as well as "that nest of thieves, the Indian Bureau, with its thieving agents and favorites as Indian traders, and its mock humanity and pretense of piety."[18] The *Indianapolis Sentinel* attacked Grant's "timid, vacillating, indecisive" Indian policy, "with its concomitant curses of swindling agents and corrupt rings."[19] The Democratic-controlled House of Representatives drew criticism as well. *Harper's Weekly* ran a front-page Thomas

TRIBUNE EXTRA.

Price 25 Cents.

BISMARCK, D. T., JULY 6, 1876.

MASSACRED

GEN. CUSTER AND 261 MEN THE VICTIMS.

NO OFFICER OR MAN OF 5 COMPANIES LEFT TO TELL THE TALE.

3 Days Desperate Fighting by Maj. Reno and the Remainder of the Seventh.

Full Details of the Battle.

LIST OF KILLED AND WOUNDED.

THE BISMARCK TRIBUNE'S SPECIAL CORRESPONDENT SLAIN.

Squaws Mutilate and Rob the Dead

Victims Captured Alive Tortured in a Most Fiendish Manner.

What Will Congress Do About It?

Shall This Be the Beginning of the End?

11. *Bismarck Tribune Extra*, 6 July 1876.

12. *Despise Not Your Enemy.* In *Punch; or, The London Charivari*, vol. 76, 1 March 1879, p. 91. N. 2706 d. 10. Courtesy the Bodleian Library, University of Oxford.

Nast cartoon on July 29, 1876, accusing the House of conspiring with the Sioux to cut army expenditures, thus assuring Custer's defeat (illus. 13).[20]

Custer, on the other hand, who as a soldier had failed to endear himself to many of his fellow army officers and troops, was celebrated as a martyr. The *New York Herald* went so far as to characterize Custer as a Homeric demigod.[21] In this vein, less than a month after the battle the *New York Tribune* carried Walt Whitman's poem "A Death-Sonnet for Custer:" [22]

From far Dakota's cañons,
Lands of the wild ravine, the dusky Sioux, the lonesome stretch of
    silence,
Haply to-day a mournful wail, haply a trumpet-note for heroes.

The battle-bulletin,
The Indian ambuscade, the craft, the fatal environment,
The cavalry companies fighting to the last in sternest heroism,
In the midst of their little circle, with their slaughter'd horses for
    breastworks,
The fall of Custer and all his officers and men.

Continues yet the old, old legend of our race,
The loftiest of life upheld by death,
The ancient banner perfectly maintain'd,
O lesson opportune, O how I welcome thee!

As sitting in dark days,
Lone, sulky, through the time's thick murk looking in vain for
    light, for hope,
From unsuspected parts a fierce and momentary proof,
(The sun there at the centre though conceal'd,
Electric life forever at the centre,)
Breaks forth a lightning flash.

Thou of the tawny flowing hair in battle,
I erewhile saw, with erect head, pressing ever in front, bearing a
    bright sword in thy hand,
Now ending well in death the splendid fever of thy deeds,
(I bring no dirge for it or thee, I bring a glad triumphal sonnet,)
Desperate and glorious, aye in defeat most desperate, most
    glorious,
After thy many battles in which never yielding up a gun or a color,

13. *The New Alliance* by Thomas Nast. In *Harper's Weekly*, vol. 20, 29 July 1876.
Courtesy the Bancroft Library.

> Leaving behind thee a memory sweet to soldiers,
> Thou yieldest up thyself.[23]

Whitman's depiction of Custer with flowing locks and shining saber, though melodic and melodramatic, is thoroughly inaccurate—Custer's hair was closely cropped in June 1876, and none of his troopers carried swords. Whitman's imagery passed into popular culture, however, when the Anheuser-Busch Brewing Company copyrighted an Otto Becker lithograph in 1896 and distributed 150,000 copies nationwide (illus. 14).[24] The Becker lithograph, based on a painting by Cassilly Adams, displays Custer with Whitman's erroneous details. Furthermore, Becker's representation perpetuates the image of Custer as one of the last bluecoats to survive, despite Indian testimony that "Yellow Hair" died earlier in the battle.

Unlike the Americans, the British press chose not to apotheosize the military commander responsible for Isandhlwana, namely, Lord Chelmsford. Archibald Forbes attributed the loss at Isandhlwana to "miserable blundering and helpless incapacity" and wrote in the *Daily News* that "Lord Chelmsford has failed as our Commander-in-Chief in South Africa and ought to be instantly recalled."[25] The *Pall Mall Gazette* observed that Chelmsford seemed to have no idea what "would have enabled him to avert the disaster which befell his camp."[26] *Punch* issued a "Phrase-Book for the Use of General Officers," in which Chelmsford is made to respond to Mr. Punch's various scenarios:

> *On learning that an Army has been cut to pieces.*—Dear me! You don't say so! . . .
> *On losing the Baggage-Train of a Division.*—Awkward—very!
> *On receiving an Officer who has ridden for his life twenty miles through an enemy's country, carrying Despatches.*—Very kind of you indeed!
> *On accepting an offer to head a Forlorn Hope.*—I'm afraid you are giving yourself a great deal of trouble!
> *On seeing a Regimental Camp in Flames.*—Odd! Isn't it?
> *On receiving a pair of Regimental Colours, recovered after a desperate struggle.*—I'm afraid you must have found them rather heavy!
> *On learning that a Regiment is "missing."*—Fellows should take more care—they should, really! . . .
> *On finding a position turned.*—I call this quite too provoking!
> *On receiving the news that the troops under his command have been out-generalled and cut to pieces*—Now, who *is* responsible for this?[27]

14. *Custer's Last Fight.* Chromolithograph by Otto Becker from a painting by Cassilly Adams, 1896. Amon Carter Museum, Fort Worth.

Mr. Punch also provides an imaginary final chapter for Chelmsford's pamphlet on rules for conducting hostilities in Africa. *Punch* entitles it "Chapter Last—How to Insure a Defeat, and How to Behave under It." In it, a prospective officer is reminded "that a strongly-fortified camp is the key and nucleus of defence against this vigilant and active enemy." Knowing this, "the commanding officer should quietly move off with the bulk of his force, leaving the tents unentrenched, and the wagons unparked." The officer is also advised that should he return and "find the camp destroyed, the stores plundered, and its defenders slaughtered to a man . . . he should lose no time in instituting a strict Official Inquiry [on] how the mischief has come about." *Punch* then points out that "should it be proved by supplementary testimony, (furnished by officers of his personal staff) that the Commander-in-Chief is not responsible, and that somebody else has been to blame, all the better for the Commander-in-Chief, and all the worse for somebody else." Mr. Punch concludes:

> Should the colonists chafe, and the indignant British Lion growl, he may suggest that an officer of rank should be sent out immediately to assist him, and, if need be, to take his place. He may at the same time remember that for a very long time he has not been at all

well. Lastly, should the growl of the British Lion get so loud as to be annoying, if he feels that more responsibility is being thrown upon him than he can bear, there will be nothing for it but to pack up his cocked hat and writing-desk and come home![28]

The Disraeli government, reproached by the Liberal opposition in Parliament,[29] took its lumps in the press as well. The liberal *Daily News* characterized the ultimatum sent to Cetshwayo as "monstrous," and wrote "that if the Ministry has consented to [Frere's] ultimatum it will not retain office a day after the next meeting of Parliament."[30] The *Spectator* labeled Disraeli's latest crisis in South Africa as "foolishly rash if not radically unjust."[31] *Punch* contrasted Disraeli's diplomatic triumph at the Congress of Berlin in 1878 with the Isandhlwana defeat in a poem entitled "Another Star Gone Out, I Think":

At Berlin, Dizzy's star, in the ascendant,
On tinsel, "Peace with Honour" shone resplendant;
Now with Zulus and Bartle Frere to master,
His star is dimmed, and must be spelt Diz-aster.[32]

In addition to conveying hasty, misleading accounts of Isandhlwana and the Little Bighorn, as well as politicizing the conflicts by assigning scapegoats, the print media fashioned images of the conquerors that passed swiftly into popular culture. The convention of simultaneously glamorizing and dehumanizing the Zulu and Sioux—of portraying each as fearless opponents as well as "inhuman, death-dealing monsters"[33]—is best illustrated in contemporary poetry, paintings, and prints. For example, Robert Buchanan's poem "The Battle of Isandúla," which appeared in the *Contemporary Review* in April 1879, characterized the Zulu as "savage swarms," "screaming devils," "wolves," and "tigers":

In the wilds of Isandúla, far away,
The little band of British soldiers lay,
When a warning voice cried, "Fly!
For the savage swarms are nigh!
See, they loom in war-array
Against the sky!
Ere they come in all the might
Of their legions black as night,
Form in order and take flight from Isandúla. . . ."

15. *Lord Chelmsford* by "Spy." In *Vanity Fair*, vol. 27, 3 September 1881. Per. 2288 b. 46. Courtesy the Bodleian Library, University of Oxford.

So an English cheer arises wild and shrill,
As they form and face the onset with a will,
For clearly now each one
Can see the black hordes run
Swift as wolves across the hill
In the sun —
They can see the host at last
Coming terrible and vast,
Like a torrent, rolling fast on Isandúla. . . .

Soon upon them in their living thousands fell
The blacks like screaming devils out of Hell,
Swarming down in mad desire
As our gunners open'd fire —
At that thunder, with shrill yell,

They swept nigher!
"Fire!" again the order ran,
As the bloody strife began
With the lion-hearted van, at Isandúla. . . .

But 'tis only for an instant they refrain,
At the challenge of that cheer they shriek again,
They swarm on every hand.
O'er the little steadfast band,
Till again, the crimson rain
Makes them stand!
Like a torrent—nay, a sea!—
They roll onward bloodily,
But no white man turns to flee from Isandúla!

Still as stone, our soldiers face the savage crew—
"Fix your bayonets! die as English soldiers do!"
It is done—all stand at bay—
But their strength is cast away;
And the black swarms shriek anew
As they slay!
Ah God! the battle-throes!
With their dead as shields, they close,—
Where the slaughter ebbs and flows, in Isandúla!

And as fast as one form falls, another springs—
They are tigers, not like human-hearted things—
Surging onward they abound,
With a clangour of shrill sound,
With a clash of shields, like wings
Waving round!
As our brave men one by one
Fall death-smitten in the sun,
O'er their corpses legions run, in Isandúla![34]

Poets in the United States immortalized the Little Bighorn battle by seeking "to convert defeat into a kind of moral victory, a glorious if vague triumph of Americanism."[35] The Sioux became a literary convenience toward this end. In his poem "The Revenge of Rain-in-the-Face," for example, Henry Wadsworth Longfellow, like Buchanan, depicted his

16. *Zulu Method of Advancing to the Attack* by Melton Prior. In *The Illustrated London News*, vol. 74, 19 April 1879, p. 373. N. 2288 b. 6. Courtesy the Bodleian Library, University of Oxford.

subjects as unmerciful savages, virtually indistinguishable from the surrounding forces of nature:

> In the meadow spreading wide
> By woodland and riverside
> The Indian village stood;
> All was silent as a dream,
> Save the rushing of the stream
> And the blue-jay in the wood.
>
> In his war paint and his beads
> Like a bison among the reeds,
> In ambush the Sitting Bull
> Lay with three thousand braves
> Crouched in the clefts and caves,
> Savage, unmerciful! [36]

In his poem, written shortly after the Little Bighorn battle, Longfellow reinforced the myth that Rain in the Face extracted Custer's heart, though

17. *Custer's Last Stand.* Watercolor by Charles M. Russell. Courtesy National Cowboy Hall of Fame and Western Heritage Center.

Custer's body was found unmutilated. Ironically, by the late nineteenth century Rain in the Face, who in Longfellow's poem shouted "revenge upon all the race of the white chief with yellow hair," experienced the same fate as many other Indians of note "by being displayed as a curio for white audiences" in Wild West shows.[37]

The poetic imagery of noble savagery was reinforced in contemporary paintings and prints. In April 1879, for example, the *Illustrated London News* exhibited a print based on a sketch by Melton Prior entitled "Zulu Method of Advancing to the Attack" in an extra supplement edition (illus. 16). It depicts athletic Zulu warriors in phalanx formation, equipped with traditional assegais, cowhide shields, and guns, advancing suicidally against British rifles.[38] Prior's sketch of advancing Zulu warriors compares with Charles Marion Russell's painting "Custer's Last Stand" (illus. 17). The "last stand" is obscured by a large group of faceless Sioux whirling about the hapless soldiers. In keeping with this "wild" imagery, Russell's painting was used in 1903 to illustrate William Allen's *Adventures with Indians and Game.*[39]

Prior sketched the Zulu warriors on location during the Anglo-Zulu War. The war artist for the *Graphic*, however, lacking even a map of the battlefield, portrayed what he imagined to be the height of the battle of Isandhlwana. A print published in mid-March 1879 depicts two mounted British soldiers surrounded by an impersonal mass of Zulu warriors (illus. 18). Symbolically, the contemporary viewer saw the representatives of "civilization" beating back the forces of savagery and barbarism.[40] Similar imagery prevails in William Cary's "The Battle on the Little Big Horn River—The Death Struggle of General Custer," which appeared in the *New York Graphic and Illustrated Evening Newspaper* on July 19, 1876 (illus. 19). Cary, who had been sketching Indians and soldiers for *Harper's Weekly, Leslie's,* and *St. Nicholas* since 1861, based his woodcut on the earliest telegraphed reports of the battle. His portrayal centers on Custer, who makes his "last stand" amid a mass of marauding Indians.[41] Cary's woodcut set the standard for Cassilly Adams's famous twelve-by-thirty-two-foot painting "Custer's Last Fight," completed about 1885 and the model for Becker's Anheuser-Busch lithograph (illus. 20). Custer, the symbol of civilization and progress, stands at the center of the painting. In the foreground, Adams displays savages hacking barbarously at Custer's hapless troopers.[42]

18. *Isandhlwana: The Height of Battle.* From *The Graphic,* 15 March 1879, p. 265. Reprinted in Sonia Clarke, ed., *Zululand at War, 1879* (Johannesburg: Brenthurst Press, 1984), p. 101. 621.16 s. 7. Courtesy the Bodleian Library, University of Oxford.

19. *The Battle of the Little Big Horn River — The Death Struggle of General Custer* by William Cary. Courtesy the Library of Congress.

The battle at Isandhlwana contributed to the Liberal party's victory over the Conservatives in 1880. Disraeli anticipated the political fallout. Shortly after news of the battle reached him he wrote: "I am greatly stricken. Everybody was congratulating me on being the most fortunate of Ministers, when there comes this terrible disaster!" [43] In contrast, the Republicans held on to defeat the Democrats in the controversial election of 1876, despite Little Bighorn, widespread corruption, and economic depression. The major political casualty of "Custer's Last Stand" was President Grant's Peace Policy. In the Indian Appropriations Act of August 15, 1876, Congress gave reservation Sioux the option of selling the Black Hills and their rights to the unceded Indian territory or receiving no additional annuities. A number of Sioux leaders signed the "agreement" under duress — far fewer, however, than the "three fourths of all the adult male Indians" required by the Treaty of 1868 — and Congress ratified the bill on February 27, 1877. [44]

The Zulu experienced their share of skulduggery as well. Bishop Colenso's biographer, Sir George Cox, writing in 1880, characterized the Anglo-Zulu War as a "disgrace," in which nothing was gained and nothing settled. "No greater shame," he wrote, "can be incurred by a people than the guilt of unjust wars unjustly waged."[45] Cox failed to be taken in by the popular images of noble savagery, and instead saw the war for what it was—the road to national ruin for the Zulu people. The twilight of the frontier signaled a similar catastrophe for the Sioux, marked by the dissolution of their reservation and the disaster at Wounded Knee Creek. A generation after the deaths of Big Foot and his people, the poet John G. Neihardt depicted Wounded Knee as an epic tragedy in *Song of the Messiah:*

> . . . A gun-shot ripped the hush. The panic roar
> Outfled the clamor of the hills and died.
>
> And then—as though the whole world, crucified
> Upon the heaped Golgotha of its years,
> For all its lonely silences of tears,
> Its countless hates and hurts and terrors, found
> A last composite voice—a hell of sound
> Assailed the brooding heavens. Once again
> The wild wind-roaring of the rage of men,
> The blent staccato thunders of the dream,
> The long-drawn, unresolving nightmare scream
> Of women and of children over all!
> Now—now at last—the peace of love would fall,

20. *Custer's Last Fight* by Cassilly Adams. Courtesy the Library of Congress.

And in a sudden stillness, very kind
The blind would look astonished on the blind
To lose their little dreams of fear and wrath. . . .

Around the writhing body still,
Beneath the flaming thunders of the hill,
That fury heaped the dying and the dead.
And where the women and the children fled
Along the gully winding to the sky
The roaring followed, till the long, thin cry
Above it ceased.
The bugles blared retreat.
Triumphant in the blindness of defeat,
The iron-footed squadrons marched away.

And darkness fell upon the face of day.
The mounting blizzard broke. All night it swept
The bloody field of victory that kept
The secret of the Everlasting Word.[46]

The frontier era ended tragically, not romantically, for the Sioux and the Zulu. Following a century of expansion, collaboration, resistance, defeat, and dissolution, however, each society was fixed in popular culture as the quintessence of noble savagery. The Zulu and Sioux paid dearly indeed for their triumph of a day.

N a final effort to open the South African frontier, the Zulu staged a rebellion against the imposition of a poll tax in Natal in 1906. The new tax came on the heels of various measures enacted by white Natalian colonists to squeeze African tenants off the land and into the labor market, completing the process of proletarianization inaugurated by the Anglo-Zulu War. The so-called Bambatha Rebellion of 1906, named after a chief who organized the resistance, ended in a decisive battle at Mome Gorge on June 10. Altogether, between three thousand and four thousand Africans lost their lives in the uprising, seven thousand taken prisoner, and over four thousand flogged. Twenty-four whites perished. Dinuzulu, whom whites believed to have instigated and coordinated the violence despite overwhelming evidence to the contrary, was arrested and tried on twenty-three counts of treason. Convicted on three counts, the Zulu king was exiled once again; he died five years later in the Middleburg district of the Transvaal.[1]

Dinuzulu's precarious position in the aftermath of the Bambatha Rebellion presaged a century in which Zulu leaders would experience, in Shula Marks's words, "the ambiguities of dependence."[2] Confronted by a coercive system of racial hostility, passbooks, compounds, and labor migration, some of the Zulu leadership, including the monarchy, turned to a "refurbished traditionalism," an ethnic nationalism built upon the past glories of the Zulu kingdom. Their efforts were supported by the central government after 1910 as a strategy of social control. White bureaucrats in the Department of Native Affairs preferred an ethnocentric Zulu nationalism for stabilizing the rural African labor base in Natal to a pan-African socialism that might radicalize it. The founding of Inkatha kaZulu (the

Zulu National Council) in the early 1920s by Solomon, Dinuzulu's son, and its regeneration by Solomon's nephew Mangosuthu Gatsha Buthelezi in 1975, institutionalized Zulu ethnic nationalism.[3]

Despite the striking similarities between Kwazulu and Pine Ridge in the twentieth century—poverty, dependence, malnutrition, and high infant mortality—traditional Lakotas embraced pan-Indianism rather than an ethnically based nationalism. In 1972 many Lakotas turned to a faction of the American Indian Movement (AIM) led by Dennis Banks and Leonard Peltier. AIM, founded in 1968 to address the plight of urban Indians, gained popular support at Pine Ridge when it protested the murder case of Raymond Yellow Thunder in 1972. Yellow Thunder died in Gordon, Nebraska, following a beating by a group of whites in February of that year. As a result of AIM's efforts to publicize the case, Yellow Thunder's attackers received six-year prison sentences, a more severe punishment than whites would normally receive in the beating death of an Indian. The subsequent alliance between AIM and Sioux traditionalists at Pine Ridge brought the organization into conflict with tribal chairman Dick Wilson, who interpreted AIM's popularity as a threat to his own authority. A showdown ensued.

In contrast with South Africa's treatment of Inkatha, the American government regarded AIM as an agency of international communism. The confrontation between Wilson and AIM culminated in AIM's occupation of Wounded Knee for seventy-one days in 1973. The federal government supported Wilson in trying to end the seizure by supplying Bureau of Indian Affairs (BIA) police, U.S. marshalls, and FBI agents. In a trial following the Wounded Knee occupation, AIM leadership was acquitted after the presiding judge accused the FBI of tampering with witnesses. Undeterred, the FBI stepped up its efforts to subvert the AIM movement. During a virtual civil war that erupted between Wilson supporters and AIM in 1975, two FBI agents died in a firefight. The government tried and convicted Leonard Peltier for the killings, despite his claim of innocence. Undermined by the relentless harassment of the FBI, the AIM movement retrogressed.[4]

The Sioux wars of the 1970s summon parallels from the nineteenth century—struggles between "progressives" and "nonprogressives," divide-and-rule strategies, official malfeasance—and also raise issues of comparative significance.[5] This book has compared the historical transformations of the Zulu and Sioux and the processes of interaction between those groups and whites in the nineteenth century, in order to identify the similarities and differences between British and American imperialism. What major themes have emerged?

Most importantly, the similarities pose a further challenge to American exceptionalism. For a number of reasons, the United States' violent encounter with the Sioux in the nineteenth century cannot be dismissed as a tragic interlude peculiar to the American frontiering experience. First, one must examine the conflict, in the words of Paul Kennedy, in the context of the "spectacular growth of an integrated global economy, which drew ever more regions into a transoceanic and transcontinental trading and financial network centered upon western Europe, and in particular upon Great Britain."[6] Although the Lakotas did not provide the unskilled labor supply that significantly influenced the British in their dealings with Africans in South Africa, Sioux control over the agricultural and mineral potential of the northern central plains preoccupied the soldiers and bureaucrats who initiated war in 1876. Second, the U.S.-Sioux War can also be seen as part of a global pattern of intensified conflict in the latter half of the nineteenth century leading to Western domination of over 80 percent of the globe by the eve of the First World War. The contest over land, labor, and resources between western powers and less technologically developed peoples such as the Zulu and Sioux, together with the consignment of native peoples to factionalized, poverty-stricken reserves, further exaggerated the economic disparity between the conquerors and the conquered.[7] Finally, these conflicts arose during the "breechloader revolution," a process that transformed warfare in the second half of the nineteenth century. The weapons technology that contributed to Custer's demise, the defense at Rorke's Drift, and the carnage at Wounded Knee foreshadowed the age of industrial slaughter.[8]

The subjugation of the Zulu and Sioux did not depend entirely on the extraneous forces of industrial capitalist expansion and great power politics. The role of indigenous collaborators and resisters in shaping the frontier process was also important. The Lakota and Zulu pursued their own diplomatic and economic interests, often from positions of strength. Not only did their concerns frequently transcend the "white threat," but their decisions to cooperate, accommodate, negotiate, bluster, cajole, and resist whites—decisions constrained by the stability of their own polities—shaped the course and timing of events as much as externalities. In effect, the subimperialisms of the Zulu and Sioux explain a great deal about the closing frontier in North America and South Africa.

We have also seen that "traditional" peoples such as the Zulu and

Sioux are far from the static entities of scholarly convention. Instead, both peoples underwent profound transformations in the centuries prior to western contact. In both cases, for example, long-distance trade and adaptations to ecological constraints and opportunities gave rise to a number of changes that scholars have regarded as "classic" features of the Sioux and Zulu societies. Both the Zulu and Sioux became aggressive, expansionist powers, dominating and subjugating other indigenous peoples according to calculated interests. At the same time, the Lakotas and Zulu developed complex systems of kinship, belief, politics, and economics, practices often unintelligible to white observers. The white peoples encountered by the Lakotas and Zulu did not monopolize aggression, ethnocentrism, and arrogance—but on the other hand, neither did whites patent human culture, despite pretensions to the contrary.

Westerners have compensated for their lack of an understanding of Zulu and Sioux history and culture by constructing images of the "Other"[9] in accordance with their own hopes and fears. Each people was reconstructed into quintessential noble savages, admired because their martial virtuosity seemed almost westernlike, reviled for their "barbarous" instincts. In the nineteenth century, journalists, poets, novelists, and artists purveyed imagery that transformed these real societies and their famous battles into myths. Filmmakers in the twentieth century have perpetuated that tradition. The barbarous Zulu appeared in such films as *Untamed*, a 1952 production starring Tyrone Power and Susan Hayward in which heroic Boer pioneers battle hordes of savage Zulu. A more romanticized version of the Zulu people appears in the 1964 production *Zulu*, although the film dwells at length on the British soldiers at Rorke's Drift, especially the officers played by Stanley Baker and Michael Caine, despite the film's title. The most recent trend in American filmmaking is to idealize the Sioux. Kevin Costner's Academy Award–winning *Dances with Wolves* was a brilliant cinematographic feat. In depicting the Lakotas as innocent victims of the Pawnees, however, the film glosses over the Sioux legacy of aggressive expansion.

Despite similarities in the Sioux and Zulu experiences—civil war, partition, and national disintegration—key differences clearly emerge. Economically, the Sioux were marginalized by their encounter with the United States, made "useless" to the economic growth of the country. A defeated Zululand, on the other hand, transformed itself into a reservoir of cheap labor, a highly desireable commodity to the British and later to South African whites. The destruction of the Zulu kingdom thus paved the way for the proletarianization of its people and for the promotion of legal white supremacy in South Africa in the twentieth century. The result, tragic for the Zulu people, represented the logical outcome of British imperial policy in South Africa.

American policy toward the Sioux bore tragic results as well, yet suffered, ironically, from a lack of Britain's imperial resolve. Riddled with contradictions and shifting goals, the U.S. reservation program led to widespread poverty, anger, and despair. Between 1887 and 1934 Indians lost 60 percent of their remaining land and two-thirds of their allotted lands.[10]

Spanning this era of conflict, subjugation, and impoverishment, the life of the Lakota holy man Black Elk personifies the dream among vanquished peoples that frontiers may open again. Black Elk witnessed the Little Bighorn battle, participated in the Ghost Dance, and appeared in Buffalo Bill's Wild West shows. Despite his conversion to Catholicism in the early 1900s, Black Elk maintained a loyalty to Lakota traditions throughout his lifetime. He turned increasingly to old beliefs in his later years, in fact, as his despair over the spiritual powerlessness and economic distress of his people deepened. In one instance, Black Elk invoked the Great Spirit in a ceremony performed on Harney Peak, the same promontory Custer ascended during his famous expedition to the Black Hills in 1874. "Hear me, O Great Spirit," Black Elk summoned, "that my people will get back into the sacred hoop and that the tree may bloom and that my people will live the ways you have set for them, and if they live, they may see the happy days and the happy land that you have promised." Black Elk then raised his voice to a wail and sang: "In sorrow I am sending a voice, O six powers of the earth, hear me in sorrow. With tears I am sending a voice. May you behold me and hear me that my people may live again."[11]

N O T E S

INTRODUCTION

1. Department of the Army, *The Medals of Honor of the United States Army* (Washington, D.C.: Government Printing Office, 1948), pp. 235–37.
2. James Gump, *The Formation of the Zulu Kingdom in South Africa, 1750–1840* (San Francisco: Mellen Research University Press, 1990).
3. Howard Lamar and Leonard Thompson, eds., *The Frontier in History: North America and Southern Africa Compared* (New Haven, Conn.: Yale University Press, 1981), pp. 7–8.
4. Robin W. Winks, "The Idea of American Imperialism," unpublished manuscript, 1984, p. xi.
5. Ronald Robinson, "Non-European Foundations of European Imperialism: Sketch for a Theory of Collaboration," in Roger Owen and Bob Sutcliffe, eds., *Studies in the Theory of Imperialism* (London: Longman, 1972).
6. George M. Fredrickson, "Comparative History," in *The Past before Us: Contemporary Historical Writing in the United States*, ed. Michael Kammen (Ithaca, N.Y.: Cornell University Press, 1980), p. 458.
7. Quoted in Lamar and Thompson, eds., *Frontier in History*, p. 35.
8. Richard White, *"It's Your Misfortune and None of My Own": A New History of the American West* (Norman: University of Oklahoma Press, 1991), p. 91.
9. Paul Kennedy, *The Rise and Fall of the Great Powers* (New York: Random House, 1987), pp. 143–50.
10. Morton N. Cohen, *Rider Haggard: His Life and Work*, 2nd ed. (London: Macmillan, 1968), p. 227.

I THE LITTLE BIGHORN IN COMPARATIVE PERSPECTIVE

1. Cited in James R. Walker, *Lakota Belief and Ritual*, ed. Raymond J. DeMallie and Elaine A. Jahner (Lincoln: University of Nebraska Press, 1980), p. 29.
2. Testimony of Little Wound, American Horse, and Lone Star, cited in Walker, *Lakota Belief*, pp. 181–82.
3. Raymond J. DeMallie, ed., *The Sixth Grandfather: Black Elk's Teachings Given to John G. Neihardt* (Lincoln: University of Nebraska Press, 1984), pp. 80–81.

4. Stanley Vestal, *Warpath: The True Story of the Fighting Sioux Told in a Biography of Chief White Bull* (Boston: Houghton Mifflin, 1934; reprint, Lincoln: University of Nebraska Press, 1984), p. 87.

5. Edgar I. Stewart, *Custer's Luck* (Norman: University of Oklahoma Press, 1955), pp. 193–94.

6. Ibid., p. 195.

7. John S. Gray, *Centennial Campaign: The Sioux War of 1876* (Ft. Collins, Colo.: Old Army Press, 1976), pp. 308–20.

8. "General Godfrey's Narrative," in W. A. Graham, ed., *The Custer Myth: A Source Book of Custeriana* (Harrisburg, Pa.: Stackpole, 1953; reprint, Lincoln: University of Nebraska Press, 1986), p. 135.

9. Testimony of Red Star, in O. G. Libby, ed., *The Arikara Narrative of the Campaign against the Hostile Dakotas, June 1876* (Glorieta, N.M.: Rio Grande Press, 1976), pp. 78–79.

10. "Godfrey's Narrative," in Graham, ed., *Custer Myth*, p. 135.

11. Gray, *Centennial Campaign*, p. 151.

12. Letter from E. W. Smith to Lt.-Col. Custer, 22 June 1876, manuscript copy in the Bancroft Library, University of California, Berkeley.

13. Gump, *Formation of the Zulu Kingdom, c. 1750–1840*, p. 144.

14. Killie Campbell Africana Library, James Stuart Papers (cited hereinafter as KCL SP), vol. 59, evidence of Lunguza, 13 March 1909.

15. KCL SP, vol. 12, evidence of Ndukwana, 21 June 1903.

16. Magema M. Fuze, *The Black People and Whence They Came*, trans. H. C. Lugg (Pietermaritzburg: University of Natal Press, 1979), p. 106.

17. Ibid., p. 106.

18. British Parliamentary Papers (cited hereinafter as BPP), C-2222, vol. 52, Frere to Hicks Beach, 10 December 1878.

19. Quoted in Reginald Coupland, *Zulu Battle Piece: Isandhlwana* (London: Collins, 1948), p. 50.

20. Donald Morris, *The Washing of the Spears: A History of the Rise of the Zulu Nation under Shaka and Its Fall in the Zulu War of 1879* (New York: Random House, 1965), p. 329.

21. Cited in E. H. Brookes and C. de B. Webb, eds., *A History of Natal* (Pietermaritzburg: University of Natal Press, 1965), p. 138.

22. Morris, *Washing of the Spears*, p. 332.

23. Daphne Child, ed., *The War Journal of Colonel Henry Harford* (Hamden, Conn.: Archon Books, 1980), p. 25.

24. J. Y. Gibson, *The Story of the Zulus* (London: Longmans, Green, 1911), p. 175.

25. Evidence of Mpatshana in C. de B. Webb and John Wright, eds, *The James Stuart Archive of Recorded Oral Evidence Relating to the History of the Zulu and Neighbouring Peoples* (cited hereinafter as *JSA*), vol. 3, p. 301.

26. Gray, *Centennial Campaign*, p. 159.

27. "The Statements of Scout Herendeen," in Graham, ed., *Custer Myth*, p. 262.

28. "Fighting the Indians," in ibid., p. 342.

29. "The Statements of Scout Herendeen," in ibid., p. 262.

30. Testimony of Red Star in Libby, ed., *Arikara Narrative*, p. 90.

31. Ibid., pp. 91–92.

32. Stewart, *Custer's Luck*, p. 261.

33. Gray, *Centennial Campaign*, p. 170.
34. "Benteen's Narrative," in Graham, ed., *Custer Myth*, pp. 179–80.
35. Stewart, *Custer's Luck*, p. 320.
36. Gray, *Centennial Campaign*, p. 183.
37. Stewart, *Custer's Luck*, p. 324.
38. Ibid., pp. 325–26.
39. Gray, *Centennial Campaign*, p. 176.
40. Ibid., p. 177.
41. W. A. Graham, "Come On! Be Quick! Bring Packs!," in Graham, ed., *Custer Myth*, p. 290.
42. Gray, *Centennial Campaign*, p. 178.
43. Brookes and Webb, *History of Natal*, p. 139.
44. Morris, *Washing of the Spears*, p. 337.
45. Cited in Coupland, *Zulu Battle Piece*, p. 135.
46. Child, ed., *Zulu War Journal*, p. 28.
47. Cited in Morris, *Washing of the Spears*, p. 340.
48. Ibid., p. 341.
49. Child, ed., *Zulu War Journal*, p. 30.
50. Horace Smith-Dorrien, *Memories of Forty-Eight Years' Service* (London: Murray, 1925), pp. 10, 11.
51. War correspondent Archibald Forbes characterized these proceedings as a "solemn mockery." Cited in Rupert Furneaux, *The Zulu War: Isandhlwana and Rorke's Drift* (London: Weidenfeld and Nicolson, 1963), p. 147.
52. Durnford served on a boundary commission in 1878 that adjudicated a territorial dispute between the Zulu kingdom and the Transvaal. In late 1878 the commission awarded the bulk of disputed territory to the Zulu. See chapter 5.
53. Edward Durnford, *A Soldier's Life and Work in South Africa, 1872–1879* (London: Sampson Low, Marston, Searle and Rivington, 1882), p. 4.
54. Ibid., pp. 199–205; Robert B. Edgerton, *Like Lions They Fought: The Zulu War and the Last Black Empire in South Africa* (New York: Free Press, 1988), pp. 82–84.
55. Coupland, *Zulu Battle-Piece*, pp. 135–36.
56. Morris, *Washing of the Spears*, p. 357.
57. J. P. C. Laband and P. S. Thompson, *A Field Guide to the War in Zululand, 1879* (Pietermaritzburg: University of Natal Press, 1979), p. 41.
58. Morris, *Washing of the Spears*, p. 364.
59. "Crazy Horse Speaks," in *Custer Myth*, ed. Graham, p. 63.
60. Gray, *Centennial Campaign*, p. 357.
61. Stewart, *Custer's Luck*, p. 434.
62. Stanley Vestal, *Sitting Bull: Champion of the Sioux* (Norman: University of Oklahoma Press, 1932), p. 161.
63. "General Godfrey's Narrative," in Graham, ed., *Custer Myth*, p. 139.
64. Stewart, *Custer's Luck*, p. 435.
65. "Low Dog's Account of the Custer Fight," in Graham, ed., *Custer Myth*, p. 75.
66. Stewart, *Custer's Luck*, pp. 435–37.
67. "The Story of War Chief Gall of the Uncpapas," in Graham, ed., *Custer Myth*, p. 88.
68. See "General Hugh L. Scott's Interviews with the Crows 'Curley' and 'White Man Runs Him,' and the Minneconjou 'Feather Earring,' " in ibid., pp. 12–18.

69. George Bird Grinnell, *The Fighting Cheyennes* (New York: Scribner's, 1915), p. 340.

70. "General Custer's Last Fight As Seen By Two Moon," in Graham, ed., *Custer Myth*, p. 103.

71. Douglas D. Scott and Richard A. Fox, *Archaeological Insights into the Custer Battle* (Norman: University of Oklahoma Press, 1987), p. 112.

72. "The Story of War Chief Gall of the Uncpapas," in Graham, ed., *Custer Myth*, p. 88.

73. Robert Paul Jordan, "Ghosts on the Little Bighorn," *National Geographic*, December 1986, pp. 796–97.

74. "Crow King's Story of the Fight," in Graham, ed., *Custer Myth*, p. 77.

75. George E. Hyde, *Red Cloud's Folk: A History of the Oglala Sioux Indians* (Norman: University of Oklahoma Press, 1937; rev. ed., 1957), p. 272.

76. Angus McBride, *The Zulu War* (London: Osprey, 1976), pp. 17–18; Laband and Thompson, *Field Guide*, p. 41.

77. Laband and Thompson, *Field Guide*, pp. 41–42.

78. Smith-Dorrien, *Forty-Eight Years*, p. 13.

79. Daniel R. Headrick, *The Tools of Empire: Technology and European Imperialism in the Nineteenth Century* (New York: Oxford University Press, 1981), pp. 96–104.

80. Morris, *Washing of the Spears*, p. 373.

81. Ibid., pp. 373–88.

82. This figure is taken from Laband and Thompson, *Field Guide*, p. 42.

83. Evidence of Mpatshana in *JSA*, 3:303.

84. C. de B. Webb and J. B. Wright, eds., *A Zulu King Speaks: Statements Made by Cetshwayo kaMpande on the History and Customs of His People* (Pietermaritzburg: University of Natal Press, 1978), p. 31.

85. Morris, *Washing of the Spears*, pp. 400–402, 417–18.

86. Cited in Furneaux, *Zulu War*, p. 163.

87. Fuze, *Black People*, p. 113.

88. Jeff Guy, *The Destruction of the Zulu Kingdom: The Civil War in Zululand, 1879–1884* (London: Longman, 1979; reprint, Johannesburg: Ravan Press, 1982), pp. 55–56.

89. Cornelius Vijn, *Cetshwayo's Dutchman* (London: Longmans, Green, 1880; reprint, New York: Negro Universities Press, 1969), p. 142.

90. Furneaux, *Zulu War*, p. 125.

91. See Thomas W. Dunlay, *Wolves for the Blue Soldiers: Indian Scouts and Auxiliaries with the United States Army, 1860–90* (Lincoln: University of Nebraska Press, 1982). The British employed between seven thousand and eight thousand African troopers, including Durnford's Frontier Light Horse, the Edendale Troop, several hundred disaffected Zulu under the command of Mvubi, and the Natal Native Contingent. See Robert B. Edgerton, *Like Lions They Fought*, pp. 56–57.

92. *Daily Telegraph*, 11 March 1879, p. 5.

2 FRONTIERS OF EXPANSION

1. These popular characterizations are discussed in chapter 7.

2. Stephen E. Feraca and James H. Howard, "The Identity and Demography of the Dakota or Sioux Tribe," *Plains Anthropologist* 8, no. 20 (May 1963): 81–83.

3. Royal B. Hassrick, *The Sioux: Life and Customs of a Warrior Society* (Norman: University

of Oklahoma Press, 1964), p. 6. I here use the three terms more or less synonymously.

4. These seven bands are further divided into three major divisions: the eastern or Santee (Mdewakanton, Wahpekute, Sisseton, and Wahpeton), the middle or Wiciyela (Yankton and Yanktonai), and the western (Teton).

5. James R. Walker, *Lakota Society*, ed. Raymond J. DeMallie (Lincoln: University of Nebraska Press, 1982), pp. 4–5.

6. P. Richard Metcalfe, "The Political Evolution of the Teton-Lakotah," seminar paper, Yale University, n.d., pp. i–iii.

7. David I. Bushnell, *Tribal Migrations East of the Mississippi*, Smithsonian Miscellaneous Collections, vol. 89, no. 12 (Washington, D.C.: Smithsonian Institution, 1934).

8. Gideon D. Scull, ed., *Voyages of Peter Espirit Radisson* (Boston: The Prince Society, 1885; reprint, New York: Burt Franklin, 1967), p. 207.

9. Cited in Mildred Mott Wedel, "Le Sueur and the Dakota Sioux," in Elden Johnson, ed., *Aspects of Upper Great Lakes Anthropology: Papers in Honor of Lloyd A. Wilford* (St. Paul: Minnesota Historical Society, 1974), pp. 165–66.

10. Frank Raymond Secoy, *Changing Military Patterns on the Great Plains* (Locust Valley, N.Y.: Augustin, 1953), p. 66.

11. Gary C. Anderson, "Early Dakota Migration and Intertribal War: A Revision," *Western Historical Quarterly* 11, no. 1 (January 1980): 18–19.

12. Cited by John C. Ewers, "Intertribal Warfare as the Precursor of Indian-White Warfare on the Northern Great Plains," *Western Historical Quarterly* 6, no. 4 (October 1975): p. 399.

13. Secoy, *Changing Military Patterns*, pp. 71–72.

14. Scudder Mekeel, "A Short History of the Teton-Dakota," *North Dakota Historical Quarterly* 10, no. 3 (July 1943): 154–56; Hyde, *Red Cloud's Folk*, p. 8; Richard White, "The Winning of the West: The Expansion of the Western Sioux in the Eighteenth and Nineteenth Centuries," *Journal of American History* 65, no. 2 (September 1978): 322.

15. Hyde, *Red Cloud's Folk*, p. 15.

16. White, "Winning of the West," p. 323.

17. Hyde, *Red Cloud's Folk*, pp. 15–16.

18. Secoy, *Changing Military Patterns*, pp. 74–75.

19. A. P. Nasatir, ed., *Before Lewis and Clark: Documents Illustrating the History of the Missouri, 1785–1804*, vol. I (St. Louis: St. Louis Historical Documents Foundation, 1952), p. 299.

20. Annie Heloise Abel, ed., *Tabeau's Narrative of Loisel's Expedition to the Upper Missouri* (Norman: University of Oklahoma Press, 1939), pp. 130–31.

21. White, "Winning of the West," p. 327.

22. St. Louis merchants at this time often characterized the Sioux as "plunderers" and "extortionists."

23. James P. Ronda, *Lewis and Clark among the Indians* (Lincoln: University of Nebraska Press, 1984), pp. 28–30.

24. Reuben Gold Thwaites, ed., *Original Journals of the Lewis and Clark Expedition*, vol. 6 (New York: Dodd, Mead, 1904–5; reprint, New York: Antiquarian Press, 1959), p. 98.

25. Guy, *Destruction of the Zulu Kingdom*, p. xvii.

26. The most exhaustive effort, A. T. Bryant's *Olden Times in Zululand* (London: Longmans, Green, 1929; reprint, Cape Town: C. Struik, 1965), is frequently cited as the

standard account of the origins of the pre-Shakan peoples. Bryant's work, however, is based on the uncritical use of oral traditions and must be used with caution.

27. Patrick Harries, "The Roots of Ethnicity: Discourse and the Politics of Language Construction in South-east Africa," *African Affairs* 87, no. 346 (January 1988): pp. 36–37.

28. John Wright, "Politics, Ideology, and the Invention of the 'Nguni,'" seminar paper, University of Natal, Pietermaritzburg, 1983, p. 14.

29. Ibid., p. 27.

30. C. R. Boxer, ed., *The Tragic History of the Sea, 1589–1662* (Cambridge: Cambridge University Press, 1959), pp. 123–24.

31. Ibid., pp. 70–71.

32. Elizabeth A. Eldredge, "Sources of Conflict in Southern Africa, c. 1800–30: The 'Mfecane' Reconsidered," *Journal of African History* 33, no. 1 (1992): 29.

33. James Gump, "Origins of the Zulu Kingdom," *Historian* 50, no. 4 (August 1988): 521–34. Cf. Henry Slater, "Transitions in the Political Economy of South-east Africa before 1840" (D.Phil. thesis, University of Sussex, 1976); and David W. Hedges, "Trade and Politics in Southern Mozambique and Zululand in the Eighteenth and Early Nineteenth Centuries" (D.Phil. thesis, University of London, 1978).

34. Hedges, "Trade and Politics," p. 61.

35. Ibid., p. 41.

36. A. T. Bryant, *The Zulu People as They Were before the White Man Came* (Pietermaritzburg, Natal: Shuter and Shooter, 1949), p. 313.

37. Martin Hall, "The Myth of the Zulu Homestead: Archaeology and Ethnography," *Africa* 54, no. 1(1984): 65–80.

38. George McCall Theal, ed., *Records of South Eastern Africa*, vol. 8 (reprint; Cape Town: C. Struik, 1964), p. 205.

39. Jeff Guy, "Analysing Pre-Capitalist Societies in Southern Africa," *Journal of Southern African Studies* 14, no. 1 (October 1987): 29.

40. Monica Wilson, "The Nguni People," in Monica Wilson and Leonard Thompson, eds., *The Oxford History of South Africa* (cited hereinafter as *OHSA*), vol. 1 (New York: Oxford University Press, 1969), pp 107–8.

41. Jeff Guy, "Production and Exchange in the Zulu Kingdom," *Mohlomi: Journal of Southern African Historical Studies* 2 (1978): 105.

42. Guy, "Ecological Factors," p. 105–9.

43. Martin Hall, "The Ecology of the Iron Age in Zululand" (Ph.D. thesis, University of Cambridge, 1980), p. 274.

44. John Ayliff and Joseph Whiteside, *History of the Abambo* (Butterworth, 1912; reprint, Cape Town: C. Struik, 1962), p. 9.

45. James Gump, "Ecological Change and Pre-Shakan State Formation," *African Economic History* 18 (1989): 57–71.

46. Ibid.

47. Ayliff and Whiteside, *Abambo*, p. 8.

48. KCL SP, vol. 59, evidence of Mabonsa, 27 January 1909.

49. Bryant, *Olden Times*, p. 641.

50. Ibid., p. 641.

51. John Wright, "Pre-Shakan Age-Group Formation among the Northern Nguni," *Natalia* 8 (December 1978): 26.

52. Guy, "Analysing Pre-Capitalist Societies," pp. 21–22.

53. Guy, "Production and Exchange," p. 102.

54. Ibid., pp. 102–3. Cf. Eldredge, "The 'Mfecane' Reconsidered," p. 27. Eldredge argues that no convincing evidence suggests that the marriage age of women, "the only factor relevant to birth rates," was postponed under Shaka.

55. Hedges, "Trade and Politics," pp. 178–87.

56. Metcalfe, "Political Evolution," p. ii.

57. Abel, ed., *Tabeau's Narrative*, pp. 104–5.

58. See chapter 3.

59. Raymond J. DeMallie, "Sioux Ethnohistory: A Methodological Critique," *Journal of Ethnic Studies* 4, no. 3 (Fall 1976): 81.

60. Ibid., p. 82.

61. Jeanette Mirsky, "The Dakota," in Margaret Mead, ed., *Cooperation and Competition among Primitive Peoples* (New York: McGraw-Hill, 1937), pp. 393–97.

62. Clark Wissler, "Societies and Ceremonial Associations in the Oglala Division of the Teton-Dakota," *American Museum of Natural History Anthropological Papers* 11, pt. 1 (1912): 9–10.

63. Hassrick, *The Sioux*, pp. 16–17.

64. Abel, ed., *Tabeau's Narrative*, p. 116.

65. Wissler, "Societies and Ceremonial Associations," p. 10.

66. See ibid., pp. 52–74.

67. *JSA* 1:342.

3 INDIGENOUS EMPIRES

1. Hyde, *Red Cloud's Folk*, pp. 12–19. Cf. Harry Anderson, "An Investigation of the Early Bands of the Saone Group of Teton Sioux," *Journal of the Washington Academy of Sciences* 46 (1956): 87–94.

2. Ferdinand V. Hayden, *Contributions to the Ethnography and Philology of the Indian Tribes of the Missouri Valley* (American Philosophical Society Transactions, vol. 12, no. 2 (Philadelphia: The Society, 1862), pp. 372–74.

3. Ibid., p. 371; Henry Atkinson, *Expedition up the Missouri, 1825*, 19th Congress, 1st session, House Doc. 117 (Washington, D.C., 1826), pp. 9–10; Thaddeus A. Culbertson, *Journal of an Expedition to the Mauvaises Terres and the Upper Missouri in 1850*, ed. John Francis McDermott, Bureau of American Ethnology Bulletin 147 (Washington, D.C.: The Bureau, 1952), p. 137; Reuben Gold Thwaites, ed., *Early Western Travels 1748–1846*, vol. 22, part 1 of *Maximilian, Prince of Wied's Travels to the Interior of North America, 1832–1834* (Cleveland: Clark, 1906), p. 304; White, "Winning of the West," pp. 329–30.

4. Edwin T. Denig, *Five Indian Tribes of the Upper Missouri: Sioux, Arickaras, Assiniboines, Crees, Crows*, ed. John C. Ewers (Norman: University of Oklahoma Press, 1961), p. 19.

5. White, "Winning of the West," pp. 329–30.

6. John C. Ewers, *Teton Dakota: Ethnology and History* (Berkeley, Calif.: U.S. Department of the Interior, 1937), pp. 75–76.

7. Hiram Martin Chittenden, *The American Fur Trade of the Far West*, vol. 2 (New York: Harper, 1902), p. 865–66.

8. White, "Winning of the West," p. 330; Hyde, *Red Cloud's Folk*, p. 62.

9. Mekeel, "Short History," p. 175.

10. George Catlin, *Letters and Notes on the Manners, Customs, and Condition of the North American Indians*, vol. 1 (London: Tosswill and Myers, 1841), p. 256; also see Fanny Kelly, *Narrative of My Captivity among the Sioux Indians* (Cincinnati: Wilstach, Baldwin, 1871), p. 76.

11. Ewers, *Teton Ethnology and History*, pp. 76–77; White, "Winning of the West," p. 330.

12. White, "Winning of the West," pp. 332–33; Denig, *Five Indian Tribes*, p. 57; Hyde, *Red Cloud's Folk*, pp. 36–38.

13. White, "Winning of the West," pp. 333–34.

14. Bryant, *Olden Times*, pp. 62–63.

15. This account of Shaka's early years is derived largely from the trader Henry Francis Fynn. See *The Diary of Henry Francis Fynn*, ed. J. Stuart and D. Mck. Malcolm (Pietermaritzburg, Natal: Shuter and Shooter, 1950), pp. 12–13.

16. J. D. Omer-Cooper, *The Zulu Aftermath: A Nineteenth-Century Revolution in Bantu Africa* (London: Longman, 1966), p. 33.

17. Bryant, *Olden Times*, pp. 194–95, 588–94.

18. Ibid., pp. 196–201; Testimony of Jantshi in *JSA* 1:182–83.

19. Julian Cobbing, "The Case against the Mfecane," seminar paper, University of the Witwatersrand, 1984, p. 1.

20. The refugees who fled south from the Zulu were known as the Mfengu. The Mfengu became important auxilliaries for the British during the long series of Anglo-Xhosa wars in the nineteenth century.

21. In addition to "The Case against the Mfecane," Cobbing has written "The Myth of the Mfecane," seminar paper, University of Durban-Westville, 1987; "The Mfecane as Alibi: Thoughts on Dithakong and Mbolompo," *Journal of African History* 29 (1988): 487–519; and "Grasping the Nettle: The Slave Trade and the Early Zulu," seminar paper, University of Natal, Pietermaritzburg, 1990.

22. See the insightful critiques of Cobbing by Eldredge, "The 'Mfecane' Reconsidered," p. 2; and especially Carolyn Anne Hamilton, " 'The Character and Objects of Chaka': A Reconsideration of the Making of Shaka as 'Mfecane' Motor," *Journal of African History* 33, no. 1 (1992): 38.

23. Leonard Thompson, *A History of South Africa* (New Haven, Conn.: Yale University Press, 1990), p. 84.

24. *JSA* 1:187.

25. Nathaniel Isaacs, *Travels and Adventures in Eastern Africa*, ed. Louis Herman and Percival R. Kirby (London: Edward Churton, 1836; reprint, Cape Town: C. Struik, 1966), p. 156.

26. Percival R. Kirby, ed., *Andrew Smith and Natal* (Cape Town: Van Riebeeck Society, 1955), p. 93.

27. Stuart and Malcolm, eds., *Diary of Fynn*, p. 18.

28. *JSA* 2:296.

29. Leonard Thompson, "The Zulu Kingdom," in *OHSA* 1:344.

30. Isaacs, *Travels and Adventures*, p. 151.

31. J. J. Guy, "Production and Exchange in the Zulu Kingdom," in J. B. Peires, ed., *Before and after Shaka: Papers in Nguni History* (Grahamstown, South Africa: Rhodes Institute of Social and Economic Research, 1981), p. 41.

32. Stuart and Malcolm, eds., *Diary of Fynn*, pp. 62, 71, 73, 95, 123, 284; Bryant, *Olden Times*, pp. 644–45; Baleka in *JSA* 1:12.

33. J. J. Guy, "Production and Exchange," pp. 28–46.

34. Bryant, *Zulu People*, p. 438.

35. P. J. Colenbrander, "The Zulu Political Economy on the Eve of the War," in Andrew Duminy and Charles Ballard, eds., *Anglo-Zulu War: New Perspectives* (Pietermaritzburg: University of Natal Press, 1981), p 80.

36. Stuart and Malcolm, eds., *Diary of Fynn*, pp. 283–84.

37. John Omer-Cooper, "Political Change in the Nineteenth-Century Mfecane," in Leonard Thompson, ed., *African Societies in Southern Africa* (London: Heinemann, 1969), p. 211.

38. Bryant, *Olden Times*, p. 531.

39. Stuart and Malcolm, eds., *Diary of Fynn*, p. 73.

40. Alan R. Booth, ed., *Journal of the Rev. George Champion* (Cape Town: C. Struik, 1967), p. 115.

41. Testimony of Madikane in *JSA* 2:51.

42. KCL SP, vol. 58, evidence of Mtshapi, 1 April 1918.

43. Ibid., vol. 60, evidence of Ndukwana, 21 June 1903.

44. Ibid., vol. 62, evidence of Sivivi, 6 March 1907.

45. Ibid., vol. 55, evidence of Baleni, 14 May 1914.

46. Denig, *Five Indian Tribes*, p. 21.

47. Ibid., pp. 24–29; White, "Winning of the West," p. 331.

48. Ewers, "Intertribal Warfare," p. 406.

49. Sioux winter counts reveal numerous attacks on the Crows as well as the Pawnees between c. 1800 and 1850. See Garrick Mallery, *Picture-Writing of the American Indians*, Smithsonian Institution Bureau of American Ethnology Annual Report no. 10, (Washington, D.C.: Smithsonian Institution, 1893; reprint, New York: Dover, 1972), 1:266–328.

50. White, "Winning of the West," pp. 336–39.

51. Denig, *Five Indian Tribes*, p. 204.

52. White, "Winning of the West," p. 337; Gene Weltfish, *The Lost Universe* (New York: Basic Books, 1965), p. 3.

53. George Bird Grinnell, *Two Great Scouts and Their Pawnee Battalion* (Cleveland: Clark, 1928), pp. 62–67, 162.

54. Weltfish, *Lost Universe*, p. 103.

55. White, "Winning of the West," pp. 338–39; Grinnell, *Two Great Scouts*, pp. 57–58; Hyde, *Red Cloud's Folk*, p. 202; and Weltfish, *Lost Universe*, p. 4.

56. Wissler, *Societies and Ceremonial Associations*, pp. 5–12; William K. Powers, *Oglala Religion* (Lincoln: University of Nebraska Press, 1977), pp. 40–41; Stephen E. Feraca, *The History and Development of Oglala Sioux Tribal Government*, Bureau of Indian Affairs Report (Washington, D.C.: The Bureau, 1964), pp. 7–8; Ewers, *Teton Dakota*, pp. 63–64.

57. Symmes C. Oliver, *Ecology and Cultural Continuity as Contributing Factors in the Social Organization of the Plains Indians* (Berkeley and Los Angeles: University of California Press, 1962), pp. 17, 52–56.

58. Francis Parkman, *The Oregon Trail: Sketches of Prairie and Rocky-Mountain Life*, 8th ed. (Boston: Little, Brown, 1925), p. 135.

59. Denig, *Five Indian Tribes*, pp. 21–22.

60. Hyde, *Red Cloud's Folk*, pp. 40, 43–46, 53.

61. Feraca, *Oglala Sioux Tribal Government*, p. 11.

62. James C. Olson, *Red Cloud and the Sioux Problem* (Lincoln: University of Nebraska Press, 1965), pp. 21–22; Hyde, *Red Cloud's Folk*, pp. 53–55.

63. Hyde, *Red Cloud's Folk*, p. 56.

64. On his way to London to publish his memoirs, the trader Nathaniel Isaacs wrote to Henry Fynn: "Make [the Zulu kings] out as blood-thirsty as you can and endeavour to give an estimate of the number of people they murdered during their reign, and also describe the frivolous crimes people lose their lives for. It all tends to swell up the work and make it interesting." Cited in Christopher Saunders, ed., *Illustrated History of South Africa: The Real Story* (Pleasantville, N.Y.: Reader's Digest Association, 1988), p. 87. See also Hamilton, " 'The Character and Objects of Chaka,' " passim.

65. Stuart and Malcolm, eds., *Diary of Fynn*, p. 19.

66. Testimony of Madikane in *JSA* 2:62; Baleka in *JSA* 1:10; Jantshi in *JSA* 1:198.

67. Testimony of Lunguza in *JSA* 1:311.

68. Stuart and Malcolm, eds., *Diary of Fynn*, pp. 132–36; Isaacs, *Travels and Adventures*, pp. 108ff.

69. Stuart and Malcolm, eds., *Diary of Fynn*, pp. 28, 83–86, 132–36, 142–43, 155–57; Isaacs, *Travels and Adventures*, pp. 140–45; Bryant, *Olden Times*, pp. 606–14, 658–64.

70. See Leonard Thompson, *The Political Mythology of Apartheid* (New Haven, Conn.: Yale University Press, 1985).

4 COLLABORATORS OF A KIND

1. Parkman, *Oregon Trail*, p. 109.

2. Hyde, *Red Cloud's Folk*, p. 84.

3. See ibid., ch. 5.

4. James H. Howard, *The Warrior Who Killed Custer: The Personal Narrative of Chief Joseph White Bull* (Lincoln: University of Nebraska Press, 1968), pp. 19–22.

5. Mallery, *Picture-Writing*, 1:324–27.

6. Walker, *Lakota Society*, pp. 142–48.

7. Robert A. Trennert, Jr., *Alternative to Extinction: Federal Indian Policy and the Beginnings of the Reservation System, 1846–51* (Philadelphia: Temple University Press, 1975).

8. Frances Paul Prucha, *The Great Father: The United States Government and the American Indians*, vol. 1 (Lincoln: University of Nebraska Press, 1984), pp. 319–35.

9. Cited in ibid., pp. 324, 324–25.

10. Stuart and Malcolm, eds., *Diary of Fynn*, p. 31.

11. Kirby, ed., *Andrew Smith and Natal*, pp. 5–6.

12. Ibid., p. 55.

13. D. J. Kotze, ed., *Letters of the American Missionaries, 1835–1838* (Cape Town: Van Riebeeck Society, 1950), p. 218.

14. Allen F. Gardiner, *Narrative of a Journey to the Zoolu Country in South Africa* (London: William Crofts, 1836; reprint, Cape Town: C. Struik, 1966), pp. 289–90.

15. Thompson, "The Zulu Kingdom" 1:355–56.

16. Ibid., p. 358.

17. John Bird, ed., *The Annals of Natal: 1495 to 1845*, vol. 1 (Cape Town: T. Maskew Miller, 1888; reprint, Cape Town: C. Struik, 1965), p. 362.

18. Ibid., p. 366; Kotze, *Letters*, p. 235.

19. Bird, *Annals of Natal*, 1:233, 241–43, 370–73, 403–8, 463.

20. Thompson, "The Zulu Kingdom" 1:360. Dingane told the American missionary Henry Venable that, though the Zulu "did not wish for war" against the Boers, he had "ascertained their intention to attack" Venable. See Kotze, *Letters*, p. 238.

21. Paul Hedren, *The Massacre of Lieutenant Grattan and his Command by Indians* (Glendale, Calif.: Clark, 1983), pp. 50, 33.

22. Ibid., p. 18.

23. Lloyd E. McCann, "The Grattan Massacre," *Nebraska History* 37, no. 1 (March 1956): 20. Also see the accounts by Hyde, *Red Cloud's Folk*, pp. 48–53, and Robert M. Utley, *Frontiersmen in Blue: The United States Army and the Indian, 1848–1865* (Lincoln: University of Nebraska Press, 1967), pp. 113–15.

24. Utley, *Frontiersmen in Blue*, p. 115.

25. Ibid., pp. 115–16; Hyde, *Red Cloud's Folk*, p. 79.

26. Ray H. Mattison, "The Harney Expedition against the Sioux: The Journal of Capt. John B. S. Todd," *Nebraska History* 43, no. 2 (June 1962): 111, 112, 113.

27. Ibid., p. 114.

28. Ibid.

29. Hyde, *Red Cloud's Folk*, pp. 79–80; Utley, *Frontiersmen in Blue*, pp. 115–17.

30. Evan S. Connell, *Son of the Morning Star: Custer and the Little Bighorn* (San Francisco: North Point Press, 1984), p. 305.

31. Doane Robinson, "A Comprehensive History of the Dakota or Sioux Indians," *South Dakota Historical Collections* 2 (1904): 225.

32. Mari Sandoz, *Crazy Horse: The Strange Man of the Oglalas* (Lincoln: University of Nebraska Press, 1961), p. 77.

33. Hyde, *Red Cloud's Folk*, p. 82. On Harney's treaty, see Mekeel, "A Short History of the Teton-Dakota," pp. 180–81, and Utley, *Frontiersmen in Blue*, pp. 117–20.

34. J. G. Bantjes, "Journal of the Expedition," in Bird, ed., *Annals of Natal* 1:445.

35. Thompson, *Political Mythology*, ch. 5.

36. Ibid., p. 448.

37. Thompson, "The Zulu Kingdom" 1:362.

38. Edgar H. Brookes and Colin de B. Webb, *A History of Natal* (Pietermaritzburg: University of Natal Press, 1965), p. 35.

39. Gibson, *Story of the Zulus*, p. 102.

40. Thompson, "Zulu Kingdom" 1:362–63.

41. John Wright and Ruth Edgecombe, "Mpande kaSenzangakhona," in Christopher Saunders, ed., *Black Leaders in Southern African History* (London: Heinemann, 1979), p. 49.

42. Leonard Thompson, *A History of South Africa* (New Haven, Conn.: Yale University Press, 1990), p. 92.

43. John S. Galbraith, *Reluctant Empire: British Policy on the South African Frontier, 1834–1854* (Berkeley and Los Angeles: University of California Press, 1963), p. 194.

44. Brookes and Webb, *History of Natal*, p. 63; Wright and Edgecombe, "Mpande kaSenzangakhona," p. 52.

45. Quoted in Brookes and Webb, *History of Natal*, p. 49.

46. Jeff Guy, "Cetshwayo kaMpande, c. 1832–84," in Saunders, ed., *Black Leaders*, p. 75.

47. Quoted in George W. Cox, *The Life of John William Colenso*, vol. 2 (London: W. Ridgway, 1888), p. 451.

48. BPP, C-1137, vol. 53, Shepstone's Report on the Installation of Cetshwayo, August 1873.
49. Wright and Edgecombe, "Mpande kaSenzangakhona," pp. 55–56; Brookes and Webb, *History of Natal*, p. 94.
50. Ibid., pp. 94–96.
51. Robinson, "Comprehensive History," p. 227.
52. Ibid., p. 351.
53. On November 29, 1864, a Colorado militia led by Colonel John M. Chivington attacked Black Kettle's Cheyenne village at Sand Creek. Black Kettle, a friendly chief whose safety had been assured by the commander at Fort Lyon, hoisted a white flag and an American flag at the outset of the assault. Determined to destroy the village, Chivington's militia slaughtered and mutilated Cheyenne men, women, and children.
54. Ibid., pp. 351–53.
55. Olson, *Red Cloud*, pp. 23–24. Cf. Hyde, *Red Cloud's Folk*, p. 97.
56. Robert M. Utley, *The Indian Frontier of the American West, 1846–1890* (Albuquerque: University of New Mexico Press, 1984), p. 99.
57. Olson, *Red Cloud*, pp. 23–25.
58. Ibid., pp. 35–38.
59. Utley, *Frontier Regulars*, ch. 7.
60. Ibid., p. 52.
61. In July 1867 Sherman wrote that "instead of talking with the Indians who did the deed, I would have preferred to have followed the savages to their own country and to have avenged the massacre in such a way that it would not have invited a repitition [sic], but congress in its wisdom, with a full knowledge of all the facts, and all its connecting circumstances has preferred to send out Civil Peace Commissioners to confer with the perpetrators" (National Archives [cited hereinafter as NA], M619, R.G. 94, Sherman to A.A.G.–U.S. Army, 1 July 1867).
62. Utley, *Indian Frontier*, pp. 108–9.
63. Quoted in Prucha, *Great Father*, 1:488.
64. John W. Bailey, *Pacifying the Plains: General Alfred Terry and the Decline of the Sioux, 1866–1890* (Westport, Conn.: Greenwood Press, 1979), p. 49.
65. Gray, *Centennial Campaign*, p. 12.
66. *Proceedings of the Great Peace Commission* (Washington, D.C.: Institute for the Development of Indian Law, 1975), p. 117.
67. Raymond J. DeMallie, "Touching the Pen: Plains Indian Treaty Councils in Ethnohistorical Perspective," in Frederick C. Luebke, ed., *Ethnicity on the Great Plains* (Lincoln: University of Nebraska Press, 1980).
68. Utley, *Indian Frontier*, p. 125. See Robert Wooster, *The Military and United States Indian Policy* (New Haven, Conn.: Yale University Press, 1988), ch. 4.

5 AGENTS OF EMPIRE

1. Utley, *Indian Frontier*, p. 229.
2. Quoted in Paul Andrew Hutton, *Phil Sheridan and His Army* (Lincoln: University of Nebraska Press, 1985), p. 246.
3. Quoted in Mekeel, "Short History," p. 188.
4. The Grant administration adopted a "Peace Policy" in 1869, but the principles on

which it stood, in the words of Francis Paul Prucha, "antedated 1869 and continued to the end of the century and beyond." Grant's interior secretary, Columbus Delano, listed the aims of the "Peace Policy" in 1873: (1) to place Indians on reservations; (2) to supply "all needed severity, to punish [Indians] for their outrages according to their merits, thereby teaching them that it is better to follow the advice of the Government, live upon reservations and become civilized, than to continue their native habits and practices"; (3) to furnish Indians high-quality and reasonably priced supplies; (4) to procure "competent, upright, faithful, moral, and religious" agents to aid the Indians in civilizational uplift; and (5) to provide churches and schools to lead Indians to appreciate "the comforts and benefits of a Christian civilization and thus be prepared ultimately to assume the duties and privileges of citizenship." In Prucha, *Great Father* 1:481–82.

5. Utley, *Frontier Regulars*, p. 239.
6. P. Richard Metcalfe, "Sitting Bull," in Howard R. Lamar, ed., *The Reader's Encyclopedia of the American West* (New York: Crowell, 1977), pp. 1119–20.
7. Cited in T. A. Bland, *A Brief History of the Late Military Invasion of the Home of the Sioux* (Washington, D.C.: National Indian Defence Association, 1891), p. 27.
8. Cited in Vestal, *Sitting Bull*, pp. 91, 113.
9. Cited in Bland, *Brief History*, p. 28.
10. Connell, *Son of the Morning Star*, p. 217.
11. Utley, *Frontier Regulars*, p. 240.
12. Hutton, *Phil Sheridan*, p. 290.
13. Peter Colenbrander, "The Zulu Political Economy on the Eve of the War," in Duminy and Ballard, eds., *Anglo-Zulu War*, pp. 78–86; Guy, *Destruction of the Zulu Kingdom*, p. 21.
14. Ibid., p. 82.
15. Charles Ballard, "John Dunn and Cetshwayo: The Material Foundations of Political Power in the Zulu Kingdom, 1857–1878," *Journal of African History* 21, no. 1 (1980): 75–91; Charles Ballard, "Sir Garnet Wolseley and John Dunn: The Architects and Agents of the Ulundi Settlement," in Duminy and Ballard, eds., *Anglo-Zulu War*, pp. 131–32; Brookes and Webb, *History of Natal*, p. 99.
16. J. P. C. Laband, "Cohesion of the Zulu Polity under the Impact of the Anglo-Zulu War: A Reassessment," *Journal of Natal and Zulu History* 8 (1985): 38.
17. J. B. Peires, "'Soft' Believers and 'Hard' Unbelievers in the Xhosa Cattle-Killing," *Journal of African History* 27 (1986): 443–61. Also see Peires's *The Dead Will Arise: Nongqawuse and the Great Xhosa Cattle-Killing Movement of 1856–7* (Johannesburg: Ravan Press, 1989).
18. Quoted in David Welsh, *The Roots of Segregation: Native Policy in Colonial Natal, 1845–1910* (Cape Town: Oxford University Press, 1971), p. 22.
19. Ibid., chs. 1, 2.
20. Welsh, *Roots of Segregation*, ch. 8.
21. Brookes and Webb, *History of Natal*, ch. 12.
22. C. W. de Kiewiet, *The Imperial Factor in South Africa* (Cambridge: Cambridge University Press, 1937), p. 34; Norman A. Etherington, "Labour Supply and the Genesis of South African Confederation in the 1870s," *Journal of African History* 20, no. 1 (1979): 235–53.

23. Quoted in Jeff Guy, *The Heretic: A Study of the Life of John William Colenso, 1814–1883* (Johannesburg: Ravan Press, 1983), p. 224.

24. Norman A. Etherington, "Anglo-Zulu Relations, 1856–1878," in Duminy and Ballard, eds., *Anglo-Zulu War*, p. 32.

25. R. L. Cope, "Political Power within the Zulu Kingdom and the 'Coronation Laws' of 1873," *Journal of Natal and Zulu History* 8 (1985): 11–31.

26. Ibid., p. 16.

27. William T. Sherman Papers, Library of Congress (cited hereinafter as Sherman Papers), letter to the *New York Herald*, 17 April 1873, reel no. 46.

28. Quoted in Richard Slotkin, *The Fatal Environment: The Myth of the Frontier in the Age of Industrialization, 1800–1890* (New York: Atheneum, 1985; reprint, Middletown, Conn.: Wesleyan University Press, 1986), p. 380.

29. De B. Randolph Keim, *Sheridan's Troopers on the Borders: A Winter Campaign on the Plains* (Lincoln: University of Nebraska Press, 1985), p. 103.

30. Robert M. Utley, *Cavalier in Buckskin: George Armstrong Custer and the Western Military Frontier* (Norman: University of Oklahoma Press, 1988), pp. 65–67.

31. Benteen penned an anonymous letter to a St. Louis newspaper that attributed Elliot's death to Custer's criminal abandonment. Incensed, Custer summoned his officers before him, vowing to horsewhip the perpetrator. Benteen, brandishing his pistol, stepped forward to claim responsibility. Custer backed off. See Utley, *Cavalier in Buckskin*, p. 75.

32. Ibid., p. 107.

33. G. A. Custer, "Battling With the Sioux on the Yellowstone," *The Galaxy* 22, no. 1 (July 1876): 91.

34. Slotkin, *Fatal Environment*, p. 393.

35. NA, M1495, R.G. 393, Custer to O. D. Greene, 15 August 1873; Utley, *Frontier Regulars*, pp. 242–43; Slotkin, *Fatal Environment*, p. 412.

36. Hutton, *Phil Sheridan*, p. 19.

37. Ibid., p. 181.

38. Philip H. Sheridan Papers, Library of Congress (cited hereinafter as Sheridan Papers), Sheridan to E. D. Townsend, 1 November 1869, reel no. 80.

39. Ibid.

40. Bailey, *Pacifying the Plains*, p. 94; Sheridan justified the expedition to the interior secretary in the following terms: "A good, strong post in the Black Hills will do much to take the hostile backbone out of these unruly savages." NA, M666, R.G., Sheridan to Delano, 25 November 1874.

41. NA, M1495, R.G. 393, Sheridan to Terry, 4 September 1874.

42. NA, M1495, R.G. 393, Custer to Terry, 30 May 1874; Bailey, *Pacifying the Plains*, p. 103; Wooster, *Military and United States Indian Policy*, p. 161.

43. Quoted in Slotkin, *Fatal Environment*, p. 417.

44. Ibid.

45. NA, M1495, R.G. 393, Cowan to Bennington, 8 September 1874.

46. Ibid., Terry to A.A.G.—Military Division of the Missouri, 9 March 1875.

47. Hyde, *Red Cloud's Folk*, p. 209; Olson, *Red Cloud*, pp. 208–9.

48. Watkins to Smith, 9 November 1875, Senate Executive Document no. 52, 44th Congress, 1st session.

49. Hutton, *Phil Sheridan*, p. 299.
50. NA, M1495, R.G. 393, Sheridan to Sherman, 4 February 1876.
51. Quoted in C. F. Goodfellow, *Great Britain and South African Confederation, 1870–1881* (Cape Town: Oxford University Press, 1966), p. 117.
52. Quoted in de Kiewiet, *Imperial Factor*, p. 69. Jeff Guy attributes the quote to Edward Fairfield, Carnarvon's assistant undersecretary. See Guy, *Heretic*, p. 225.
53. BPP, C-1342-I, vol. 52, Wolseley to Carnarvon, 12 May 1875.
54. The diversion of laborers to the Kimberley diamond mines exacerbated labor short-ages in Natal. A Durban "Labour League" enlisted Shepstone in the early 1870s to as-sist them in securing labor supplies for the colony. See Etherington, "Labour Supply," p. 241.
55. BPP, C-1137, vol. 53, Shepstone's Report of the Coronation of August, 1873.
56. *Fortnightly Review* 29 (1 June 1878): 945.
57. Cited in ibid., p. 948.
58. Etherington, "Labour Supply," pp. 235–53.
59. Colonial Office Correspondence (cited hereinafter as CO), 1879/12, African 147, Shep-stone to Carnarvon, 1 December 1877.
60. CO 879/13, African 150, Shepstone to Carnarvon, 22 December 1877.
61. CO 879/13, African 150, Shepstone to Carnarvon, 5 January 1878.
62. Cited in Guy, *Heretic*, p. 261.
63. Ibid., p. x.
64. Ibid., p. 356.
65. Goodfellow, *South African Confederation*, p. 152.
66. Frere, posted to India in 1842 as private secretary to Sir George Arthur, served as Resi-dent in Sattara from 1847 to 1850 and as commissioner of the Sind province through-out the 1850s. In 1859 Frere was selected to join the viceroy's Council in Calcutta, followed by the highlight of his Indian career, appointment as governor of Bombay between 1862 and 1867. See W. J. de Kock and D. W. Kruger, eds., *Dictionary of South African Biography*, vol. 2 (Cape Town and Johannesburg: Tafelberg-Uitgewers, 1972), pp. 243–46.
67. BPP, C-2222, vol. 52, Frere to Hicks Beach, 14 December 1878.
68. CO 879/14, African 166, Confidential notes to the Cabinet by Frere, 3 February 1879.
69. See Etherington, "Labour Supply," p. 238.
70. BPP, C-2220, vol. 52, Frere to Hicks Beach, 30 September 1878.
71. Cited in John Martineau, *The Transvaal Trouble, How It Arose: Being an Extract from the Biography of the Late Sir Bartle Frere* (London: John Murray, 1900), p. 61.
72. Etherington, "Anglo-Zulu Relations," pp. 39–41; Guy, *Heretic*, p. 256.
73. BPP, C-2220, vol. 52, Frere to Hicks Beach, 30 September 1878.
74. Durnford, *A Soldier's Life and Work*, p. 17.
75. BPP, C-2220, vol. 52, Hicks Beach to Frere, 17 October 1878.
76. Cited in Goodfellow, *South African Confederation*, p. 161.
77. De Kiewiet, *Imperial Factor*, p. 230.
78. Ibid.
79. The ultimatum consisted of ten points, including the requirements that Cetshwayo disband his army and that he accept a British Resident in Zululand.
80. BPP, C-2222, vol. 52, Frere to Hicks Beach, 10 December 1878.

81. Frere withheld the report from the Colonial Office until January 2, 1879, nine days before the outbreak of the war.
82. BPP, C-2252, vol. 53, Frere to Hicks Beach, 24 January 1879.

6 PATTERNS OF IMPERIAL OVERRULE

1. See Wooster, *Military and United States Indian Policy*, passim.
2. Utley, *Frontier Regulars*, pp. 267–71.
3. Ibid., p. 277.
4. E. A. Brininstool, "The Story of Crazy Horse," *Nebraska History* 12, no. 1 (January–March 1929): 7; John G. Bourke, *On the Border with Crook* (Lincoln: University of Nebraska Press, 1971), p. 413.
5. He Dog's interview with Eleanor H. Hinman in "Oglala Sources on the Life of Crazy Horse," *Nebraska History* 57, no. 1 (Spring 1976): 13–16.
6. Bourke, *On the Border*, p. 415.
7. Utley, *Frontier Regulars*, pp. 281–82; He Dog in "Oglala Sources," pp. 19–22; Robert A. Clark, ed., *The Killing of Chief Crazy Horse* (Glendale, Calif.: Clark, 1976), pp. 15–38.
8. Connell, *Son of the Morning Star*, pp. 73–74.
9. Utley, *Frontier Regulars*, p. 272.
10. C. T. Binns, *The Last Zulu King* (London: Longmans, 1963), p. 153; Brookes and Webb, *History of Natal*, p. 142.
11. Adrian Preston, ed., *The South African Journal of Sir Garnet Wolseley, 1879–1880* (Cape Town: A. A. Balkema, 1973), p. 40. In addition, Wolseley superceded Frere, being appointed governor of Natal and the Transvaal and high commissioner for the adjacent territories.
12. *Punch* 76 (7 June 1879): 261. For *Punch*'s attacks on Chelmsford, see chapter 7.
13. Brookes and Webb, *History of Natal*, pp. 142–44; Morris, *Washing of the Spears*, pp. 536–38.
14. Binns, *Last Zulu King*, pp. 166–67; Brookes and Webb, *History of Natal*, pp. 144–45.
15. Quoted in Binns, *Last Zulu King*, p. 169.
16. Ibid., p. 173.
17. Cited in Preston, *Journal of Wolseley*, p. 53.
18. Under Gladstone's government Britain withdrew from the Transvaal in 1881, following a Boer uprising there. The vague peace convention signed in August provided the Transvaal "complete self-government, subject to the Suzerainty of Her Majesty."
19. Guy, *Heretic*, p. 234.
20. Leonard Thompson, "The Subjection of the African Chiefdoms, 1870–1898," in *OHSA* 2:265–66.
21. Cited in Brookes and Webb, *History of Natal*, p. 148.
22. Quoted in Guy, *Destruction of the Zulu Kingdom*, p. 71.
23. Preston, *Journal of Wolseley*, p. 53.
24. CO 879/16, African 204, Wolseley to Hicks Beach, 9 October 1879.
25. Mpatshana in *JSA* 3:210.
26. BPP, C-3247, vol. 67, Robinson to Kimberley, 16 May 1882.
27. See, for example, BPP, C-3247, vol. 47, Lady Florence Dixie to Lord Kimberley, 24 May 1882.
28. Binns, *Last Zulu King*, pp. 189–92.

29. CO 879/13, African 304, Edward Fairfield, 4 August 1885, "Vacillation in Policy in South Africa."

30. Jeff Guy, "The Role of Colonial Officials in the Destruction of the Zulu Kingdom," in Duminy and Ballard, eds., *Anglo-Zulu War*, pp. 158–59.

31. Binns, *Last Zulu King*, p. 196.

32. Guy, "Role of Colonial Officials," p. 159.

33. Ibid., p. 198.

34. Ibid., p. 149.

35. BPP, C-4913, vol. 61, Havelock to Granville, 11 April 1886.

36. BPP, C-4980, vol. 61, Sir Theophilus Shepstone, 21 February 1887, "Memorandum on the Zulu Situation."

37. See, for example, BPP, C-4913, vol. 61, Granville to Havelock, 11 March 1886.

38. Frederick E. Hoxie, *A Final Promise: The Campaign to Assimilate the Indians, 1880–1920* (Lincoln: University of Nebraska Press, 1984), chs. 1, 2; Robert F. Berkhofer, Jr., *The White Man's Indian: Images of the American Indian from Columbus to the Present* (New York: Random House, 1978), pt. 4.

39. Quoted in Prucha, *Great Father* 2:619.

40. Hoxie, *Final Promise*, pp. 13–15.

41. Ibid., p. 640.

42. Morgan (1818–81) was America's preeminent anthropologist in the nineteenth century. His most famous work, *Ancient Society*, posits an evolutionary theory of social development, including transformations in the idea of property.

43. The reservation police represented an adaptation of Lakota *akicita* societies. On the Indian police see William T. Hagan, *Indian Police and Judges* (New Haven, Conn.: Yale University Press, 1966).

44. Robert M. Utley, *The Last Days of the Sioux Nation* (New Haven, Conn.: Yale University Press, 1963), ch. 3; Olson, *Red Cloud*, ch. 13.

45. George E. Hyde, *Spotted Tail's Folk: A History of the Brulé Sioux* (Norman: University of Oklahoma Press, 1961), pp. 3, 32–35, 127–28; idem, *A Sioux Chronicle* (Norman: University of Oklahoma Press, 1956), ch. 1.

46. Hyde, *Sioux Chronicle*, ch. 2.

47. What motivated Spotted Tail to send the children to Carlisle in 1879 in the first place is far from clear. Hyde suggests that the Brulé chief, who disliked the boarding school concept, agreed to send the youngsters because Carlisle's director, R. H. Pratt, offered a lucrative position to Spotted Tail's white son-in-law, Charles Tackett. The chief's motives for withdrawing the children are more straightforward. Within the scope of one year, the children had been given Christian names, baptized Episcopalians, and on frequent occasions subjected to physical punishment for disciplinary reasons. The old chief, strongly attached to a Lakota culture that included benign child-rearing practices, could stomach no more. See Hyde, *Sioux Chronicle*, pp. 51–56.

48. Ibid., ch. 2.

49. Julia B. McGillycuddy, *McGillycuddy Agent* (Palo Alto, Calif.: Stanford University Press, 1941), pp. 103–4; Olson, *Red Cloud*, pp. 265–66.

50. Olson, *Red Cloud*, p. 269.

51. Ibid., ch. 14.

52. Hyde, *Sioux Chronicle*, pp. 104–6.

53. Utley, *Last Days*, pp. 17, 31.

54. Ibid., ch. 4; Prucha, *Great Father* 2:640.
55. Commissioner of Indian Affairs Annual Report (cited hereinafter as CIAAR), House Executive Documents, 51st Congress, 2nd session, 1890–91, vol. 12, p. 49.
56. Wovoka was a Paiute shaman from western Nevada who experienced a vision during the solar eclipse of January 1, 1889. He claimed to have traveled to heaven, returning as the Indian Messiah and holding a divine mandate to rescue the Indian people from their predicament.
57. See Raymond J. DeMallie, "The Lakota Ghost Dance: An Ethnohistorical Account," *Pacific Historical Review* 51 (November 1982): 385–405. The classic account of the Ghost Dance and events leading to the Wounded Knee massacre is James Mooney, *The Ghost-Dance Religion and the Sioux Outbreak of 1890*, Smithsonian Institution, Bureau of American Ethnology, Annual Report no. 14, pt. 2 (Washington, D.C.; 1896; reprint, Chicago: University of Chicago Press, 1965).
58. Cited in Bland, *Brief History*, p. 8.
59. CIAAR (1891), McLaughlin to Morgan, 18 June 1890 and 17 October 1890, pp. 328–29.
60. Utley, *Last Days*, pp. 146–66.
61. Ibid., p. 103.
62. CIAAR (1891), Royer to Morgan, 15 November 1890, p. 128.
63. Thomas C. Leonard, "Red, White, and the Army Blue: Empathy and Anger in the American West," *American Quarterly* 26, no. 2 (May 1974): 176–90.
64. Utley, *Last Days*, p. 126.
65. Ibid., chs. 7, 8.
66. Ibid., p. 177.
67. Ibid., ch. 10.
68. Ibid., ch. 12.
69. Cited in Richard E. Jensen, R. Eli Paul, and John E. Carter, *Eyewitness at Wounded Knee* (Lincoln: University of Nebraska Press, 1991), p. 18.
70. CIAAR (1891), p. 180.
71. Mooney, *Ghost-Dance Religion*, pp. 116–17.
72. Ibid., p. 118.
73. Jensen et al., *Eyewitness at Wounded Knee*, p. 19; Utley, *Last Days*, ch. 10.
74. Utley, *Frontier Regulars*, p. 408.
75. David Humphreys Miller, *Ghost Dance* (New York: Duell, Sloan, and Pearce, 1959; reprint, Lincoln: University of Nebraska Press, 1985).
76. Brookes and Webb, eds., *History of Natal*, p. 155; Guy, "Role of Colonial Officials," p. 163.
77. CIAAR (1891), p. 409.
78. Guy, *Destruction of the Zulu Kingdom*, p. 239.

7 IMAGES OF EMPIRE

1. Slotkin, *Fatal Environment*, p. 19.
2. See Richard White, "Race Relations in the American West," *American Quarterly* 38, no. 3 (1986): 396–416; Thomas C. Leonard, "Red, White, and the Army Blue"; and Slotkin, *Fatal Environment*.
3. Morris, *Washing of the Spears*, p. 443.
4. Ibid.

5. Stephen Koss, *The Rise and Fall of the Political Press in Britain: The Nineteenth Century* (Chapel Hill: University of North Carolina Press, 1981), pp. 38–39.

6. Morris, *Washing of the Spears*, p. 443.

7. Lucy Brown, *Victorian News and Newspapers* (Oxford: Clarendon Press, 1985), p. 30.

8. Morris, *Washing of the Spears*, p. 443.

9. Robert M. Utley, *Custer and the Great Controversy: The Origin and Development of a Legend* (Los Angeles: Westernlore Press, 1962), p. 29; Slotkin, *Fatal Environment*, pp. 3–12.

10. Utley, *Custer and the Great Controversy*, pp. 30–31.

11. Ibid., pp. 37–38.

12. Slotkin, *Fatal Environment*, pp. 458–68.

13. *Saturday Review* 47 (1 February 1879): 129; (10 May 1879): 574.

14. Cited in Furneaux, *Zulu War*, p. 142.

15. London *Daily Telegraph*, 11 March 1879, p. 5.

16. Alexander Allardyce, "The Zulu War," *Blackwood's Edinburgh Magazine*, March 1879, p. 376.

17. *Punch* 76 (1 March 1879): 91.

18. Cited in Utley, *Custer and the Great Controversy*, p. 39.

19. Ibid., p. 40. The reference to thievery and "corrupt rings" stems from the profiteering associated with (1) the supplying of government Indian agencies with oftentimes inferior and inadequate goods at inflated prices, and (2) the exorbitant costs of transporting supplies from eastern markets to remote western reservations. Such profit making contributed to speculation regarding conspiratorial "rings" of suppliers and Indian agency personnel. See Prucha, *Great Father* 1:586–89, and George H. Phillips, "The Indian Ring in Dakota Territory, 1870–1890," *South Dakota History* 2 (Fall 1972): 345–76.

20. See the commentary by Brian W. Dippie in "'What Will Congress Do about It?' The Congressional Reaction to the Little Big Horn Disaster," *North Dakota History* 37, no. 3 (Summer 1970): 163.

21. Ibid., p. 120.

22. This poem first appeared in the seventh edition of *Leaves of Grass* (1881) as "From Far Dakota's Cañons (June 25, 1876)." See Brian W. Dippie, "Bards of the Little Big Horn," *Western American Literature* 1, no. 3 (Fall 1966): 184.

23. Walt Whitman, *Complete Poetry and Collected Prose*, ed. Justin Kaplan (New York: Literary Classics of the United States, 1982), pp. 592–93.

24. Paul A. Hutton, "From Little Bighorn to Little Big Man: The Changing Image of a Western Hero in Popular Culture," *Western Historical Quarterly* 7, no. 1 (January 1976): 25, 29; Robert Taft, "The Pictorial Record of the Old West," *Kansas Historical Quarterly* 14, no. 4 (November 1946): 361–90.

25. Cited in Furneaux, *Zulu War*, p. 147.

26. "The Disaster at Isandula," *Pall Mall Gazette*, 6 March 1879, p. 1.

27. *Punch* 76 (15 March 1879): 109.

28. *Punch* (5 April 1879): 153.

29. William Gladstone referred to the conflict as "a monstrously unjust war: one of the most monstrous in point of policy, and one of the most clearly indefensible in point of principle." See Frederic MacKarness, "What England Has Done for the Zulus," *Fortnightly Review* 42 (September 1884): 392.

30. "Our Zulu War Policy," London *Daily News*, 1 March 1879, p. 6.
31. "Great Britain and South Africa," *Spectator*, 1 March 1879, p. 264.
32. *Punch* 76 (26 April 1879): 192.
33. Robert B. Edgerton, *Like Lions They Fought*, p. 214.
34. Robert Buchanan, "The Battle at Isandúla," *Contemporary Review* 35 (April 1879): 153–55.
35. Dippie, "Bards of the Little Big Horn," p. 175.
36. Ibid., p. 177.
37. Hutton, "Little Bighorn to Little Big Man," p. 26.
38. *Illustrated London News* 74 (19 April 1879): 373.
39. Don Russell, *Custer's Last* (Ft. Worth: Amon Carter Museum of Western Art, 1968), p. 42.
40. London *Graphic*, 15 March 1879, p. 265.
41. Russell, *Custer's Last*, p. 15.
42. Hutton, "Little Bighorn to Little Big Man," p. 29.
43. Cited in Goodfellow, *Great Britain and South African Confederation*, pp. 168–69.
44. See chapter 6.
45. George W. Cox, "The English Nation and the Zulu War," *Fraser's Magazine* 21 (February 1880): 261, 271.
46. John G. Neihardt, *The Song of the Messiah* (New York: Macmillan, 1935), pp. 108–10.

CONCLUSION

1. Shula Marks, *Reluctant Rebellion: The 1906–8 Disturbances in Natal* (Oxford: Clarendon Press, 1970).
2. Shula Marks, *The Ambiguities of Dependence in South Africa: Class, Nationalism, and the State in Twentieth-Century Natal* (Baltimore: Johns Hopkins University Press, 1986).
3. Ibid.
4. Peter Mathiessen, *In the Spirit of Crazy Horse* (New York: Viking Press, 1983); White, *New History*, pp. 586–88.
5. Given the preference of Lakota traditionalists for a pan-ethnic nationalism in the twentieth century, a useful comparison might be made with the South African Xhosa or the Maori of New Zealand.
6. Kennedy, *Rise and Fall*, p. 143.
7. Ibid., pp. 148–50.
8. Headrick, *Tools of Empire*, pp. 83–104.
9. See Edward W. Said, *Orientalism* (New York: Random House, 1978).
10. White, *New History*, p. 115.
11. Raymond J. DeMallie, ed. *The Sixth Grandfather*, p. 296.

BIBLIOGRAPHY

MANUSCRIPT SOURCES AND PUBLIC DOCUMENTS

Bancroft Library, University of California at Berkeley. Letter from E. W. Smith to Lt.-Col. Custer, 22 June 1876.

British Parliamentary Papers. C-1137, vol. 53 (1875); C-2000, vol. 40 (1877); C-2079, C-2100, C-2144, vol. 56 (1878); C-2220, C-2222, C-2242, vol. 52 (1878–79); C-2252, C-2260, C-2269, C-2308, C-2316, C-2318, C-2367, vol. 53 (1878–79); C-2234, C-2374, C-2354, vol. 54 (1878–79); C-3113, C-3174, C-3247, C-3270, C-3293, vol. 47 (1882); C-3796, C-4645, vol. 48 (1883, 1886); C-3466, C-3616, C-3705, vol. 49 (1883); C-3864, C-4037, C-4191, vol. 58 (1884); C-4214, C-4274, C-4587, vol. 56 (1884–85); C-4913, C-4980, C-5143, vol. 61 (1887).

Colonial Office Correspondence, Public Record Office, London. CO 879/11 African 117; CO 879/12 African 142, 147; CO 879/13 African 150; CO 879/14 African 166, 169; CO 879/16 African 203, 204; CO 879/23 African 304.

House Executive Documents, 3rd Session, 46th Congress, 1880–81, vol. 9. Report of the Commissioner of Indian Affairs.

House Executive Documents, 1st Session, 51st Congress, 1889–90, vol. 12. Report of the Commissioner of Indian Affairs.

House Executive Documents, 2nd Session, 51st Congress, 1890–91, vol. 12. Report of the Commissioner of Indian Affairs.

House Executive Documents, 1st Session, 52nd Congress, 1891–92, vol. 15. Report of the Commissioner of Indian Affairs.

Killie Campbell Africana Library, University of Natal, Durban, Natal. James Stuart Papers.

Library of Congress, Washington, D.C. Philip H. Sheridan Papers, reel nos. 80–82, 87–89; William T. Sherman Papers, reel nos. 23, 45–46.

National Archives, Washington, D.C. M1495, Record Group 393, "Special Files" of Headquarters, Division of the Missouri, Relating to Military Operations and Administration, 1863–85; M619, Record Group 94, Letters Received by the Office of the Adjutant General, 1861–70; M666, Record Group 94, Letters Received by the Office of the Adjutant General, 1871–80; M983, Record Group 94, Reports and Correspondence Relating to the Army Investigations of the Battle at Wounded Knee and to the Sioux Campaign of 1890–91.

BOOKS, PAMPHLETS, AND NEWSPAPERS

Abel, Annie Heloise, ed. *Tabeau's Narrative of Loisel's Expedition to the Upper Missouri.* Norman: University of Oklahoma Press, 1939.

Anderson, Gary. *Kinsmen of Another Kind: Dakota-White Relations in the Upper Mississippi Valley, 1650–1862.* Lincoln: University of Nebraska Press, 1984.

Andrist, Ralph K. *The Long Death: The Last Days of the Plains Indians.* New York: Collier Books, 1964.

Ayliff, John, and Joseph Whiteside. *History of the Abambo.* Butterworth, Transkei: Gazette, 1912. Reprint. Cape Town: C. Struik, 1962.

Bailey, John W. *Pacifying the Plains: General Alfred Terry and the Decline of the Sioux, 1866–1890.* Westport, Conn.: Greenwood Press, 1979.

Berkhofer, Robert F., Jr. *The White Man's Indian: Images of the American Indian from Columbus to the Present.* New York: Random House, 1978.

Binns, C. T. *The Last Zulu King.* London: Longmans, 1963.

Bird, John, ed. *The Annals of Natal: 1495 to 1845.* 2 vols. Cape Town: T. Maskew Miller, 1888. Reprint. Cape Town: C. Struik, 1965.

Booth, Alan R., ed. *Journal of the Rev. George Champion.* Cape Town: C. Struik, 1967.

Bourke, John G. *On the Border with Crook.* Lincoln: University of Nebraska Press, 1971.

Brookes, E. A., and C. de B. Webb. *A History of Natal.* Pietermaritzburg: University of Natal Press, 1965.

Brown, Lucy. *Victorian News and Newspapers.* Oxford: Clarendon Press, 1985.

Bryant, A. T. *Olden Times in Zululand and Natal.* London: Longmans, Green, 1929. Reprint, Cape Town: C. Struik, 1965.

——. *The Zulu People As They Were before the White Man Came.* Pietermaritzburg: Shuter and Shooter, 1949.

Bushnell, David I. *Tribal Migrations East of the Mississippi.* Smithsonian Miscellaneous Collections, vol. 89, no. 12. Washington, D.C.: Smithsonian Institution, 1934.

Carroll, John M., ed. *Custer in Periodicals: A Bibliographic Checklist.* Fort Collins, Colo.: Old Army Press, 1975.

——. *General Custer and the Battle of the Little Big Horn: The Federal View.* New Brunswick, N.J.: Garry Owen Press, 1976.

Catlin, George. *Letters and Notes on the Manners, Customs, and Condition of the North American Indians.* Vol. 1. London: Tosswill and Myers, 1841.

Cell, John W. *The Highest Stage of White Supremacy: The Origins of Segregation in South Africa and the American South.* Cambridge: Cambridge University Press, 1982.

Child, Daphne, ed. *The War Journal of Colonel Henry Harford.* Hamden, Conn.: Archon Books, 1980.

Chittenden, Hiram Martin. *The American Fur Trade of the Far West.* 2 vols. New York: Francis P. Harper, 1902.

Clark, Robert A., ed. *The Killing of Chief Crazy Horse.* Glendale, Calif.: Clark, 1976.

Clark, Sonia. *Zululand at War, 1879.* Johannesburg: Brenthurst Press, 1984.

Colenso, Francis E. *History of the Zulu War and Its Origin.* London: Chapman and Hall, 1880.

Connell, Evan S. *Son of the Morning Star: Custer and the Little Bighorn.* San Francisco: North Point Press, 1984.

Coupland, Reginald. *Zulu Battle Piece: Isandhlwana.* London: Collins, 1948.

Cox, George W. *The Life of John William Colenso.* Vol. 2. London: W. Ridgway, 1888.

Culbertson, Thaddeus A. *Journal of an Expedition to the Mauvaises Terres and the Upper Missouri in 1850.* Edited by John Francis McDermott. Bureau of American Ethnology Bulletin 147. Washington, D.C.: The Bureau, 1952.

Custer, George Armstrong. *My Life on the Plains.* New York: Sheldon and Company, 1874. Reprint. Lincoln: University of Nebraska Press, 1966.

De Kiewiet, C. W. *The Imperial Factor in South Africa.* Cambridge: Cambridge University Press, 1937.

DeMallie, Raymond J., ed. *The Sixth Grandfather: Black Elk's Teachings Given to John G. Neihardt.* Lincoln: University of Nebraska Press, 1984.

Denig, Edwin T. *Five Indian Tribes of the Upper Missouri: Sioux, Arickaras, Assiniboines, Crees, Crows.* Edited by John C. Ewers. Norman: University of Oklahoma Press, 1961.

Dippie, Brian W. *Custer's Last Stand: The Anatomy of an American Myth.* Missoula: University of Montana Press, 1976.

Duminy, Andrew, and Charles Ballard, eds. *The Anglo-Zulu War: New Perspectives.* Pietermaritzburg: University of Natal Press, 1981.

Dunlay, Thomas W. *Wolves for the Blue Soldiers: Indian Scouts and Auxiliaries with the United States Army, 1860–90.* Lincoln: University of Nebraska Press, 1982.

Durnford, E. *A Soldier's Life and Work in South Africa, 1872–1879.* London: Sampson, Low, Marston, Searle and Rivington, 1882.

Edgerton, Robert B. *Like Lions They Fought: The Zulu War and the Last Black Empire in South Africa.* New York: Free Press, 1988.

Ewers, John C. *Teton Dakota: Ethnology and History.* Berkeley, Calif.: U.S. Department of the Interior, 1937.

Feraca, Stephen E. *The History and Development of Oglala Sioux Tribal Government.* Bureau of Indian Affairs Report. Washington, D.C.: The Bureau, 1964.

Fredrickson, George M. *White Supremacy: A Comparative Study in American and South African History.* New York: Oxford University Press, 1981.

Furneaux, Rupert. *The Zulu War: Isandhlwana and Rorke's Drift.* London: Weidenfeld and Nicolson, 1963.

Fuze, Magema M. *The Black People and Whence They Came.* Translated by H. C. Lugg. Pietermaritzburg: University of Natal Press, 1979.

Fynn, H. F. *The Diary of Henry Francis Fynn.* Edited by J. Stuart and D. Mck. Malcolm. Pietermaritzburg: Shuter and Shooter, 1950.

Galbraith, John S. *Reluctant Empire: British Policy on the South African Frontier, 1834–1854.* Berkeley and Los Angeles: University of California Press, 1963.

Gardiner, Allen F. *Narrative of a Journey to the Zoolu Country in South Africa.* London: William Crofts, 1836. Reprint. Cape Town: C. Struik, 1966.

Gibson, J. Y. *The Story of the Zulus.* London: Longmans, Green, 1911.

Goodfellow, C. F. *Great Britain and South African Confederation, 1870–1881.* Cape Town: Oxford University Press, 1966.

Graham, W. A., ed. *The Custer Myth: A Source Book of Custeriana.* Harrisburg, Pa.: Stackpole, 1953. Reprint. Lincoln: University of Nebraska Press, 1986.

The Graphic. 1879.

Gray, John S. *Centennial Campaign: The Sioux War of 1876.* Fort Collins, Colo.: Old Army Press, 1976.

Grinnell, George Bird. *The Fighting Cheyennes*. New York: Scribner's, 1915.

——. *Two Great Scouts and Their Pawnee Battalion*. Cleveland: Clark, 1928.

Gump, James O. *The Formation of the Zulu Kingdom in South Africa, 1750–1840*. San Francisco: Mellen Research University Press, 1990.

Guy, Jeff. *The Destruction of the Zulu Kingdom: The Civil War in Zululand, 1879–1884*. London: Longman, 1979. Reprint, Johannesburg: Ravan Press, 1982.

——. *The Heretic: A Study of the Life of John William Colenso, 1814–1883*. Johannesburg: Ravan Press, 1983.

Hagan, William T. *Indian Police and Judges*. New Haven, Conn.: Yale University Press, 1966.

Harper's Weekly, vol. 20. 1876.

Hassrick, Royal B. *The Sioux: Life and Customs of a Warrior Society*. Norman: University of Oklahoma Press, 1964.

Hayden, Ferdinand V. *Contributions to the Ethnography and Philology of the Indian Tribes of the Missouri Valley*. American Philosophical Society Transactions, vol. 12, no. 2. Philadelphia: The Society, 1862.

Headrick, Daniel R. *The Tools of Empire: Technology and European Imperialism in the Nineteenth Century*. New York: Oxford University Press, 1981.

Hedren, Paul. *The Massacre of Lieutenant Grattan and his Command by Indians*. Glendale, Calif.: Clark, 1983.

Hennepin, Louis. *Father Louis Hennepin's Description of Lousiana*. Translated by Marion E. Cross. Minneapolis: University of Minnesota Press, 1938.

Hoebel, E. Adamson. *The Plains Indians: A Critical Bibliography*. Bloomington: Indiana University Press, 1977.

Hoover, Herbert T. *The Sioux: A Critical Bibliography*. Bloomington: Indiana University Press, 1979.

Houghton, Walter E., ed. *The Wellesley Index to Victorian Periodicals, 1824–1900*. 3 vols. Toronto: University of Toronto Press, 1966, 1972, 1979.

Howard, James H. *The Warrior Who Killed Custer: The Personal Narrative of Chief Joseph White Bull*. Lincoln: University of Nebraska Press, 1968.

Hoxie, Frederick E. *A Final Promise: The Campaign to Assimilate the Indians, 1880–1920*. Lincoln: University of Nebraska Press, 1984.

Hyde, George E. *Red Cloud's Folk: A History of the Oglala Sioux Indians*. Norman: University of Oklahoma Press, 1937. Rev. ed., 1957.

——. *A Sioux Chronicle*. Norman: University of Oklahoma Press, 1956.

——. *Spotted Tail's Folk: A History of the Brulé Sioux*. Norman: University of Oklahoma Press, 1961.

The Illustrated London News, vols. 74–75. 1879.

Isaacs, Nathaniel. *Travels and Adventures in Eastern Africa*. Edited by Louis Herman and Percival R. Kirby. London: Edward Churton, 1836. Reprint. Cape Town: C. Struik, 1966.

Jackson, Donald. *Custer's Gold: The United States Cavalry Expedition of 1874*. New Haven, Conn.: Yale University Press, 1966. Reprint. Lincoln: University of Nebraska Press, 1972.

Johnson, Elden, ed. *Aspects of Upper Great Lakes Anthropology: Papers in Honor of Lloyd A. Wilford*. Saint Paul: Minnesota Historical Society, 1974.

Karol, Joseph S., ed. *Red Horse Owner's Winter Count: The Oglala Sioux, 1786–1968*. Martin, S.D.: Booster, 1969.

Keim, De B. Randolph. *Sheridan's Troopers on the Borders: A Winter Campaign on the Plains.* Lincoln: University of Nebraska Press, 1985.

Kelly, Fanny. *Narrative of My Captivity among the Sioux Indians.* Cincinnati: Wilstach, Baldwin, 1871.

Kennedy, Paul. *The Rise and Fall of the Great Powers.* New York: Random House, 1987.

Kirby, Percival R. *Andrew Smith and Natal.* Cape Town: Van Riebeeck Society, 1955.

Koss, Stephen. *The Rise and Fall of the Political Press in Britain: The Nineteenth Century.* Chapel Hill: University of North Carolina Press, 1981.

Lamar, Howard R., ed. *The Reader's Encyclopedia of the American West.* New York: Crowell, 1976.

Lamar, Howard, and Leonard Thompson, eds. *The Frontier in History: North America and Southern Africa Compared.* New Haven, Conn.: Yale University Press, 1981.

Lewis, Oscar. *The Effects of White Contact upon Blackfoot Culture: With Special Reference to the Role of the Fur Trade.* Seattle: University of Washington Press, 1942. Rev. ed., 1966.

Libby, O. G., ed. *The Arikara Narrative of the Campaign against the Hostile Dakotas, June, 1876.* Glorieta, N.M.: Rio Grande Press, 1976.

London *Daily News.* 1879.

London *Daily Telegraph.* 1879.

London *Times.* 1879.

Luttig, John C. *Journal of a Fur-Trading Expedition on the Upper Missouri, 1812–13.* Edited by Stella M. Drumm. Saint Louis: Missouri Historical Society, 1920.

Mallery, Garrick. *Pictographs of the North American Indians.* Smithsonian Institution, Bureau of American Ethnology, Annual Report no. 10. Washington, D.C., 1893. Reprint. New York: Dover, 1972.

Marks, Shula. *The Ambiguities of Dependence in South Africa: Class, Nationalism, and the State in Twentieth-Century Natal.* Baltimore: Johns Hopkins University Press, 1986.

Marks, Shula, and Anthony Atmore, eds. *Economy and Society in Pre-Industrial South Africa.* London: Longman, 1980.

Martineau, John. *The Transvaal Trouble, How It Arose: Being an Extract from the Biography of the Late Sir Bartle Frere.* London: John Murray, 1900.

Mathiessen, Peter. *In the Spirit of Crazy Horse.* New York: Viking Press, 1983.

McBride, Angus. *The Zulu War.* London: Osprey, 1976.

McGillycuddy, Julia B. *McGillycuddy Agent: A Biography of Dr. Valentine T. McGillycuddy.* Palo Alto, Calif.: Stanford University Press, 1941.

Mendelssohn, Sidney. *Mendelssohn's South African Bibliography.* 2 vols. London: Kegan Paul, Trench, Trubner, 1910.

Miller, David Humphreys. *Custer's Fall: The Indian Side of the Story.* New York: Duell, Sloan, and Pearce, 1957. Reprint. Lincoln: University of Nebraska Press, 1985.

——. *Ghost Dance.* New York: Duell, Sloan, and Pearce, 1959. Reprint. Lincoln: University of Nebraska Press, 1985.

Monaghan, Jay. *Custer: The Life of General George Armstrong Custer.* Boston: Little, Brown, 1959. Reprint. Lincoln: University of Nebraska Press, 1971.

Mooney, James. *The Ghost-Dance Religion and the Sioux Outbreak of 1890.* Smithsonian Institution, Bureau of American Ethnology, Annual Report no. 14, pt. 2. Washington, D.C., 1896. Reprint. Chicago: University of Chicago Press, 1965.

Morris, Donald. *The Washing of the Spears: A History of the Rise of the Zulu Nation under Shaka and Its Fall in the Zulu War of 1879.* New York: Random House, 1965.

Moulton, Gary E., ed. *The Journals of the Louis and Clark Expedition*, vols. 2, 3, and 4. Lincoln: University of Nebraska Press, 1986.

Murdock, George Peter, and Timothy J. O'Leary. *Ethnographic Bibliography of North America*. 4th ed. Vols. 1 and 5. New Haven, Conn.: Human Relations Area Files Press, 1975.

Nasatir, A. P., ed. *Before Lewis and Clark: Documents Ilustrating the History of the Missouri, 1785–1804*. Vol. 1. Saint Louis: Saint Louis Historical Documents Foundation, 1952.

Oliver, Symmes C. *Ecology and Cultural Continuity as Factors in the Social Organization of the Plains Indians*. Berkeley and Los Angeles: University of California Press, 1962.

Olson, James C. *Red Cloud and the Sioux Problem*. Lincoln: University of Nebraska Press, 1965.

Omer-Cooper, J. D. *History of Southern Africa*. London: James Currey, 1987.

——. *The Zulu Aftermath: A Nineteenth-Century Revolution in Bantu Africa*. London: Longman, 1966.

Owen, Roger, and Bob Sutcliffe, eds. *Studies in the Theory of Imperialism*. London: Longman, 1972.

Pall Mall Gazette. 1879.

Parker, John, ed. *The Journals of Jonathan Carver and Related Documents, 1766–1770*. Saint Paul: Minnesota Historical Society Press, 1976.

Parkman, Francis. *The Oregon Trail: Sketches of Prairie and Rocky-Mountain Life*. 8th ed. Boston: Little, Brown, 1925.

Peires, J. B., ed. *Before and after Shaka: Papers in Nguni History*. Grahamstown, South Africa: Rhodes Institute of Social and Economic Research, 1981.

Powers, William. *Oglala Religion*. Lincoln: University of Nebraska Press, 1977.

Preston, Adrian, ed. *The South African Journal of Sir Garnet Wolseley, 1879–1880*. Cape Town: A. A. Balkema, 1973.

Proceedings of the Great Peace Commission of 1867–1868. Introduction by Vine Deloria, Jr., and Raymond DeMallie. Washington, D.C.: Institute for the Development of Indian Law, 1975.

Prucha, Francis Paul. *The Great Father: The United States Government and the American Indians*. 2 vols. Lincoln: University of Nebraska Press, 1984.

Punch; or, The London Charivari, vol. 76. 1879.

Robinson, Doane. *A History of the Dakota or Sioux Indians*. South Dakota History Collections 2. Pierre, S.D., 1904. Reprint. Minneapolis: Ross and Haines, 1956.

Ronda, James P. *Lewis and Clark among the Indians*. Lincoln: University of Nebraska Press, 1984.

Rosenberg, Bruce A. *Custer and the Epic of Defeat*. University Park: Pennsylvania State University Press, 1974.

Russell, Don. *Custer's Last*. Fort Worth: Amon Carter Museum of Western Art, 1968.

Sandoz, Mari. *Crazy Horse: The Strange Man of the Oglalas*. Lincoln: University of Nebraska Press, 1961.

Saturday Review, vols. 47–57. 1879–84.

Schreuder, D. M. *Gladstone and Kruger: Liberal Government and Colonial "Home Rule," 1880–85*. London: Routledge and Kegan Paul, 1969.

Scott, Douglas D., and Richard A. Fox. *Archaeological Insights into the Custer Battle*. Norman: University of Oklahoma Press, 1987.

Scull, Gideon D., ed. *Voyages of Peter Espirit Radisson*. Boston: The Prince Society, 1885. Reprint. New York: Burt Franklin, 1967.

Secoy, Frank Raymond. *Changing Military Patterns on the Great Plains.* Locust Valley, N.Y.: Augustin, 1953.

Slotkin, Richard. *The Fatal Environment: The Myth of the Frontier in the Age of Industrialization, 1800–1890.* New York: Atheneum, 1985. Reprint. Middletown, Conn.: Wesleyan University Press, 1986.

Smith, Andrew. *The Diary of Dr. Andrew Smith, Director of the "Expedition for Exploring Central Africa," 1834–1836.* 2 vols. Edited by Percival R. Kirby. Cape Town: Van Riebeeck Society, 1939, 1940.

Smith, Tony. *The Pattern of Imperialism: The United States, Great Britain, and the Late-Industrializing World since 1815.* Cambridge: Cambridge University Press, 1981.

Smith-Dorrien, Horace. *Memories of Forty-Eight Years' Service.* London: John Murray, 1925.

The Spectator, vol. 52. 1879.

Stewart, Edgar I. *Custer's Luck.* Norman: University of Oklahoma Press, 1955.

Thompson, Leonard M. *A History of South Africa.* New Haven, Conn.: Yale University Press, 1990.

——. *The Political Mythology of Apartheid.* New Haven, Conn.: Yale University Press, 1985.

——, ed. *African Societies in Southern Africa.* London: Heinemann, 1971.

Thompson, Leonard, Richard Elphick, and Inez Jarrick. *Southern African History before 1900: A Select Bibliography of Articles.* Stanford, Calif.: Hoover Institute Press, 1971.

Thwaites, Reuben Gold, ed. *Early Western Travels, 1748–1846.* Vol. 22, part 1 of *Maximilian, Prince of Wied's Travels to the Interior of North America, 1832–1834.* Cleveland: Clark, 1906.

——. *Original Journals of the Lewis and Clark Expedition, 1804–1806.* Vol. 6. New York: Dodd, Mead, 1904–05. Reprint. New York: Antiquarian Press, 1959.

Trennert, Robert A. *Alternative to Extinction: Federal Indian Policy and the Beginnings of the Reservation System.* Philadelphia: Temple University Press, 1975.

Utley, Robert M. *Cavalier in Buckskin: George Armstrong Custer and the Western Military Frontier.* Norman: University of Oklahoma Press, 1988.

——. *Custer and the Great Controversy: The Origin and Development of a Legend.* Los Angeles: Westernlore Press, 1962.

——. *Frontier Regulars: The United States Army and the Indian, 1866–1891.* New York: Macmillan, 1973. Reprint. Lincoln: University of Nebraska Press, 1984.

——. *Frontiersmen in Blue: The United States Army and the Indian, 1848–1865.* New York: Macmillan, 1967. Reprint. Lincoln: University of Nebraska Press, 1967.

——. *The Indian Frontier of the American West, 1846–90.* Albuquerque: University of New Mexico Press, 1984.

——. *The Last Days of the Sioux Nation.* New Haven, Conn.: Yale University Press, 1963.

Vanity Fair, vols. 11, 27. 1874, 1881.

Vestal, Stanley. *Sitting Bull: Champion of the Sioux.* Norman: University of Oklahoma Press, 1932.

——. *Warpath: The True Story of the Fighting Sioux Told in a Biography of Chief White Bull.* Boston: Houghton Mifflin. Reprint. Lincoln: University of Nebraska Press, 1984.

Vijn, Cornelius. *Cetshwayo's Dutchman.* London: Longmans, Green, 1880. Reprint. New York: Negro Universities Press, 1969.

Walker, James R. *Lakota Belief and Ritual.* Edited by Raymond J. DeMallie and Elaine A. Jahner. Lincoln: University of Nebraska Press, 1980.

——. *Lakota Society.* Edited by Raymond J. DeMallie. Lincoln: University of Nebraska Press, 1982.

Webb, C. de B., and J. B. Wright, eds. *The James Stuart Archive of Recorded Oral Evidence Relating to the History of the Zulu and Neighbouring Peoples.* 4 vols. Pietermaritzburg: University of Natal Press, 1976, 1979, 1982, 1986.

——. *A Zulu King Speaks: Statements Made by Cetshwayo kaMpande on the History and Customs of His People.* Pietermaritzburg: University of Natal Press, 1978.

Welsh, David. *The Roots of Segregation: Native Policy in Colonial Natal, 1845–1910.* Cape Town: Oxford University Press, 1971.

Weltfish, Gene. *The Lost Universe.* New York: Basic Books, 1965.

White, Richard. *"It's Your Misfortune and None of My Own": A New History of the American West.* Norman: University of Oklahoma Press, 1991.

Whitman, Walt. *Complete Poetry and Prose.* Edited by Justin Kaplan. New York: Literary Classics of the United States, 1982.

Wilson, Monica, and Leonard Thompson, eds. *The Oxford History of South Africa.* 2 vols. New York: Oxford University Press, 1969, 1971.

Wooster, Robert. *The Military and United States Indian Policy.* New Haven, Conn.: Yale University Press, 1988.

Wright, John, and Andrew Manson. *The Hlubi Chiefdom in Zululand-Natal: A History.* Ladysmith, Natal: Ladysmith Historical Society, 1983.

ARTICLES

Allardyce, Alexander. "The Zulu War." *Blackwood's Edinburgh Magazine* 125 (March 1879): 376–94.

Anderson, Gary C. "Early Dakota Migration and Intertribal War: A Revision." *Western Historical Quarterly* 11, no. 1 (January 1980): 17–36.

Anderson, Harry. "An Investigation of the Early Bands of the Saone Group of Teton Sioux." *Journal of the Washington Academy of Sciences* 46, no. 3 (March 1956): 87–94.

Atmore, Anthony, and Shula Marks. "The Imperial Factor in South Africa in the Nineteenth Century: Towards a Reassessment." *Journal of Imperial and Commonwealth History* 3, no. 1 (1974): 105–39.

Ballard, Charles. "John Dunn and Cetshwayo: the Material Foundations of Political Power in the Zulu Kingdom, 1857–1878." *Journal of African History* 21, no. 1 (1980): 75–91.

Birmingham, David, and Shula Marks. "Southern Africa." In *The Cambridge History of Africa,* vol. 3, edited by Roland Oliver, 567–620. Cambridge: Cambridge University Press, 1977.

Brininstool, E. A., et al. "Chief Crazy Horse, His Career and Death." *Nebraska History Magazine* 12, no. 1 (January–March 1929): 4–77.

Buchanan, Robert. "The Battle of Isandúla." *Contemporary Review* 35 (April 1879): 153–56.

Carnarvon, Lord. "Imperial Administration." *Fortnightly Review* 30 (December 1878): 751–64.

Cope, R. L. "Political Power within the Zulu Kingdom and the 'Coronation Laws' of 1873." *Journal of Natal and Zulu History* 8 (1985): 11–31.

Cox, George W. "The English Nation and the Zulu War." *Fraser's Magazine* 21 (February 1880): 261–71.

Custer, G. A. "War Memoirs." *The Galaxy* 21–22 (March–November, 1876).

DeMallie, Raymond J. "The Lakota Ghost Dance: An Ethnohistorical Account." *Pacific Historical Review* 51 (November 1982): 385–405.

———. "Sioux Ethnohistory: A Methodological Critique." *Journal of Ethnic Studies* 4, no. 3 (Fall 1976): 77–83.

———. "Touching the Pen: Plains Indian Treaty Councils in Ethnohistorical Perspective." In *Ethnicity on the Great Plains*, edited by Frederick C. Luebke, 38–53. Lincoln: University of Nebraska Press, 1980.

Dippie, Brian W. "Bards of the Little Big Horn." *Western American Literature* 1, no. 3 (Fall 1966): 175–95.

———. " 'What Will Congress Do about It?' The Congressional Reaction to the Little Big Horn Disaster." *North Dakota History* 37, no. 3 (Summer 1970): 161–89.

Eldredge, Elizabeth A. "Drought, Famine and Disease in Nineteenth-Century Lesotho." *African Economic History* 16 (1987): 61–93.

———. "Sources of Conflict in Southern Africa, c. 1800–30: The 'Mfecane' Reconsidered." *Journal of African History* 33 (1992): 1–35.

Ellis, Richard. "Civilians, the Army, and the Indian Problem on the Northern Plains, 1862–1866." *North Dakota History* 37, no. 1 (Winter 1970): 20–39.

———. "The Humanitarian Generals." *Western Historical Quarterly* 3, no. 2 (April 1972): 169–78.

Etherington, Norman A. "Labour Supply and the Genesis of South African Confederation in the 1870s." *Journal of African History* 20, no. 2 (1979): 235–53.

Ewers, John C. "Intertribal Warfare as the Precursor of Indian-White Warfare on the Northern Great Plains." *Western Historical Quarterly* 6, no. 4 (October 1975): 397–410.

Feraca, Stephen E. and James H. Howard. "The Identity and Demography of the Dakota or Sioux Tribe." *Plains Anthropologist* 8, no. 20 (May 1963): 80–84.

Fredrickson, George M. "Comparative History." In *The Past before Us: Contemporary Historical Writing in the United States*, edited by Michael Kammen. Ithaca, N.Y.: Cornell University Press, 1980.

Frere, H. B. "On the Future of Zululand and South Africa." *Fortnightly Review* 38 (November 1882): 581–95.

Froude, J. A. "The South African Problem." *Quarterly Review* 147 (April 1879): 552–84.

Gibbon, John. "Hunting Sitting Bull." *American Catholic Quarterly Review* 2 (October 1877): 665–94.

———. "Last Summer's Expedition against the Sioux and Its Great Catastrophe." *American Catholic Quarterly Review* 2 (April 1877): 271–304.

Gump, James. "Ecological Change and Pre-Shakan State Formation." *African Economic History* 18 (1989): 57–71.

———. "Origins of the Zulu Kingdom." *Historian* 50, no. 4 (August 1988): 521–34.

———. "The Subjugation of the Zulus and Sioux: A Comparative Study." *Western Historical Quarterly* 19, no. 1 (January 1988): 21–36.

Guy, J. J. "Production and Exchange in the Zulu Kingdom." *Mohlomi: Journal of Southern African Historical Studies* 2 (1978): 96–106.

Guy, Jeff. "Analysing Pre-Capitalist Societies in Southern Africa." *Journal of Southern African Studies* 14, no. 1 (October 1987): 18–37.

Hall, Martin. "The Myth of the Zulu Homestead: Archaeology and Ethnography." *Africa* 54, no. 1 (1984): 65–80.

Hall, Martin, and Kathleen Mack. "The Outline of an Eighteenth-Century Economic System in South-East Africa." *Annals of the South African Museum* 91, no. 2 (January 1983): 163–94.

Hamilton, Carolyn Anne. "'The Character and Objects of Chaka': A Reconsideration of the Making of Shaka as 'Mfecane' Motor." *Journal of African History* 33 (1992): 37–63.

Harries, Patrick. "The Roots of Ethnicity: Discourse and the Politics of Language Construction in South-east Africa." *African Affairs* 87, no. 346 (January 1988): 25–52.

Hinman, Eleanor H. "Oglala Sources on the Life of Crazy Horse." *Nebraska History* 57, no. 1 (Spring 1976): 1–52.

Horsman, Reginald. "Scientific Racism and the American Indian in the Mid-Nineteenth Century." *American Quarterly* 27, no. 2 (May 1975): 152–68.

Howard, James H. "Yanktonai Ethnohistory and the John K. Bear Winter Count." *Plains Anthropologist* 21, no. 73 (August 1976): 15–78.

Hutton, Paul A. "From Little Bighorn to Little Big Man: The Changing Image of a Western Hero in Popular Culture." *Western Historical Quarterly* 7, no. 1 (January 1976): 19–46.

Laband, J. P. C. "The Cohesion of the Zulu Polity under the Impact of the Anglo-Zulu War: A Reassessment." *Journal of Natal and Zulu History* 8 (1985): 33–62.

Leonard, Thomas C. "Red, White, and the Army Blue: Empathy and Anger in the American West." *American Quarterly* 26, no. 2 (May 1974): 176–90.

MacKarness, Frederic. "What England Has Done for the Zulus." *Fortnightly Review* 42 (September 1884): 391–400.

Marks, Shula, and Richard Gray. "Southern Africa and Madagascar." In *The Cambridge History of Africa*, vol. 4, edited by Richard Gray, 384–468. Cambridge: Cambridge University Press, 1975.

Mattison, Ray. "The Harney Expedition against the Sioux: The Journal of Capt. John B. S. Todd." *Nebraska History* 43, no. 2 (June 1962): 89–130.

Mekeel, Scudder. "A Short History of the Teton Dakota." *North Dakota Historical Quarterly* 10, no. 3 (July 1943): 137–205.

Mirsky, Jeanette. "The Dakota." In *Cooperation and Conflict among Primitive Peoples*, edited by Margaret Mead, 382–427. New York: McGraw-Hill, 1937.

Monahan, Jay. "Custer's 'Last Stand': Trevilian Station, 1864." *Civil War History* 8, no. 3 (September 1962): 245–58.

Morley, John. "Further Remarks on Zulu Affairs." *Fortnightly Review* 31 (April 1879): 546–62.

———. "The Plain Story of the Zulu War." *Fortnightly Review* 31 (March 1879): 329–52.

Omer-Cooper, J. D. "The Nguni Outburst." In *The Cambridge History of Africa*, vol. 5, edited by John E. Flint, 319–52. Cambridge: Cambridge University Press, 1976.

Peires, J. B. "The Central Beliefs of the Xhosa Cattle-Killing." *Journal of African History* 28 (1987): 43–63.

———. "'Soft' Believers and 'Hard' Unbelievers in the Xhosa Cattle-Killing." *Journal of African History* 27 (1986): 443–461.

Phillips, George H. "The Indian Ring in Dakota Territory, 1870–1890." *South Dakota History* 2 (Fall 1972): 345–76.

Pine, Benjamin C. C. "The Boers and the Zulus." *Contemporary Review* 35 (June 1879): 541–70.

Sanderson, John. "The Transvaal and the Zulu Countries." *Fortnightly Review* 29 (June 1878): 937–54k.

Taft, Robert. "The Pictorial Record of the Old West: Custer's Last Stand." *Kansas Historical Quarterly* 14, no. 4 (November 1946): 361–90.

Wedel, Mildred Mott, and Raymond J. DeMallie. "The Ethnohistorical Approach in Plains

Area Studies." In *Anthropology on the Great Plains*, edited by W. Raymond Wood and Margot Liberty, 110–28. Lincoln: University of Nebraska Press, 1980.

White, Richard. "Race Relations in the American West." *American Quarterly* 38, no. 3 (1986): 396–416.

———. "The Winning of the West: The Expansion of the Western Sioux in the Eighteenth and Nineteenth Centuries." *Journal of American History* 65, no. 2 (September 1978): 319–43.

Wissler, Clark. "Societies and Ceremonial Associations in the Oglala Division of the Teton-Dakota." *American Museum of Natural History Anthropological Papers* 11, pt. 1 (1912): 3–99.

Wright, John B. "Pre-Shakan Age-Group Formation among the Northern Nguni." *Natalia* 8 (December 1978): 22–30.

THESES AND OTHER UNPUBLISHED PAPERS

Cobbing, Julian. "The Case against the Mfecane." Seminar paper, University of the Witwatersrand, March 1984.

Gump, James O. "Origins of the 'Mfecane': An Ecological Perspective." Seminar paper, University of the Witwatersrand, 1991.

———. "The Zulu and Sioux: The British and American Experience with the 'Noble Savage.'" Seminar paper, University of Texas at Austin, 1991.

Guy, J. J. "Ecological Factors in the Rise of Shaka and the Zulu Kingdom." Seminar paper, National University of Lesotho, 1976.

Hall, Martin. "The Ecology of the Iron Age in Zululand." Ph.D. thesis, University of Cambridge, 1980.

Hamilton, Carolyn, and John Wright. "The Making of the Lala: Ethnicity, Ideology and Class-Formation in a PreColonial Context." Seminar paper, University of the Witwatersrand, 1984.

Hedges, David W. "Trade and Politics in Southern Mozambique and Zululand, c. 1750–1830." D. Phil. thesis, University of London, 1978.

Metcalfe, P. Richard. "The Political Evolution of the Teton-Lakotah." Seminar paper, Yale University, n.d.

Wright, John. "Politics, Ideology, and the Invention of the 'Nguni.'" Seminar paper, University of Natal, Pietermaritzburg, 1983.

I N D E X